CITY OF THE BEAST

In memory of the women: Blackley, Brooksmith, Busch, Clarke, Donley, Falconer, de Miramar, Pickett, Speller, Wakeford and the rest.

CITY OF THE BEAST:

The London of Aleister Crowley

City of the Beast: The London of Aleister Crowley by Phil Baker
First Published by Strange Attractor Press 2022.

Text © 2022 Phil Baker
'The Mad Grey City' © 2021 Timothy d'Arch Smith
All unpublished Crowley material © 2022 Ordo Templi Orientis

Cover photograph: Regent Street 1930s, by Harold Burdekin

Book design/layout by Maïa Gaffney-Hyde
Set in Bunyan Pro

ISBN: 9781913689322

Strange Attractor Press
BM SAP
London, WC1N 3XX
UK

Distributed by The MIT Press, Cambridge, Massachusetts.
And London, England.

Printed and bound in Estonia by Tallinna Raamatutrükikoda.

"I dreamed I was paying a visit to London. It was a vivid, long, coherent, detailed affair of several days, with so much incident that it would make a good-sized volume."

– Crowley in Cefalu, Sicily, 8 June 1920.

CONTENTS

THE MAD GREY CITY:
a Foreword by Timothy d'Arch Smith

Do what thou wilt shall be the whole of the Law.

Around 1908-9 Crowley was delivered of a Holy Book, Liber 65, *Liber cordis cincti serpente*. Chapter V, verse 3, reads:

> Yea, cried the Holy One, and from Thy spark will I the Lord
> kindle a great light; I will burn through the grey city in the old
> and desolate land; I will cleanse it from its great impurity.

Crowley commented on this book in 1923:

> The Angel spontaneously promises 666 that his True Will shall
> be made operative... This Book was written down in London,
> and the apparent reference in the first instance is to that
> city. The text may mean that in some way or other 666 will
> become 'a great light,' a portentous phenomenon pregnant with
> destruction in the eyes of its inhabitants... it would appear that
> some such event is still in the future.
>   'Commentary to Liber 65,' (*The Equinox*, IV, 1, 1996 e.v.)

In the same place, he goes on to wonder what the numerical equivalent of 'grey city,' φαιά πόλις (phaia polis) would be, employing Greek kabbalah. The answer is that it adds up to 902. Another word with the same number in this particular system, one that decrees that similarity to be of thought-provoking significance and not mere coincidence, is the word παρανούζ (paranoia): mad.

As we read Dr Baker's gripping guide to Crowley in London, it becomes clear that this is a fair enough description of the 'grey city' where he lived, and moved, and had his being; and at the date these words are written perhaps an even fairer one.

Love is the law, love under will.

Timothy d'Arch Smith

☉ in 14° ♎ : ☽ 19° ♋ : An. V$_6$: 7 October 2020 e.v.

INTRODUCTION: MAGUS ABOUT TOWN

Aleister Crowley hated London, or claimed to:

> The very streets testify against the city. On the one hand we have pale stunted hurrying pygmies jostling each other in the bitter search for bread; an ant heap is a miracle of beauty and dignity in comparison. On the other, when it comes to excitement or amusement, we see perspiring brutes belching the fumes of beer; course, ugly parodies of apes. Nature affords no parallel to their degradation. There is no open air life, physical or mental, and there is the ever-abiding sense of sin and shame to obsess these slaves.

But at the same time, it was the capital of the civilization that produced him: he would never have been the man he was without the rich matrix of late Victorian culture behind him. Crowley believed in the invocation of gods and the channelling of spirits, but not least of the forces that spoke through him was the darker genius of Victorian and Edwardian Britain, and its cultural and sexual discontents.

Crowley felt a particular antipathy to Queen Victoria and everything she represented. She died in 1902 while he was on a climbing expedition in Mexico with his friend Eckenstein, and a well-meaning Mexican had to give them the sad news; he was then astonished to see the two Englishmen break into singing and dancing. Crowley's formative years were those of a Victorian anti-Victorian, a cultural revolt that was particularly associated with the 1890s. It is a decade remembered as the era of Wilde, Beardsley, absinthe, the Café Royal, and the decadent periodical *The Yellow Book*. Like the Swinging Sixties, a decade with which it has some affinity, the 1890s had its centre in London, and just as the Sixties are often said to have lasted until 1974, so certain currents of the Nineties persisted well into the Edwardian period, and in Crowley's case far longer; this "post-decadent" aspect was more obvious to his contemporaries.[1]

+

I have drawn extensively on Crowley's unpublished diaries, dense with London detail, which give an exceptionally intimate and human picture of his day-to-day life. In a world of trigger warnings, I should add that they have something to offend everyone, even to appal, and that I don't intend to labour this aspect; Crowley can speak for himself. When he writes in a 1913 letter that "speaking as a man of the world, I am a reactionary Tory of the most bigoted type" he wasn't being flippant. His diaries, letters and even published work are strewn with unapologetically "bigoted" and defiantly transgressive comments, like a product of political Tourette's. As the world dumbs down, it is likely that in fifty years many readers will assume that this is just 'what people in Britain were like, then'. It is not. Crowley was well out on a limb and deliberately provocative, like a caricature of the mad Tory squire from Hell, and he was aware that he was doing it.

Crowley can joke about transgressive contents when he sends an early diary to a friend to read, "in privacy and confidence. There's about 114, 278, 394 years penal servitude in it if sent to Plowden."[2] But one of the curious things about his diaries is that he wrote them knowing they would be read, and read at various levels. At a personal level he can disguise women's addresses to conceal them from the woman he was living with, so Sinclair Gardens in Hammersmith becomes *Jardins de Ste.-Clair*, and a horizontal oval with four circles

---

1   I have written about this in more detail in an afterword, 'A Word in Wilde Haste', but relegated it to the back so as not to let this dense essay come between the reader and the book.

2   Alfred Chichele Plowden (1844-1914) was the once well-known Metropolitan Police Magistrate at Marlborough Street Magistrates Court – one of London's major courts – in Great Marlborough Street, off Regent Street.

above it – from the standard heraldic image of a baron's crown – stands in for the Baron in Baron's Court Road.[3] More actively, going beyond simple discretion, on another occasion he writes a fictional entry for his current partner to find, almost like an alibi or at least 'his version of events', and later notes this when he corrects it.

This aspect of writing-for-others is relevant to the testimonials (as they effectively are) that he writes for his own health products, his Amrita rejuvenation pills, and for the rapid effectiveness of magical practices. It might also shed light on his almost inexplicable account of triumph in a court case that he has in fact lost, or another lost court case where he implies that he might have won, if only asthma hadn't "stopped me spilling the beans in the witness box". These are attempts to present 'his side' for posterity, perhaps feeling his diaries would be read long after the day's court reportage had been forgotten.

There is an acute moment in this matter of future readership when Crowley finds himself missing some manuscripts. He then wonders if, rather than someone thieving them for gain, it might be his supernatural masters the Secret Chiefs who were behind their disappearance, as a form of censorship: "There were a great many entries in some of the diaries, for example, which would no doubt be very dangerous to print. I do not think so, myself..."

The man who emerges from the diaries is acutely alive: after a bath he records having "the 'cat-feeling' – direct pleasure in the body as such." Crowley was a great writer on meditation, magic, drug experiences and dreams, his "untrodden regions of the mind" – the whole dimension that has been termed "inner experience", as a successor to mysticism[4]

---

3   With reference to Pat Harvey of Sinclair Gardens, and Ruby, probably Ruby Butler, of Baron's Court Road. See sites 69 and 75.

4   "Therefore we set out diligently to map and explore these 'untrodden regions of the mind'" is Crowley's loose quote at the start of his 1908 magical diary, adapting John Keats's "untrodden region of my mind" from his 1819 poem 'Ode to Psyche' ("Yes, I will be thy priest, and build a fane" – a temple or ☞

– and there are many flashes of this same intelligence in the diaries. Alternating between exultation and depression, he is also dogged by moments of rather passive superstition ("An awful day. Eleven things went wrong in the queerest way") while on the other hand there are small gifts of good luck: accidentally "long-changed" by ten shillings in Soho restaurant Chez Victor, he writes "a really charming gesture of the Gods. Made complete difference to my whole day." Ten shillings was worth having in 1938, but he can also be candidly and almost endearingly small-time. Every day he threw the *I Ching* for guidance, interpreting his day in the light of it, and one day he observes "'Small restraint' [Hexagram 9, *Hsiao Khu*] at South Kensington Station about my Cheap Day Return ticket. Very curious incident."

Crowley was financially hard-up for most of his life, but even when he was down on his luck he lived as a gentleman (in the sense of class, rather than good behaviour). Writing from a brief stay in Portugal, where life was cheaper, he says "If I'm in London I have to swank". London, particularly the West End, was a playground for the Victorian and Edwardian gent, dining well and pursuing women, and Crowley never lost caste or quite fell from the idea of this atavistic, old school, man-about-town: a character we might now see with a dash of Aubrey Beardsley's 'Diabolic Dandy' about him.

Crowley was nostalgic for his days as a young man in the West End, as he explained in the 1940s to an occult student. After she complains about the tone of flippancy in the personal correspondence course she is paying for, he first refers her to Max Beerbohm's 1904 caricature of Matthew Arnold, the famously high-minded Victorian, with his little niece asking him why he won't be more serious. Then he looks back to the days of greater freedom, before the forces of social progress cracked down on prostitution and drinking, and particularly to the Nineties pleasure zone of the Leicester Square area:

shrine – "In some untrodden region of my mind"). For "inner experience" see Georges Bataille, *Inner Experience* (NY, SUNY, 1988) [*L'Experience Interieure*, 1943]. Other writers in this area, but without Crowley's esoteric apparatus, must include William James and Aldous Huxley.

Far-off indeed those sunny days when life in England was worth living... when we complained that closing time was twelve-thirty a.m.; when there was little or no class bitterness, the future seemed secure, and only Nonconformists failed to enjoy the fun that bubbled up on every side. Well, in those days there were Music-halls; I can't hope to explain to you what they were like, but they were jolly... At the Empire, Leicester Square, which at that time actually looked as if it had been lifted bodily from the "Continong" (a very wicked place) there was a promenade, with bars complete (drinking bars, my dear child, I blush to say) where one might hope to find "strength and beauty met together, Kindle their image like a star in a sea of glassy weather." There one might always find London's "soiled doves" (as they revoltingly called them in the papers) of every type: Theodora (celebrated "Christian" Empress) and Phryne, Messalina and Thais, Baudelaire's swarthy mistress, and Nana, Moll Flanders and Fanny Hill.[5]

"But the enemies of life were on guard," says Crowley, "They saw people enjoying themselves...". In particular, he cites Christian feminist and social reformer Mrs. Ormiston Chant, who led protests against prostitution and general immorality at the Empire (now the Leicester Square Cineworld) in what became a famous case of 1894, leading to greater restraint.

---

5   Crowley's "strength and beauty" quotation is from Shelley's poem, 'A Bridal Song'. The Empire itself was the subject of *fin-de-siècle* poems by Arthur Symons and Theodore Wratislaw, both focused on women: Wratislaw describes "The calm and brilliant Circes who retard / Your passage with the skirts and rouge that spice / The changeless programme of insipid vice, / And stun you with a languid strange regard".
    Following "Soiled doves" in Crowley's next line, a sentimental Victorian euphemism for prostitutes, he gives a spread of women from history and fiction: Byzantine empress and former prostitute Theodora, played on stage by Sarah Bernhardt; Greek Phryne; vicious and depraved Roman empress Messalina, famously drawn by Beardsley; Thaïs, fourth-century Egyptian prostitute with a pure spiritual heart, subject of Jules Massenet's 1894 opera *Thaïs*; Baudelaire's Haiti-born "Black Venus" Jeanne Duval; and the fictional Nana, Moll Flanders and Fanny Hill from Zola, Defoe and John Cleland respectively.

And now, he says, his student complains he is not serious, but Magick is the subject that takes him back to the gay days of his youth. He set out almost half a century earlier to find "The Stone of the Wise, the *Summum Bonum*, True Wisdom and Perfect Happiness", and now "I have plenty of trouble in life, and often enough I am in low enough spirits to please anybody; but turn my thoughts to Magick – the years fall off. I am again the gay, quick, careless boy to whom the world was gracious."

✛

The world was definitely more gracious to Crowley in certain districts. Bernard Bromage, an acquaintance of the Thirties and Forties, noticed "there must still have been supporters, overt and secret. He did not live, in these last crumbling years, in Seven Dials or Poplar or Peckham but in Jermyn Street…".

Crowley in Peckham would hardly have been Crowley. Writing about navigation in 1909, he cheerfully claims not to know the whereabouts of Haggerston, a poor district in east London just north of Bethnal Green:

> Suppose I were to start from Scott's [restaurant] and walk… to Haggerston Town Hall (wherever Haggerston may be; but say it's N.E.), thence to Maida Vale. From Maida Vale I could take a true line for Piccadilly again and not go five minutes' walk out of my way, bar blind alleys, etc., and I should know when I got close to Scott's again before I recognised any of the surroundings.

Not far from the Empire theatre, between Leicester Square and Piccadilly Circus, his starting point here is 'Scott's Oyster and Supper Rooms' on Coventry Street ("the hub of the West End of London" says *The Gourmet's Guide to London* of 1914). It was just behind the Trocadero and the building still has its 'S' motifs, with seashells higher up (it is currently Five Guys fast food). A year earlier, as he tells it, Crowley picked up a newly published novel by Somerset Maugham – whom he had known quite well in Paris – entitled *The*

Magician, and took it to Scott's, where he was so pleased to recognise the main character was quite closely modelled on himself "I think I ate two dozen oysters and a pheasant, and drank a bottle of No.III [champagne]... Yes, I did myself proud, for the Magician, Oliver Haddo, was Aleister Crowley..."

The Piccadilly area is a definite nexus in Crowley's London. Just south of Scott's is Haymarket, where he stayed in Yeoman House at number 31-32 in the late Twenties, obtained tobacco from Fribourg and Treyer at 34, and heroin from Heppell's chemist next door at 35. At the top of the north-south sloping road was the long-gone Haymarket Stores (25, 26, 29 Coventry Street) where he shopped on account – lobster, pineapple, pheasant, sherry, Stilton, crystallised fruit – until they pursued him for unpaid bills, and in 1934 he stayed briefly at Mapleton House, 'Bachelor Flats', 39 Coventry Street.

Just across the Circus he had a more sustained association with Jermyn Street, just south of Piccadilly, over three decades and several lodgings, and he banked with Barclay's (home branch Piccadilly Circus, 52 Regent Street) and Westminster (home branch Piccadilly, 63-65 Piccadilly). He was a regular at the Café Royal, where Regent Street meets the Circus, and at Oddenino's restaurant almost next door ("Oddie's", where he also stayed at Oddenino's hotel). Regent Street was another well-worn path, and he also knew Bond Street well – like Jermyn Street, an old-style, high-class shopping street, but on a grander scale – where he stayed faithful year after year to 'Royal Court' diaries from Smythson's intensely upmarket stationery shop; still there and still expensive.

Inevitably he also knew Soho, for its restaurants and sex trade (and stayed there occasionally) as well as the more down-at-heel and equivocal Paddington and other districts near railway termini. After reduced circumstances forced him into digs in Paddington Green during the 1930s, where he had a brush with what would soon be known as 'bedsit-land', he was relieved to escape to the more pleasant quarter of Chelsea, another favoured district along with Piccadilly and Mayfair. Crowley took an interest in the metropolis (telling an American friend he wished he could take him "exploring odd bits of London") and he was alert to the particular atmospheres, nuances and social gradations of these areas, writing – by way of a metaphor – that "Brixton need not envy Bayswater, or Bayswater Belgravia, if it would only be itself".

✝

I started this book as a diversion during the 2020 lockdown, not intending much more than a gazetteer of addresses, but it grew into a biography by sites. As well as the social nuances and atmospheric qualities of place, there is a peculiar magic about knowing someone walked through this doorway, looked into that shop window, walked up those stairs. Years ago, spellbound by a novel which mentioned a particular door on Soho's Dean Street, I was driven to go for a walk that night to see if this door really existed, and if so what it was like (very Georgian, as it turned out). Finding it not only added something to the experience of the book, but also transformed that particular corner of Soho with a slightly dreamlike sensation.

One way of thinking about this is through the idea of what has been called "transitional space", a term describing an area that is not only in the mind or wholly in the external world, but lies in an overlap between the two. This region which is neither totally subjective nor objective is part of why people want to see the *Mona Lisa*: not because it is beautiful but because they already have it in their heads, so the novelty of finally seeing the real thing brings inner and outer together with a feeling that can be almost uncanny (however banal it might sometimes be in practice). The idea of transitional space is also relevant to the fascination and strange sensation of being in film locations – finding a village pub that is in *The Avengers*, or a Dickensian alley in Fitzrovia that is in Michael Powell's *Peeping Tom* – and to the popularity of psychogeography, particularly in psychogeography's more 'cultural-historical' aspect and the long tradition of books such as E. Beresford Chancellor's 1933 *Literary Ghosts of London* (nothing supernatural).

Back in the world of reality, at least relatively, trailing Crowley into a bygone London is also a revealing exploration of social history. Bohemia, prostitution, restaurants, ordinary life during the Blitz and much more all come into focus through Crowley's reportage, as he prowls through the city in his role of the esoteric gentleman at large.

Just as it is hard to imagine Buddhism without the great accretion of Asian culture entwined with it, so Crowley is virtually inseparable from his 'English gentleman' aspect. And London, is, par excellence, this particular gent's terrain. Never quite as leisurely or disinterested as the Parisian-style flaneur, he traversed the city on a myriad personal missions, ultimately in service of the long spiritual quest he always dated from one night in Covent Garden in 1898. And as he wrote later, apologizing for not setting an account of his magical adventures in remote exotic Asia, "there are just as many miracles in London as in Luang Prabang."[6]

6   City in Laos famed for Buddhist temples.

I

TOMB OF BURTON, MORTLAKE:
The perfect pioneer

Sir Richard Burton, first of the "Three Immortal Memories" to whom Crowley's *Confessions* are dedicated, lies in the churchyard of St. Mary Magdalen in this curious tomb. It is an Arab tent in stone, with a ladder and a window to peer in at the two coffins – Sir Richard and his wife Lady Isabel – mouldering gloriously inside. Like Crowley, Burton was a great Victorian malcontent who incarnated the genius and stranger undercurrents of Victorian Britain even as he was transgressing against mainstream Victorian values.

Burton was an Orientalist, explorer, writer and anthropologist with an unfailing ability to shock his contemporaries. Asked by a vicar if it was true he had killed a man in the Arabian desert, he said "Sir, I am proud to say that I have committed every sin in the Decalogue".[1] When a doctor asked him roughly the same question – "How do you feel when you have killed a man?" – he replied "Quite jolly, what about you?"

Burton had a genius for languages, speaking about thirty, and a talent for deep disguise: along with pseudonyms such as Frank Baker he created whole identities such as Haji Abdu el-Yezdi and Sheikh Abdullah, a wandering Sufi dervish who practised medicine (so successfully that he built up a flourishing business as part of the disguise). It was as Sheikh Abdullah that he achieved his most celebrated feat, risking death to visit the forbidden city of Mecca and bring back detailed ethnographic reportage.

---

1   (i.e. the Ten Commandments). Disguised as a Muslim pilgrim, Burton was widely believed to have killed a young Arab who saw that he was an impostor in disguise.

Burton also investigated Mormonism in America, interviewing Brigham Young, and his miscellaneous travels range from South America to Iceland, but Africa was a more central interest. He searched unsuccessfully for the source of the Nile, but he did become the first European to see Lake Tanganyika (he "discovered" it, as we used to say) and survived a murderous attack by Somalis at two in the morning. Taking a javelin through the face, he lost four teeth and part of his palate but escaped and made it to the sea, where the spear was removed on board a friendly ship. He also attempted to suppress the slave trade in Dahomey.

Burton's early adventures – smoking opium, sleeping with local women, alligator-riding – are well within acceptable Victorian extremes, but he was felt to have trodden more dubious ground with his exploration of male brothels in Sind (now part of Pakistan). This was undertaken on Empire business, as part of a larger British attempt to stamp out wife-murdering, infanticide and paederasty in the region. Among many eyebrow-raising details, Burton reports of boys and eunuchs that the boys cost twice as much, because "the scrotum of the unmutilated boy could be used as a kind of bridle for directing the movement of the animal."

Burton's Eastern experiences fed into his unexpurgated adult edition of *The Book of the Thousand Nights and a Night* ("The Arabian Nights"), published in sixteen volumes (1885-1888). Burton's interest in sexuality led him to found the Kama Shastra Society, ostensibly (for legal reasons) a distant organisation in Benares, northern India, but in fact Burton and his friend Foster Fitzgerald Arbuthnot. They published the *Kama Sutra* (1883), and *The Perfumed Garden* (1886). At the time of his death he was working on a book called *The Scented Garden*: "I have put my whole life and all my life blood into that Scented Garden," he wrote, "...It is the crown of my life." He was a day from finishing it when he died, and his wife burned the thousand-page manuscript to protect public morality.

Burton wrote over forty books ("not one dull paragraph", says Crowley) and he was a friend of the poet Swinburne and of Bram Stoker. Stoker admired him immensely and used him – particularly his unusual canine teeth – as a model for the appearance of Count Dracula. For Edward Said, the opponent of Western 'Orientalism', Burton was a wicked imperialist villain,[2] but for Crowley he was "the perfect pioneer of spiritual and physical adventure".

---

2   A "totemic pantomime demon", even, to borrow the title of John Wallen's trenchant defence of Burton, 'Sir Richard Burton as Totemic Pantomime Demon in Postcolonial Theory', *International Journal of Applied Linguistics and English Literature*, Vol.6 no.4, July 2017.

2

THISTLE GROVE, KENSINGTON:
Disapproval of the universe in general

Crowley had a repressive Christian upbringing: his family were Plymouth Brethren, and his father was an evangelist who refused to buy railway shares because there were no trains in the Bible. Nevertheless Crowley admired him, and during his lifetime young Crowley's sense of their religion was less about sin and stifling morality and more about being a member of a vanguard spiritual elite. Along with his later revolt against Christianity, this was another lifelong legacy.

The Crowleys had lived happily enough in Redhill, Surrey, but in 1887, when Crowley was eleven, his father died and his world changed. His mother Emily took him to live with her brother Tom Bond Bishop in Drayton Gardens (formerly Thistle Grove), Kensington, off Old Brompton Road. She had lived there before her marriage in the Bishop family house – their mother's – at number 71, now numbered 20. It was in this new household that Crowley's loathing of Christianity really set in (along with his time at the hateful Plymouth Brethren boarding school of the Reverend Champney D'Arcy, in Cambridge). Bishop was another evangelist, founder of the Children's Scripture Union and the Children's Special Service Mission. "No more cruel fanatic, no meaner villain, ever walked this earth", says Crowley in his *Confessions*, and in an 'obituary' – published while Bishop was still alive – he writes "To the lachrymal glands of a crocodile he added the bowels of compassion of a cast-iron rhinoceros; with the meanness and cruelty of a eunuch he combined the calculating avarice of a Scotch Jew...". And on top of all that, Bishop had "a horror of what he called sin which was exaggerated almost to the point of insanity."

Built in the 1840s, Drayton Gardens is an attractive and classically Victorian street of terraced townhouses with Doric-columned portico front doors. But by the standards of 1880s London, Crowley considered it "nondescript... neither upper nor lower middle-class", and more than that "The dinginess of my uncle's household, the atmosphere of severe disapproval of the universe in general, and the utter absence of the spirit of life, combined to make me detest my mother's family." This was the mother who called him the Beast 666 when he was naughty.

Having earlier lived at 71 (20), by 1885 Bishop had moved to 43 (now 48). Crowley remembers the road as Thistle Grove,[1] and writes "The name has since been changed to Drayton Gardens, despite a petition enthusiastically supported by Bishop; the objection was that a public house in the neighbourhood was called the Drayton Arms." To the likes of Bishop, and Emily Crowley, the very idea of a public house would have meant a den of iniquity, and been 'common' with it. Happily it is still there, splendidly rebuilt in 1891, on the corner with Old Brompton Road.

+

When Tom Bishop moved to Streatham, Crowley's mother followed, and took him to number 7 Polworth Road, in what was then a distinctly unfashionable suburb. This was more *déclassé*, and Crowley – who fully shared the prejudice against suburbs – refers to it contemptuously as "London's most suburban 'subbub'"

---

1   It was already officially Drayton Gardens, since 1884, but the earlier name probably persisted for a while. The address has a confusing history because (as well as being totally renumbered in the 1890s, and renamed twice from Drayton Grove to Thistle Grove to Drayton Gardens) there is still a Thistle Grove, a much smaller thoroughfare just on the other side of Old Brompton Road, which was called Thistle Grove Lane until 1907.

3

ROYAL ARCADE, OLD BOND STREET: LEONARD SMITHERS
What all the others are afraid to touch

While still at school, Crowley had developed interests in chess and rock climbing; his talent for chess was precocious, and he devised a manoeuvre where the pawns attack the bishop.[1] The horrors of boarding school took their toll on him, and he took up climbing to build his fitness after being bullied; away from the world of school, it must have offered an intimation of transcendence.

In 1895 he went to Trinity College, Cambridge (studying chemistry, and playing chess for the university) and it was during this period that two new interests developed, in poetry and magic.

Crowley published his first volume of poetry, *Aceldama: A Place to Bury Strangers In* ("A Philosophical Poem by a Gentleman of the University of Cambridge") in 1898 with Leonard Smithers, the quintessential 1890s publisher, at 4 & 5 Royal Arcade, Bond Street. He had chosen the right man. "Publisher to the decadents", Smithers prided himself on publishing "what all the others are afraid to touch". He published Oscar Wilde and Aubrey Beardsley, and Wilde described him as a publisher of very limited editions: one for himself, one for the author, and one for the police.

When Wilde's 1895 arrest led to a general backlash against decadence, Beardsley was fired from *The Yellow Book* (the famous decadent journal published by John Lane), but he bounced back with a new journal, *The Savoy*, also published by Smithers; his original cover design featured a cherub urinating on *The Yellow Book*. Smithers had also known Richard Burton, and published an edition

1   He later realised he had unknowingly re-invented something called the Tarrasch Trap.

of his *Thousand and One Nights*. Smithers had a murky reputation for publishing erotica, and some of the stock was kept under the counter in Gladstone bags, so that it could be spirited away in the event of a police raid (the drill was to take it to a railway station and leave it in Left Luggage).

With all that in mind, Smithers was again just the right man to publish Crowley's second book, later in 1898 (this time under the pseudonym of Bishop): *White Stains: The Literary Remains of George Archibald Bishop, a Neuropath of the Second Empire*. A tour of the perversions, it was Crowley's response to Krafft-Ebing. Peter Fryer, an authority on erotica (and author of *Private Case – Public Scandal*, a study of pornography in the British Library) considered it the filthiest book in the English language. It was clandestinely printed by Smithers in Amsterdam, and many copies were destroyed by the British customs.

Crowley had liked Smithers (and presented him with a copy of *Aceldama*, inscribed in the Malory-style mediaevalism of the era "...from Aleister Crowley, hys fyrst booke")[2] but there was later a cooling off, and there is a vicious picture of him in Crowley's short story 'At The Fork of the Roads'. Crowley later described *Aceldama* as produced not by the famous Smithers but by an obscure "jobbing printer in the Brompton Road." This was the printer Smithers had used, Francis Edwin Murray, at 180 Brompton Road, a firm associated with gay material who sometimes traded as the "Middlesex Press", a pun of the time.

Crowley's love of finely and even talismanically produced books was lifelong. Smithers had employed the Chiswick Press as printers, and Crowley continued using them on and off from 1898 until 1944. Founded in 1789 and trading as Chiswick since 1811, they were one of the best printers in Britain. In Crowley's heyday they were in Took's Court, Holborn.

---

2   This 'olde' style was popular after Sir Thomas Malory's *Morte D'Arthur*, first printed in the fifteenth century but newly in vogue after the Aubrey Beardsley edition of 1894. Crowley went on to write his own tale after Malory, *Good Sir Palamedes* (1912), after the knight in Malory who follows "The Questing Beast".

Crowley liked to get special copies of his books bound by the fine bookbinder Zaehnsdorf who were at 144-146 Shaftesbury Avenue, including some books in his own library, and he later used the famous firm of Sangorski and Sutcliffe (whose bindings include a *Rubaiyat of Omar Khayyam* with over a thousand jewels; it sank with the Titanic). They had started in Bloomsbury but were at 1-5 Poland Street by the time he asked them to bind *The Book of Thoth* in 1944; he also recommended them to a disciple in the 1940s as a place to find vellum for talismans.

Smithers was by far the most distinguished of the publishers Crowley dealt with in a prolific writing career. He was a key player in the culture of the Nineties, and one of the figures in his circle was Herbert Pollitt, whom Crowley already knew from Cambridge. Pollitt was a noted female impersonator, performing as Diane de Rougy. He had a relationship with Crowley – Crowley even writes that he lived as Pollitt's wife for six months – and introduced him to the work of Beardsley, whom he knew, Whistler, Felicien de Rops and the decadent current of the period in general.

Their relationship foundered, seemingly because Pollitt ("the only person with whom I had ever enjoyed truly spiritual intercourse") failed to share Crowley's growing interest in mysticism. It ended unhappily on Bond Street in the autumn of 1898 (when at least one of them was quite likely going to or from Royal Arcade). Crowley says he simply failed to see Pollitt, but Pollitt thought he was deliberately 'cutting' him, "and our destinies drew apart." And that was the end; "It has been my lifelong regret, for a nobler and purer comradeship never existed on this earth."

4

WATKINS BOOKSHOP, CECIL COURT
Great Mysteries

Crowley's *Aceldama* is prefaced with a short prose fantasy.

> It was a windy night... when this philosophy was born in me. How
> the grave old Professor wondered at my ravings! I had called at
> his house, for he was a valued friend... and I felt strange thoughts
> and emotions... Ah! how I raved!... We passed together into the
> stormy night. I was on horseback, how I galloped round him in
> my phrenzy, till he became the prey of a real physical fear! How I
> shrieked out I know not what strange words! And the poor good
> old man tried all he could to calm me; he thought I was mad! The
> fool! I was in the death struggle with self: God and Satan fought
> for my soul those three long hours. God conquered – now I have
> only one doubt left – which of the twain was God?

Which indeed? While at Cambridge, Crowley developed an interest
in what could vulgarly be called Satanism ("The forces of good
were those which had constantly oppressed me. I saw them daily
destroying the happiness of my fellow-men. Since, therefore, it was
my business to explore the spiritual world, my first step must be to
get into personal communication with the devil..."). It was a revolt
against his Plymouth Brethren background, going deeper than the
fashionable diabolism of the time, and it led him to buy A.E. Waite's
newly published *Book of Black Magic and Pacts*. This had been
published in 1898 by George Redway, based in York Street, Covent
Garden, a publisher with an interest in the esoteric who employed
Arthur Machen as a cataloguer and compiler. It is a compendium of
old school magical grimoires, including the *Enchiridion* of Pope Leo,
The Key of Solomon, The Lesser Key of Solomon, The Sacred Magic of

Abramelin (skimmed over in three pages), the *Grimorium Verum* and the *Grimoire of Honorius*.

Ironically Arthur Edward Waite was a staunch Christian, albeit of an esoteric and mystical bent, and his main motive in putting the book together seems to have been to show what a dismal business it all is; these books of "foolish mysteries of old exploded doctrines... interesting assuredly, but only as curiosities of the past". But it caught Crowley's imagination, particularly when Waite hinted in the preface that there exist certain transcendent occult sanctuaries, run by mysterious initiates. He wrote to Waite, who wrote back encouraging him to read *The Cloud Upon the Sanctuary* by von Eckartshausen. This expounded the idea that behind the mundane Christian church, the outer church, is a secret inner church: a Secret Sanctuary of the spiritual elite that has existed since time immemorial. This idea fascinated Crowley.

Despite his somewhat prosaic day job – he was editor of *Horlicks' Magazine and Home Journal*, the malted milk publication – Waite was a genuine scholar of the esoteric, as well as a friend of Arthur Machen and a member of the Golden Dawn, but his later relations with Crowley were not cordial. Crowley ridiculed him as mediocre – "a pompous, ignorant and affected dipsomaniac from America... the most ponderously platitudinous and priggishly prosaic of pretentiously pompous pork butchers of the language" – and caricatured him as Arthwait in his novel *Moonchild*. But he later conceded "if it had not been for Waite, I doubt if, humanly speaking, I should ever have got in touch with the Great Order."

Waite and Eckartshausen led Crowley into magical reading, which led him to visit Watkins, London's oldest surviving occult bookshop, originally linked to the Theosophical Society and frequented by members of the Golden Dawn. It was founded in the early 1890s by John Watkins as a result of his association with Madame Blavatsky (he attended her Sunday afternoon tea-parties, and helped to see the first edition of *The Secret Doctrine* through the press). It was once at 26 Charing Cross Road (long since replaced by an Edwardian mansion block) but in 1901 it moved just around the corner into Cecil Court, where it has been ever since, and where Yeats was a regular visitor.

Writing in 1938, Waite himself describes Watkins's window as "emblazoned over, within and without, on the hither side and the further with Signs, Sigils and Talismans, telling of Great Mysteries", and in *The Long Trip: A Prehistory of Psychedelia*, Paul Devereux remembers Watkins in the occult revival of the late Sixties. He saw Mick Jagger (whose favourite bedside reading at the time was Richard Cavendish's 1967 bestseller *The Black Arts*) wearing a white suit and leaving the shop with "a stack of occult books."

The Cecil Court shop is the site of a characteristic Crowley magic story, related by John Symonds. When John Watkins challenged Crowley to show him some magic, Crowley told him to close his eyes and open them again, whereupon the shop's entire stock had vanished; in another blink, closed and opened, it was all back on the shelves.

Or so we're told.

5

DOUGLAS ROAD, CANONBURY: HOUSE OF OSCAR ECKENSTEIN
The quality of the phantasmal

Oscar Eckenstein is another dedicatee of Crowley's *Confessions*, the man "who trained me to follow the trail". Eckenstein (1859-1921) was a pioneering mountaineer and Crowley's mentor in climbing. He was also a Burton enthusiast – "Sir Richard Burton was my hero and Eckenstein his modern representative", writes Crowley – and he collected Burton books and documents, eventually donating them to the Royal Asiatic Society.

Formidably intelligent and equally fit, Eckenstein climbed around the world, but his strangest adventure took place while walking home to this family house in 29 Douglas Road, Canonbury, Islington.[1] There was "an immense amount in his life mysterious and extraordinary beyond anything I have ever known" and one of the mysteries was a series of murderous attacks, lasting several years, which led him to believe his assailants must be mistaking him for someone else.

One night, after beating off an attack in Soho or Fitzrovia, he took an unfamiliar route to shake off anyone trailing him, but somewhere around the Caledonian Road he realised two men were following. Dodging into an alleyway behind some houses, he let himself into a back garden, hoping to explain himself to the householder and be let out by the front door on to a different street.

---

1   Eckenstein lived at this address, which had been his parents' house, until he was in his thirties. In later life he lived with his sister at 34 Greencroft Gardens, South Hampstead. That he was going north-east to Douglas Road, from the Euston Road/King's Cross area towards Islington (or at least thinking of it, in what may be a very embroidered tale) is suggested by the mention of the Caledonian Road; Greencroft Gardens is north-west, over Regents's Park.

Inside the house was a beautiful woman in evening dress, who asked him to stay for supper. He noticed the quality of the pictures – some Monets, and some drawings or etchings by Whistler – and found a cold supper for two already laid out, with no servants visible. It was delightful, and as morning broke he left with the understanding that he would return that evening. Unfortunately he was delayed and didn't make it, but twenty-four hours later he was back at last, only to find the house dark, shut up, and "To Let". He knocked, but there was no answer. Returning with the letting agent, he found it was the right house, but emptied, with the wallpaper less faded where the bookcase and pictures had been. The agent assured him it had been vacant for three months, while the elderly owner was in France. Now obsessed, Eckenstein kept watch on the house. In a month or so two servants reappeared and told him that the owner would be back in the spring, but the woman he described made no sense to them. A while later he received an anonymous letter, which said in vague terms that there was no hope; it was impossible; but the memory would never fade. Eckenstein thought this must be from the woman.

And there the story ends. It is a dreamlike situation like something out of the *Arabian Nights*. As Crowley writes, it is

> almost as universal as the 'flying dream'. It possesses the quality of the phantasmal... an adventure which in some form or other happens to a very large number of men.

He dreams of it regularly, he says. He uses a similar idea in his own short story 'The Dream Circean', and remembers related instances in the once-famous 1883 novel *Called Back*, by Hugh Conway, and in Robert Louis Stevenson tales including 'John Nicholson', 'The Sire de Malétroit's Door', and 'A Lodging for the Night', as well as *Jekyll and Hyde*, adding "There are similar ideas in oriental and classical literature."

This oriental aspect struck Proust in Venice, wandering in a maze of alleys:

> Suddenly, at the end of one of these alleys... [a] vast and splendid campo of which, in this network of little streets, I should never have guessed the scale, or even found room for it, spread out before me surrounded by charming palaces silvery in the moonlight... it seemed to be deliberately concealed in a labyrinth of alleys, like those palaces in oriental tales whither mysterious agents convey by night a person who, brought back home before daybreak, can never find his way back to the magic dwelling which he ends by believing that he visited only in a dream.

The glimpse of a lost paradise is so archetypal we find variants of it in Coleridge's *Kubla Khan*, Keats's *Lamia*, De Quincey's story of his vanishing druggist on Oxford Street, and on into H.G. Wells's 'The Door in the Wall' (1907), Arthur Machen's 'N' (1935), and elsewhere.

Crowley relates the Eckenstein adventure to his own life, destiny, and "whole book" (his *Confessions*, in which he is telling the story), always looking for romance and hoping the incidents and apparent setbacks of life might prove to be the opening scene in some great drama. More than that, he connects it to the essence of spiritual and magical experience.

Discussing it with a magical comrade, they agreed it was not only "extraordinarily gripping" but that the whole scenario was "nodal" for the spirit of romance, i.e. that it showed the intersection of an "extraordinary number of vital threads or 'nerves' of romance." It was like a magical test or ordeal, which Eckenstein failed by not appreciating its miraculous character early enough and keeping his first appointment. "The main test is his realization that the incident is high Magick, that if he fail to grasp its importance, to understand that unless he return that night the way will shut for ever". But by failing to appreciate its full value "he had somehow missed the supreme chance of his life, as if the 'wrong house' were the gateway to another world, an inn, so to speak, on the outskirts of the City of God."

✦

On a less exalted note, Eckenstein encountered another topographical mystery when a friend asked him "Is it possible to reach Q from P (mentioning two places in London) without passing a public house?" After endless experiment, Eckenstein finally found such a route. "Good for you!" said the friend, "Here's something else. Can you get to the Horseshoe, Tottenham Court Road, from here without passing a public house?" (The Horseshoe was at number 267, next to the Dominion Theatre at the foot of the road). "I do not know how many pairs of alpine boots Eckenstein wore out on the problem, before asking his friend, 'Can it be done?'" A telegram said it could. More experimentation. Finally Eckenstein had to give up.

It's easy, said the friend. You don't pass them; you go in.

6

HOTEL CECIL AND THE STRAND:
Sky above Cecil

Crowley's magical education leaped ahead in the second half of 1898. Climbing in the alps with Eckenstein, he was in a beer hall one night when he fell into conversation with a man about alchemy, and it became clear the man knew more than he did. He introduced himself as Julian Baker, a chemist who lived in Basingstoke and had an interest in brewing (he went on to spend most his working life at the Stag Brewery, Pimlico). Influenced by Eckartshausen, Crowley was looking for the Sanctuary of Saints, and wondered if Baker could show him the way. Was Baker a 'Master'? No, he said, but he could introduce him to someone who was, back in London.

Crowley became sick, returning to London to convalesce. He took a room at the Hotel Cecil, an enormous building on the Strand at number 80, where he holed up to write drama and poetry while reading up on the occult.

In due course, in October 1898, Baker introduced him to the 'Master'. This man was George Cecil Jones, known as Cecil, another analytical chemist.[1] Jones had been brought up by his mother since his father, a bank accountant suffering from depression, had cut his throat at the bank one day when Jones was five. Jones and Baker were lifelong friends since their schooldays at City of London School, and Jones would go on to marry Baker's sister. Unknown to Crowley both men were members of the great Victorian magical society, The Order of the Golden Dawn.

Among the books that Jones recommended was *The Book of the Sacred Magic of Abramelin*, published earlier that year by Watkins.

---

1   i.e. they both worked in industry; they were not pharmacists.

Crowley had great respect for Jones, and later asked him that if he should die, then Jones was to embalm his body and entomb it in a secret place. Jones and Baker also taught him the basics of 'astral projection', which led to extraordinary visions. One night in November, in his room at the Hotel Cecil with Baker, Crowley saw a "Feminine Hermes on cubic stone of white light – intense auto-brilliance of this"; she gave them a caduceus, and then they were in a scene with a lakeside and water, until finally they returned, back down to the hotel: "I take B.'s hand and we sail through sky above Cecil."

The Hotel Cecil was a convenient if expensive base for writing and reading during this quiet but pivotal time in Crowley's life. It was the largest hotel in Europe, with 800 rooms (about three times larger than the nearby Savoy). Originally it stretched from the Strand down to the river – the riverside end was demolished to make way for Shell-Mex House – and the Strand frontage survives, now with shops in it. The grand entrance is still architecturally much as Crowley would have known it.

The Strand itself, now rather miscellaneous and characterless, was the great exciting thoroughfare of Victorian London (hence the title of the magazine *The Strand*, where Sherlock Holmes appeared; it had more theatres than any other street in London, and there was a popular Edwardian song, 'Let's All Go Down the Strand'). At night it was also associated with public drunkenness, which shocked foreign visitors, and with other deviant behaviour: there were notices in several pub windows (not intended humorously) saying "Beware of Sods", meaning sodomites. At number 417 was a decadent watering-hole, the oddly named Bun Shop, well-known to Smithers and the rest. Crowley was very familiar with the Strand – he describes an easy mountain climb by saying that even average climbers "could make as certain of strolling to the top as if it were the Strand" – and Crowley-related sites include the Savoy, Simpson's, the Tivoli Theatre, Dowie and Marshall bootmakers at 455, where he bought alpine and other boots (now a modern bank), Milliken and Lawley at 165, where he bought a skeleton, and unfortunately, the Royal Courts of Justice at number 60. As a man with romantic Jacobite leanings, he would also have known the statue of royal martyr Charles I, as celebrated in Lionel Johnson's poem 'By the statue of King Charles at Charing Cross' (this statue is the official centre of London, from where distances are measured).

In his novel *Moonchild* Crowley describes Charing Cross – the western end of the Strand and the train station – as the centre of London. London, he says, should have been painted by Goya: "The city is monstrous and misshapen; its mystery is not a brooding, but a conspiracy. And these truths are evident above all to one who recognizes that London's heart is Charing Cross."

7

FARRINGDON ROAD: MYTHIC ORIGINS
Found on a bookstall

Jones and Baker agreed Crowley was a sincere aspirant after the mysteries, and that it was time to introduce him to what Jones later described as a "club"; a place to socialise and meet one's friends. This club was The Order of the Golden Dawn; probably the most influential magical order there has ever been. Although it had a fairly large membership it managed to be a discreet, semi-secret society, and unlike Theosophy it looked to the Western hermetic tradition rather than the East, giving its members a grounding in astral projection, Kabbalah, tarot, alchemy, visualisation, and ceremonial magic. It was quasi-Masonic but unlike conventional Masonic orders it admitted women on equal terms, and its members included W.B. Yeats, Maud Gonne, Arthur Machen, tea heiress Annie Horniman, actress Florence Farr, Oscar Wilde's wife Constance, and the writer Algernon Blackwood.

It was founded in 1888 by three men with Masonic backgrounds and esoteric, Rosicrucian interests: London coroner Dr William Wynn Westcott, who lived at 396 Camden Road;[1] retired doctor Dr William Robert Woodman, who lived at 28 Greville Road, Maida Vale; and Samuel Liddell 'MacGregor' Mathers, who was effectively a professional occultist and relied on the support of patrons, notably Annie Horniman. He had lived in Great Percy Street, near King's Cross; and at Stent Lodge, Forest Hill, near the Horniman Museum (where W.B. Yeats visited him, as remembered in his 1901 essay 'Magic'); but by the time Crowley knew him he and his wife Moina were based in Paris.

---

1   Crowley calls it Hampden Road in *Moonchild*, where Westcott is Vesquit.

41

The Golden Dawn began with a manuscript, known as the Cipher Manuscript, that somehow came into the hands of Westcott in 1887; the best known version of the story says he got it from the Reverend A.F.A. Woodford, an elderly clergyman, who allegedly found it on the once legendary Farringdon Road pavement book market. This was a goldmine for old books and manuscripts, and hung on in very reduced form until 1994.[2]

More recent research suggests the Cipher Manuscript came to Westcott among the posthumous papers of Kenneth Mackenzie (1833-1886), an eminent Freemason, and that Mackenzie had written it himself (in which case the prime foundational site of the Golden Dawn might be considered Mackenzie's house out in Isleworth, the long-ago demolished 4 Wellington Villas on Wellington Road, now the A3603). Mackenzie was a man of considerable scholarship, whose works include a book on Burma and a well-respected encyclopaedia of Masonry (although his interests also included spiritualism and astrology: he had an astrological system for picking horse-race winners, and like Mathers he lived in near-poverty). He had met with the influential French occultist Eliphas Levi in Paris and, probably inspired by Levi, his magical pseudonym was Baphometus, after the alleged idol of the Templars.

The cipher was not difficult to read, and Westcott recognised that it was based on an artificial alphabet found in Johann Trithemius's *Polygraphiae*, first published in 1518. It contained skeletal rituals with a Masonic flavour for something called the Golden Dawn, so Westcott asked Mathers – who had a genius for such things – to flesh them out into workable rituals. They also invited Woodman to be the third chief, and in 1888 the three of them had the business up and running.

Westcott apparently found a further leaf of old paper in the manuscript, which mentioned a high-ranking German adept, a Fraulein Sprengel; members of her order took magical mottoes as

2   I can dimly remember it reduced to one man, the great George Jeffery, whose grandfather had been there back in the 1880s. Jeffery was admirably philosophical when he made the newspapers after selling a £42,000 book for £20.

their names, and Sprengel was Soror Sapiens Dominabitur Astris. There was even an address where she could be reached. Westcott wrote, and in due course received a series of letters from her secretary, a Frater In Utroque Fidelis, establishing the GD's heritage as the British branch of a long-established continental occult order. By June 1890 she had authorised a charter, establishing an Isis-Urania Temple No.3 of the Hermetic Order of the Golden Dawn – but then, sadly, a letter in different handwriting, from a Frater Ex Uno Disce Omnes, announced that she had died, so further enquiries were unfortunately impossible.

No one now believes this story, and on various grounds – bad German, for one – it is considered to be a hoax: a magnificently fertile hoax, almost certainly by Westcott himself, building on Mackenzie's manuscript. Nevertheless, it is the version of the story that Crowley himself knew and told ("a cipher manuscript was found on a bookstall by a Dr Woodman, a colleague in magical study of Dr W. Wynn Westcott"), giving the whole business a material origin, a solid bricks-and-mortar reference ("there is nothing dishonest about the Farringdon Road, except its inhabitants"). And so the Farringdon Road holds its place in the foundational myth of the Golden Dawn.

The Golden Dawn has been described as W.B. Yeats' "church and university", and much the same could be said of Crowley. Yeats also said that although some of the Golden Dawn material was "obvious and melodramatic", and in this it "resembled Masonic rituals", there was "much that I thought beautiful and profound." And Arthur Machen writes "it was a stumer – or stumed – to use a very old English word...3 Its originators must have had some knowledge of Freemasonry; but, so ingeniously was this occult fraud 'put upon the market' that, to the best of my belief, the flotation remains a mystery to this day. But what an entertaining mystery; and, after all, it did nobody any harm."

3   i.e. a forgery, or forged; the word stumer was also used for dud cheques well into the 1920s.

8

GREAT QUEEN STREET: THE GOLDEN DAWN
Enter the Secret Chiefs

Crowley took his impending initiation into the Golden Dawn very seriously; he asked Baker if anyone had died during the ritual. It came around on 18 November 1898, in Mark Masons' Hall, 64-65 Great Queen Street, Covent Garden.[1] The vast Masonic edifice that now stands there, dominating the street in its strangely inconspicuous way, only dates from 1927-33. The previous building that Crowley knew was completed in 1869: part of the façade survives together with the 'Tavern' portion, both now part of the Connaught Rooms, where the banqueting rooms from the 1869 building are now the Grand Hall.

Cowley was initiated as a Neophyte of the Isis-Urania Temple, taking the name Perdurabo ("I shall endure") but he found it an anticlimax. Having sworn the aspirant to Masonic-style secrecy, whereby the slightest breach of his oath would incur "a deadly and hostile current of will, set in motion by the Greatly Honoured Chiefs of the Second Order, by the which I should fall slain or paralysed, as if blasted by the lightning flash", they then entrusted him with the Hebrew alphabet, the names of the planets and their attribution to days of the week, and some very basic Kabbalah. This, he thought, was fourth-form schoolboy stuff.

Nor did the membership impress him: instead of the Sanctuary of Saints they were "an abject assemblage of nonentities... as vulgar

---

1   There has been confusion about where this was, since Mark Masons' Hall is not a building as such, but a Masonic use of a building. It is now at 86 St. James's Street, and shortly before that it was at 40 Upper Brook Street. In her 1938 memoirs, Maud Gonne seems to remember it in its Golden Dawn days on Euston Road; she may be thinking of Oakley Square.

and commonplace as any other set of average people." Crowley was not the first person to be struck by this: Maud Gonne, the beautiful and aristocratic Irish woman adored by Yeats, thought they were "the very essence of British middle-class dullness". Talking to Baker and Jones, they saw his point of view, but told him not to be too hasty. This was only the Outer Order, and he hadn't yet seen the Second Order.

The Golden Dawn was divided into eleven grades in three Orders. Members of the Outer Order were largely restricted to theory, and after Neophyte the grades went up through Zelator, Theoricus, Practicus, and Philosophus.

From Philosophus one could proceed to the Second Order. After the theory of the Outer Order, members of the more secretive Second Order were instructed in the actual practice of ceremonial and ritual magic, and Mathers named it the Ordo Rosae Rubeae et Aureae Crucis (the Order of the Rose of Ruby and Cross of Gold) or the R.R. et A.C. for short: this had three further grades, Adeptus Minor, Adeptus Major, and Adeptus Exemptus. Between 1894-96 the R.R. et A.C. Second Order met at 62 Oakley Square, a rather gloomy location north of Euston (not far from Westcott's house) and by the time of Crowley's initiation Second Order activities were held at 36 Blythe Road, Hammersmith.

The Second Order was ruled by three Adeptus Exemptus chiefs: Mathers, Westcott, and the non-existent Anna Sprengel. Above the Second Order, across the 'Abyss', were three further theoretical grades of Magister Templi, Magus, and Ipsissimus, but these were almost super-human beings. Ultimately the authority came from the Secret Chiefs, who existed largely on the astral plane and only interfered in human affairs occasionally, somewhat like the Hidden Masters of Theosophy.

9

BARROW ROAD, STREATHAM: LODGING OF ALLAN BENNETT
A mean, grim horror

One day in the spring of 1899, "at some ceremony or other" in Great Queen Street, Crowley became aware of what he felt was great spiritual and magical force emanating from another Golden Dawn member. This was Allan Bennett (Frater Iehi Aour: 'Let There Be Light'), a gaunt-looking man in his twenties with dark hair and striking eyes, who was held in awe by other Golden Dawn members – as a practical magician he was second only to Mathers, who had informally adopted him.

"Little Brother," he said to Crowley, "You have been meddling with the Goetia" (a magical grimoire).[1] Crowley claimed innocence, but Bennett wasn't convinced: "In that case," he said, "the Goetia has been meddling with you."

Next day Crowley sought Bennett out, and found him in south London at what he described as a squalid tenement ("a tiny tenement in Southwark or Lambeth – I forget which. It was a mean, grim horror"). The word tenement suggests slummy redbrick flats in several storeys, but it was a suburban house at 24 Barrow Road, Streatham, not so far from Crowley's own childhood house at Polworth Road. Bennett was lodging there with Charles Rosher (Frater Aequi Animo) and his wife Lily. Rosher – not to be confused with Charles Rosher the cinematographer and cameraman, who was his son – had travelled the world as an adventurer, "invented a patent

---

1 *The Goetia, or Lesser Key of Solomon* is a magical textbook for trafficking with demons, but the word Goetia is applied more generally to mean low magic and demonology, dealing and dabbling with low malignant forces, as opposed to the higher magic of theurgy or Theurgia.

water-closet and been court painter to the Sultan of Morocco", and he also wrote terrible poetry. "If his talents had been less varied," says Crowley, "he might have made a success of almost anything."

Crowley made Bennett an offer: if he would teach Crowley magic, he could come and lodge with him in Holborn.

10

CHANCERY LANE
Semi-solid shadows

When Crowley became serious about the Golden Dawn, he left the Hotel Cecil and took rooms at 67-69 Chancery Lane, within 'New Stone Buildings' towards the north western corner with High Holborn.

Crowley had fitted this flat out with two temples, one for white magic and one for black: the white magic room was lined with eight-foot mirrors, and the one for black magic – in a sort of cupboard – had "an altar supported by the figure of Negro standing on his hands... the presiding genius of this place was a human skeleton,[1] which I fed from time to time with blood, small birds and the like. The idea was to give it life, but I never got further than causing the bones to become covered with a viscous slime." (This was done "with the idea of creating a material and living demon servant".)

Bennett's words about the Goetia may have startled Crowley, because he had been dabbling with Goetia and more specifically with the magic of Abramelin (a system for contacting one's Holy Guardian Angel, from a manuscript Mathers had found in the Bibliothèque Nationale; Mathers's edition of the book had just been published by Watkins in 1898). As well as the HGA it involves subsidiary demons, and it has a bad reputation in magical circles. One night, says Crowley, he and Jones were working on magic and went out to eat: coming back, they saw a black cat on the stairs ("not a real cat, either") and opened the door to find the temple – or cupboard – door open and the altar upset. More than that, "Round and round the big library tramped the devils all the evening, an endless procession; 316

---

1   The presiding genius had been purchased for £5 (about £500 today) from the firm of Milliken and Lawley at 165 Strand.

of them we counted, described, named, and put down in a book. It was the most awesome and ghastly experience I had known."

Or in a variant account, "As we went out, we noticed semi-solid shadows on the stairs; the whole atmosphere was vibrating with the forces which we had been using. (We were trying to condense them into sensible images.) When we came back... the temple door was wide open, the furniture disarranged and some of the symbols flung about in the room. We restored order and then observed that semi-materialised beings were marching around the main room in almost unending procession." It is possible that Bennett knew what Crowley had been dabbling with not because evil was showing in his face, or aura, but because Jones had told him; they knew each other.

Bennett was another chemist (he worked for the firm of Dr Bernard Dyer, Analytical and Consulting Chemist, at 17 Great Tower Street EC3). Crowley got to know Bennett at Chancery Lane and found him to be one of the most remarkable men he had ever met. He had been brought up a Catholic by his mother, who had died slowly from ulcerated tuberculosis of the throat when Bennett was about ten, contributing to his horror of the flesh. Bennett later abandoned the occult for Buddhism, becoming an important early British Buddhist, but for now his passion was magic, and he taught it to Crowley, going through the invocation of gods, the evocation of spirits and demons, and the consecration of talismans. As Crowley puts it, at Chancery Lane "We made talismans that got on the job, and stayed on the job."

I I

STAFFORD STREET, MAYFAIR: LOWE'S CHEMIST
Exploring the pharmacopeia

Bennett was crucified by asthma, which had no remedy. Asthma cigarettes – or even normal cigarettes – were the nearest thing to relief, together with opiates to calm the breathing. Crowley remembers Bennett's regime:

> His cycle of life was to take opium for about a month, when the effect wore off, so that he had to inject morphine. After a month of this he had to switch to cocaine, which he took till he began to "see things" and was then reduced to chloroform. I have seen him in bed for a week, only recovering consciousness sufficiently to reach for the bottle and sponge.

Ether may also have figured. Bennett was interested in drugs not just for his health but for psycho-spiritual voyaging, visions, and what he called "clairvoyance", for which he used the herb dittany as an incense .

Bennett talked of wanting to find a Holy Grail of drugs, a drug that would "open the gates of the World behind the Veil of Matter", and Crowley refers to them both "exploring the pharmacopoeia for the means of grace." When they did this they followed what he later calls "The old Chancery Lane rule: begin with half the minimum dose of the Pharmacopeia, and if nothing happens within the expected time, double the dose. If you go on long enough, something is nearly sure to happen!"

Drugs were more freely available from chemists before the 1920 Dangerous Drugs Act, and Crowley's favourite was Lowe's at 8 Stafford Street, off Bond Street. He makes it sound almost like a salon: "My favourite rendezvous was a little chemist's shop in Stafford Street, managed by a man named E.P. Whineray, one of the most remarkable and fascinating men that I have ever met... He knew all the secrets of London... I used to haunt his shop and learned from him about London." These secrets ("People of all ranks, from the courtier and the cabinet minister, to the coachman and the courtesan, made him their father confessor") must have involved drug use and even drug addiction: "He understood human frailty in every detail and not only forgave it, but loved men for their weaknesses."

A Lancashire man with an owl-like appearance, Whineray commuted into Mayfair every day from Leyton, out on the other side of the East End. He had a serious interest in drugs, and published a pharmaceutical study of cannabis in Crowley's journal *The Equinox*. He was also well-known as a drug supplier. The English classical composer and occultist Peter Warlock[1] wrote a peculiar rhyme about him:

> There was an old sister of Binnary
> Who came to a chemist in thin array
> Just like Monna Vanna.[2] This
> Great punk wanted cannabis
> And said: 'O my dear Mr. Whinneray
> Give me some, and I'll pour all my gin away.
> What more can a sodden old sinner say?'
> But he said: 'For a tanner, miss,
> I'll sell you a can o' piss –
> Nothing else – though the chemist at Pinner may.'
> 'But I need a stiff swig to begin a day –
> Can't you get one some coke before dinner, eh?'
> 'No', he said, 'These vile practices
> Are the death of young actresses'[3] –
> So she walked with a grisly grim grin away.

---

1   Real name Philip Heseltine (1894-1930); father of the art critic Brian Sewell, he killed himself, allegedly after dabbling with Abramelin magic.

2   A striking Pre-Raphaelite portrait of a woman, by D.G. Rossetti.

3   An allusion to the Billie Carleton case; aged 22, she was found dead in the Savoy after what was reported as a cocaine overdose.

Lowe's was firmly embedded in Crowley's mental London (as such places tend to be: a friend of mine once obtained a 'legal grey area' product regularly from a particular health food shop, and whenever he thought of it the whole street seemed to have a warm sepia glow). While in Italy in 1920, he dreamed of it: "I have had a long 'wish-fulfilment' (no doubt) dream of being in Whineray's shop in London, and getting large quantities of cocaine from him."

In the winter of 1924 Crowley was becoming very anxious about his heroin supply and asked a disciple to get in touch with the ever-understanding Whineray; Crowley knew he had retired, but thought Lowe would have his home address. Whether Whineray would have helped or not (he'd had some trouble with the police in the meantime) we shall never know; it turned out that he had just recently died, that September.

Whineray was also sympathetic to magicians, and when he reviewed a book called *The Chronicles of Pharmacy*[4] he noted "To the student of the occult it ought to appeal strongly, as the author gives a long list of drugs used in religious ceremonies in different ages...". As well as drugs, Whineray supplied Crowley with ingredients for magical preparations "such as *kyfi*, the mysterious incense of the ancient Egyptians; the perfume and oil of Abramelin, the *unguentum Sabbati*, and the like. In particular," (says Crowley in his *Confessions*) "he was at one time able to supply *onycha*". Mentioned in the Book of Exodus, this was an incense material so rare and obscure there has been uncertainty as to what it was: it is believed to be derived from the shell of a particular mollusc.

In 1926 Crowley delegated his young disciple Tom Driberg to buy some items from Lowe's only to find the shop had moved and things were not what they were: they had become incorporated into Blake Sandford and Blake, round the corner at 49 Dover Street. Crowley wanted lignum aloes, the exquisitely scented agarwood, but unfortunately Driberg allowed himself to be fobbed off with the wrong thing, and wrote a grovelling letter of apology.

4   A.C. Wootton, *The Chronicles of Pharmacy* (Macmillan, 1910). Review in *The Equinox*, Vol. No.6, Autumn 1911.

Dear Sir Aleister... it really is good of you to bother about anyone as ignorant and disappointing as myself... they gave me "black" aloes, and said it was exactly the same...

It is extraordinary to think he ended up as Chairman of the Labour Party.

12

BLYTHE ROAD, HAMMERSMITH
The battle

The Golden Dawn was already feuding when Crowley joined. Woodman had died, and Westcott had been embarrassed by a revelation of his occult activities clashing with his respectable day job as a coroner: as Crowley put it, his employers felt he should be investigating corpses and not raising them. He might also have felt the strain of keeping up the tale of Fraulein Sprengel, and the gloriously fake account of the Order he had written in his 'History Lecture for Neophytes'. This left Mathers as the unrivalled leading light.

Mathers had been briefly employed, through Annie Horniman, as a curator at her father's Horniman collection in Forest Hill (now the Horniman Museum), until he had a personality clash with Horniman senior. Since then he had been discreetly financed by Annie, who was in love with his wife Moina and subsidised them both in Paris. Annie was frustrated by Mathers's Jacobite and military fantasies distracting him from occult work and, after he rebuked her for 'undermining' his authority, she stopped supporting him. Mathers grew increasingly autocratic in response, and claimed contact with the Secret Chiefs of the Third Order ("I believe them to be human and living upon this earth; but possessing superhuman powers"). They had appeared to him in the Bois de Boulogne, he said.

The Golden Dawn was being largely held together by Florence Farr, an eminent actress and close friend of George Bernard Shaw who was also a serious occultist (with Allan Bennett she had evoked Taphthartharath, the spirit of the planet Mercury, to what they felt was visible appearance). Finally she grew tired of Mathers, and in February 1900 she suggested it was time to close the GD down. Mathers then torpedoed the London branch by revealing he had known all along that the Sprengel letters were fake, causing even more embarrassment. And as Crowley wrote at the time, if there was no authority from Sprengel then "there is no Second Order and no Golden Dawn and no nuffin'."

Things grew worse when Crowley, who had progressed through the grades of the Outer Order, expected admission to the Second Order (which was "by invitation"). The London members, notably Farr and W.B. Yeats, felt he was too unstable and delinquent; Yeats said the GD wasn't meant to be "a reformatory" (the idea of a reformatory – rather than, say, a lunatic asylum – was probably a dig at Crowley's relative youth; he was still not 25). So Crowley went to Paris and received his second order initiation directly from Mathers.

Crowley and Yeats disliked each other, and Crowley's grudge went back to the night in the spring of 1899 when he had called on Yeats at his lodgings – at 5 Woburn Walk, WC1, then known as 18 Woburn Buildings – with his play *Jephthah*, expecting praise and recognition. Yeats was polite but clearly not very interested, and Crowley saw this as concealing a "black, bilious rage" of jealousy at his own superior genius. He went on to caricature Yeats, a "lank, dishevelled demonologist", as 'Gates' in *Moonchild*.

Things came to a head in April 1900 with the Battle of Blythe Road, when Crowley returned from Paris as Envoy Plenipotentiary of Mathers and attempted to take possession of the Second Order's Vault at number 36, in a quiet backwater opposite what was then Hammersmith post office. The vault was in a room above a shop frontage (then the offices of a builder, now George's Cafe). On the 17 April Crowley persuaded the landlord to let him in, changed the locks, and also admitted himself to the Temple's Second Order by signing the roll and back-dating it to 23 January.

The Farr-Yeats faction then persuaded the landlord to change the locks back (Farr was the official tenant), and on 19 April there was a second showdown. Having recruited a pub bouncer from outside the Alhambra Theatre in Leicester Square, Crowley turned up at about 11.30 in a kilt, with a highland dagger, a large gold cross on his chest, and a black mask. Meanwhile the bouncer had got lost and failed to find Blythe Road, leaving him to be confronted by Yeats and Edmund Hunter (Frater Hora et Semper), an amateur boxer. The landlord then called the police, who told Crowley to leave.

The Battle of Blythe Road was over. Mathers and Crowley had lost. The London members now expelled them, and Yeats became Imperator of the Isis-Urania Temple. "In 1900," Crowley wrote later, "the Order in its existing form came to grief, and nobody has ever been able to pick up the pieces." The glory days of the Golden Dawn were over.

13

RANDOLPH ROAD, MAIDA VALE: HOUSE OF ELAINE SIMPSON
Magical feuding

While all this was going on Crowley was staying on and off at number 15 Randolph Road, Maida Vale, the home of his then partner Elaine Simpson (Soror Donorum Dei Dispensatio Fidelis, or Fidelis for short). The Chancery Lane menage with Allan Bennett had broken up. Bennett was moving from magic to yoga and Buddhism, and in 1900 he left for Ceylon. Crowley, meanwhile, chose to devote himself to Abramelin magic and the "knowledge and conversation" of his Holy Guardian Angel.[1] This led him to purchase a house by Loch Ness, Boleskine, as a suitable base for the operation.

Crowley had moved back to the Hotel Cecil after Chancery Lane, and also stayed at the Paddington Hotel immediately after his return from Mathers in Paris. There, according to Crowley, Mathers had been baptising dried peas with the names of the Golden Dawn rebels and then shaking them about in a sieve to cause discord and confusion in the enemy ranks.

Soror Fidelis lived at the Randolph Road apartment with her sister and her mother Alice Simpson (Soror Perseverantia et Cura

---

1 Crowley's definitions of the Holy Guardian Angel – an important part of the Golden Dawn system – varied over time and according to whom he was talking. To a disciple named Frank Bennett (a man who worked with his hands, as Crowley calls him, who suffered from pains in the head and 'voices' after a morally repressed upbringing) he explained it was the Real Self as unrepressed "subconscious" mind, throwing Bennett into ecstasies of cathartic relief. Writing to a woman named Ann Macky two decades later, he insisted it was a real separate entity. Across his writing it is variously the unconscious mind, a higher self, "mine inmost self", the incarnation of the True Will, and an entity resembling the Greek *daimon* or Golden Dawn *genius*.

Quies). Her future brother-in-law, Georg Witkowski, described the set-up there as "somewhat Bohemian; most peculiar was a large empty room painted with magical circles, squares and triangles."

Alice Simpson didn't like Crowley, and she spread rumours that he was entering her daughter's room at night in his astral body. The house – and life in general – was also affected by the results of magical feuding: horses bolted, cab lamps caught fire, the fires at Randolph Road refused to light, and a mackintosh burst into flames. Crowley blamed this on the occult machinations of Yeats.

14

GOWER STREET: THE HOROS AFFAIR
Any sin would be an act of piety

There was a postscript to the final Golden Dawn debacle with a couple of chancers named Theo and Laura Horos, an American couple who ran a short-lived, shady cult at 99 Gower Street. They mixed a smattering of occultism, picked up from their Golden Dawn contacts, with a further emphasis on sexual magic. Mrs Horos was a woman of about sixty who also went by the names of Swami Vive Ananda and Marie of the Commune (the 1870 Paris Commune), but under a pile of aliases her earliest name seems to have been Ann or Editha Salomon. Mr Horos was about thirty years younger and may have been an unfrocked priest; his real name seems to have been Frank Dutton Jackson.

Their most impressive fraud was perpetrated on Mathers, when they stayed with him in Paris and infiltrated his magical group; he believed them to be initiates of a previously unknown Golden Dawn temple in America, and Madame Horos managed to convince him that she was, in fact, the missing Fraulein Sprengel (which is to say Sprengel spoke through her; Mathers told Yeats she was "the most powerful medium living"). He was also impressed by the way she seemed to have knowledge of a conversation he'd had with the late Madame Blavatsky, when he had visited Blavatsky in Denmark Hill, suggesting Blavatsky could also speak through her. But gradually he became suspicious, not least of Madame Horos's claim that she was the illegitimate daughter of Lola Montez (a dancer and international courtesan who had been the mistress of Ludwig I of Bavaria) and Pope Pius IX.

Crowley was very aware of the Horos case, and his particular take on them was that they were "vampires" (by which he meant that they practised oral sex, supposedly taking energy from the recipient, or 'victim').[1] In a more prosaic form of vampirism the Horoses sponged hospitality and money from Mathers – who had hoped they might be moving money in the other direction, towards him – along with ritual documents which helped their later career.

In September 1901 the Horoses were arrested and appeared in Marylebone Police Court as Frank and Edith Jackson, charged with fraud, theft, and procuring young women for immoral purposes. They had been running a cult called The Order of Theocratic Unity at 99 Gower Street, and victims Vera Croysdale, Olga Rowson and Daisy Adams, a sixteen-year-old whom Frank Jackson was accused of raping, had come forward. Vera Croysdale remembered Frank had told her he was Christ, and that any sin with him would be an act of piety. She had also undergone an impressive initiation ritual beginning "I, Vera Croysdale, in the presence of the Lord of the Universe and in the Hall of the Neophytes in the Order of the Golden Dawn..."

It transpired that girls were being hypnotised, drugged, and given whisky for breakfast. This was the first that the great newspaper-reading public had heard of the already disintegrating Golden Dawn, and it did the Order's reputation no favours. Suddenly it, or its Horos version, was even being celebrated in comic songs ("Way down upon the Swami River..."). The public galleries at the trial were packed, and the Horoses provided rich entertainment by conducting their own defence; at one stage Mr Horos turned to the gallery and shouted "Keep quiet, you reptiles!". The trial moved to the Old Bailey, where Mrs Horos – the prime mover – received seven years and her unfortunate husband fifteen.

1   Discussed as "a method of vampirism" in *De Arte Magica* [1914], section XVIII, 'Of a certain other method of Magick [...]' where Crowley notes "The practice was held to be dangerous. (It was used by the late Oscar Wilde, and by Mr. and Mrs. 'Horos'; also in a modified and marred form by S.L. Mathers and his wife, and by E.W. Berridge. The ineptitude of the three latter saved them from the fate of the three former.)"

15

CAFÉ ROYAL, REGENT STREET
Pagan and painted

Crowley was a life-long habitué of the Café Royal at the Piccadilly Circus end of Regent Street towards the Soho corner at number 68 (now only a hotel), just a few doors along from Oddenino's – another familiar haunt – at 60-62, the grander building on the circus itself with pillars and Roman-style rustication. Crowley started going to the Café Royal around 1897 and continued right through to the 1940s. Modelled on the great Paris cafes of the mid-nineteenth century Second Empire, with the Napoleonic 'N' still featuring on its façade, it was the enduring centre of 1890s culture in London, frequented by Oscar Wilde, Beardsley, and Smithers, along with painters Walter Sickert, Gerald Kelly and Augustus John.

It was also well known to the writer and caricaturist Max Beerbohm, the great chronicler of the era, who makes his quintessential Nineties character Enoch Soames thoroughly at home there, "in that exuberant vista of gilding and crimson velvet set amidst all those upholding mirrors and upholding caryatids, with fumes of tobacco ever rising to the pagan and painted ceiling." The author of two volumes of verse entitled *Negations* and *Fungoids*, Soames is also a devil-worshipper (or thereabouts: "It's not exactly worship... It's more a matter of trusting and encouraging") and as he drinks his absinthe he explains to Beerbohm that here is no such thing as good and bad: "Of course in Art there is the good and the evil. But in Life – no"; "In Life, there are illusions of evil, but..." (and his voice trails away to a murmur).

Crowley felt so at home in the Café Royal that he put adverts for it in his occult journal *The Equinox* – probably unpaid and unsolicited – announcing "EPICURES are invited to taste the special dishes invented by ALEISTER CROWLEY. This can be done at the CAFÉ ROYAL, REGENT STREET, W. Pivots d'Amour Cro-Cro, Pilaff de Moules a la Santa Chiara, Crowley Mixed Grill, Soufflé Aleister Crowley etc etc.",

The Café had a more Modernist revamp at the end of the 1920s and continued to be popular with later figures such as Wyndham Lewis. The model Betty May contrasts this smarter and grander Café Royal with the earlier one, which had garish gilt, sawdust on the floor, and marble-top tables (which in those days meant hardwearing cheapness; pie and mash shops also had them).

Crowley had been outraged by the French authorities putting a butterfly-shaped piece of metal over the genitals of Jacob Epstein's new sculpture for Oscar Wilde's grave in Père Lachaise cemetery, so after a guerrilla unveiling of the statue, pulling the tarpaulin off before a crowd of about twenty people recruited from the Left Bank, he hacked it off and then strode into the Café Royal one night wearing it like a codpiece. In Crowley's own telling of the story, Epstein himself was in the Café and appreciated the gesture (Epstein's own telling of the story is less enthusiastic, but confirms it really happened).

On another occasion Crowley is alleged to have entertained a party of guests royally, excused himself from the table to go the gents, and absconded down Regent Street in a taxi, dodging the bill. A no less characteristic and at least semi-apocryphal Crowley story has him practising invisibility – one of the powers in Abramelin – at the Café Royal. He was parading about between tables in full regalia (or in one version wearing a conical hat with stars on it), not catching anyone's eye, when a non-regular asked a waiter what was going on. "Don't worry," said the waiter: "That's just Mr. Crowley being invisible."

16

ST. MARY'S TERRACE, PADDINGTON: LIFE WITH ROSE
Obvious from the style

The few years after the Blythe Road confrontation were the most extraordinary of Crowley's life, spent largely abroad and burning through an inheritance. After visiting Mathers again in Paris, he then went to Mexico via New York, and his Victorian-Edwardian travels include Ceylon, Burma, India, Vietnam, Hong Kong (where he visited Elaine Simpson, now married, and found her using her Golden Dawn robes in a fancy dress contest), China, Japan, and Tangier. With Eckenstein he climbed Popocatepetl volcano in Mexico, where he rejoiced over the death of Queen Victoria, and he made two unsuccessful attempts on the Himalayan mountain Kanchenjunga, the second badly mishandled with four deaths and the ruin of his reputation in mountaineering circles.

He studied yoga, meditation and Buddhism with Allan Bennett, and magically he practised Abramelin magic, Enochian magic (after Dr John Dee's late renaissance attempts to communicate with angels in their own language), and published an edition of Mathers's manuscript of *The Goetia*.

In Scotland he met Rose Kelly, the unstable sister of his friend Sir Gerald Kelly the painter, and married her. While honeymooning in Cairo, travelling as Prince and Princess Chioia Khan (with Rose also known as Ouarda the Seer) he made contact with an entity named Aiwass, who dictated the text that became known as *The Book of The Law*, a Nietzschean screed that trampled on other religions in general and Christian values in particular ("With my Hawk's head I peck at the eyes of Jesus as he hangs upon the cross"; "I flap my wings in the face of Mohammed and blind him"; "...I spit on your crapulous creeds.") Crowley always insisted that he hadn't written it himself, taking dictation from a voice that seemed to be coming from behind his left shoulder while he wrote; it wasn't an 'inspired' or 'automatic' writing, coming from his unconscious, but the work of an external entity, a disembodied intelligence he variously identified with his Holy Guardian Angel, with Set, an Egyptian adversarial 'bad' god prefiguring Satan, and even straightforwardly with Satan himself. The 1904 revelations also involved a long-dead Egyptian priest, Ankh-f-n-Khonsu (whose stele – a painted plaque – was catalogued as item 666 in Cairo Museum), and whose reincarnation Crowley came to believe he was ("in the 26th Dynasty... I was Ankh-f-n-khonsu and brought about the Aeon of Osiris to replace that of Isis".)

The Book of the Law became the foundation of Crowley's new religion, and he considered it the greatest event of his life. It combines the style of *fin-de-siècle* decadence – "To worship me take wine and strange drugs whereof I will tell my prophet, & be drunk thereof!" – with a belief that might is right, and the joy of strength: "The kings of the earth shall be Kings forever: the slaves shall serve"; "We have nothing with the outcast and the unfit: let them die in their misery. For they feel not. Compassion is the vice of kings: stamp down the wretched and the weak: this is the law of the strong: this is our law and the joy of the world." It embodies the essence that British writer Cyril Connolly crystallised when he wrote that Crowley "bridges the gap between Wilde and Hitler."

Crowley and Rose had a daughter born at Boleskine, Nuit Ma Ahathoor Hecate Sappho Jezebel Lilith Crowley (Lilith for short), and continued to travel, but while journeying back through China alone – he'd sent Rose home separately with the infant – Crowley felt he didn't love them, and that they were a distraction from his destiny. Reaching Liverpool, he found that the baby had meanwhile died in Rangoon; Crowley's friend and early bibliographer Louis Duncombe-Jewell said the unfortunate child must have succumbed to "acute nomenclature".

Crowley and Rose were unhappy, but in October 1906 they moved to 106 St. Mary's Mansions, an upmarket Victorian mansion block in St. Mary's Terrace, Paddington, and in December Rose had another daughter, Lola Zaza Crowley. Crowley loved Rose in his fashion and wrote pornographic poetry to amuse her, but their marriage was tense. He was unfaithful (Lola seems to have been named after his mistress);[1] by his own account he kicked his mother-in-law downstairs and threw her out when she visited them here; and he continued to experiment alone with hashish and tincture of peyote (with characteristic introspection he was able to relate his mescaline colour visions to having earlier looked at an opal matrix in a jeweller's window on New Bond Street, possibly Hunt and Roskell at 156). He also continued his deferential magical association with George Cecil Jones, asking permission to take a vow of silence and being instructed more specifically to cut his arm with a razor whenever he unthinkingly answered a question. Rose thought this was ridiculous and hated it.

Rose was unhappy and drinking heavily – leading to a spell in a Leicestershire sanatorium for alcoholics – and on the weekend of 23-24 March 1907 Crowley moved out. While living there he also wrote the 'Proem' to his play *The World's Tragedy* (the tragedy is Christianity), leading to his inscrutable reference to it a couple of years later as something "which was written long ago when I lived, as will be obvious from the style, in Paddington."

---

1   Actress and beauty Vera Snepp, known in her later career as Vera Neville; Crowley called her Lola, and her name is entwined in his poetry around this time.

17

WARWICK ROAD, WEST KENSINGTON
Pure prestidigitation

After a brief spell in Chancery Lane, Crowley moved alone to rooms on the fourth floor of 60 Jermyn Street, a good address associated with restaurants and gentlemen's retailing – shirtmakers, shoemakers, scent, barbering – just south of Piccadilly and on the edge of clubland. Number 60 itself has a quietly magnificent doorway. He would have a life-long association with Jermyn Street, handy for Piccadilly, Regent St, Bond St, Whineray, and the Café Royal; there were also Turkish baths at number 76, and he later used the Savoy Turkish Baths at number 92 (opened 1910). He would return to Jermyn Street in 1942 for his last London address.

Crowley went to Tangier in 1907 with his student the Earl of Tankerville (a paranoid cocaine user or 'coke fiend' whom he'd met at Whineray's: Crowley calls him "the Earl of Coke and Crankum") and on his return he found Rose's bill for 150 bottles of whisky in five months. Rose's unhappiness was made worse by knowledge of Crowley's infidelities, including the birth of an illegitimate son with a girl he had met in Soho named Jenny Zwee, who worked as a milliner in Burlington Arcade.

Nevertheless from February 1908 they made one last attempt to live together again at 21 Warwick Road, West Kensington. Crowley's library-study was in the ground floor room at the front, overlooking the main road, with the dining room and kitchen in the basement, and Crowley recounts his surprise at the speed and stealth with which Rose could nip downstairs and surreptitiously throw back a glass of whisky: "It was an act of prestidigitation and nothing else."

By June he was writing to her doctor, a W. Murray Leslie of 74 Cadogan Place, that life with Rose is intolerable while she locks me out of the house, insults her own guests at my table, uses foul language to servants, reels up Bond Street charging into passers-by, goes from crisis to crisis of hysteria, tells people wild and impossible lies about me etc etc etc ad nauseam... Rose is subject to insane delusions. I will not live in a house alone with her and a drunken ex-Piccadilly prostitute (called a servant, God knows why...)

This same servant would later testify in court that Crowley hit Rose, and entertained a short, dark, heavily jewelled woman overnight while Rose was absent, and in 1909 they divorced.

18

VICTORIA STREET: CROWLEY'S FLAT, & TEMPLE OF THE ASTRUM ARGENTEUM
The most sinister atmosphere

Crowley continued his magical work with George Cecil Jones, and while staying with him in Surrey achieved the crowning of the Abramelin system, contact with his Holy Guardian Angel. Jones now insisted that Crowley, having ascended the Outer Order in the Great Queen Street days, and then been initiated into the Second Order by Mathers in Paris (and ascended through that to his own satisfaction), had now jumped from the Second Order – becoming a "Babe of the Abyss" and crossing it – to the mysterious Third Order. He was now a Magister Templi, a Master of the Temple, required to put all worldly things behind him including his dead child, and vowing to interpret everything that happened to him as the direct dealing of god with his soul.

A further responsibility of a Magister Templi was to found a temple, and this was what Jones was inspiring Crowley to do, but they needed a third man. This was Captain – later to be Major-General – J.F.C. Fuller, an admirer of Crowley's writing. Crowley had offered a £100 prize for the best essay on his work, which Fuller had won (he was the only entrant). Crowley then managed not to produce the prize money, but Fuller's admiration was undimmed, and the two men had met (with Rose) at the Hotel Cecil. Fuller was a steely intellect and a visionary of warfare, particularly tank combat and *blitzkrieg* tactics. He would attend German manoeuvres as a guest in 1935, and was one of only two Englishmen invited to Hitler's fiftieth birthday celebrations in 1939. Meanwhile he wrote books on yoga and the Kabbalah.

Fuller lived at 80 Overstrand Mansions, Prince of Wales Drive, Battersea, and after they fell out Crowley lampooned him as "The

Bismarck of Battersea" (where after "abyss after abyss" of Hell, we reach "The ledge labelled 'Battersea', supreme word of malignity in the tongue of the pit"). But for now he was the great Crowley enthusiast, publishing his prize essay as *The Star in the West* (1907) and coining the word "Crowleyanity" for the new religion he hoped would supplant Christianity. This was the man Jones and Crowley needed: the three of them became the founding members of a new magical order, the discreetly named A∴A∴ (generally thought to mean the Argenteum Astrum or Silver Star).

Compared to the Golden Dawn's mixture of artistic talent and Masonic-mystical burghers, the A∴A∴ was less high-minded: esoteric historian R.A. Gilbert describes the A∴A∴ members as "self-centred moral pygmies", and overall they were less distinguished. Along with just a couple of higher-powered magical members, notably Fuller and Charles Stansfeld Jones, members included novelist Ethel Archer, salonist Gwen Otter, poet Victor Neuburg, psychic researcher Everard Feilding, model Nina Hamnett, and the palmist Cheiro.

Crowley had a short spell living in Coram Street, Holborn, but in the early days of the A∴A∴ he took a flat, five flights up at 124 Victoria Street, which also served as the A∴A∴ temple. It was next door to the Victoria Palace Theatre (on the theatre's left; or on the right, if you're looking from the road) and only demolished recently.[1]

A∴A∴ members would dance around an altar in the flat, which Gwen Otter described as having "the most sinister atmosphere I have ever known". One night, as Crowley tells it, there was dancing with the room dimly lit and heavy with incense, when several participants felt an extra person was present; "there was one too many." The spell was broken when someone grabbed for the light: "No stranger was to be seen... We all agreed about the appearance of the visitor. We had all been impressed with the same feeling that he did not belong to the human species." In the best traditions of occult fiction, the identity of this visitor is not spelled out.

---

1   I remember its final days, with a charity shop and then a betting shop in the ground floor; in Crowley's time it housed a branch of Lyons Cafes.

There is a fictionalised description of Victoria Street in Ethel Archer's 1932 novel *The Hieroglyph*, based on Crowley as she'd known him around 1910: "A room, she reflected, betrays the character of its owner and occupant, and this was far from being a common one... the semi-ecclesiastical austerity side by side with evidences of strange perversity and barbarity." The bare floor is painted black, with a leopard skin rug before the fireplace. A large stuffed crocodile grins from the corner of the room. From the ceiling hangs a "wonderful silver lamp or censer" and above the mantelpiece is a Byzantine crucifix, while on the mantelpiece itself are several images of Buddha, together with Chinese and Egyptian gods. On the wall is a scarlet silk hanging embroidered with gold letters, "the spoil of a Tibetan temple." On the bookshelves are first editions of Verlaine, Baudelaire, Swinburne, and Wilde, with some Rodin busts on top of the bookcases, and on the wall beside the fireplace are "drawings by Beardsley and Osman Spare."

19

HENRIETTA STREET, COVENT GARDEN: NORTHAM'S ROBE MAKERS
Fitted for the infernal rites

Members of the Argenteum Astrum needed ceremonial robes, which could be obtained from the firm of W. Northam at 9 Henrietta Street. These were available in different ranks, from Probationer at five pounds and Neophyte at six pounds, through to Magister Templi at fifty pounds (around £5000 today; so even the Neophyte robe would be around £600).

Northam's advertisement was clearly written by Crowley himself, with mysteries of which Northam's knew nothing. The Dominus Liminis robe, for example, was "fitted for the infernal rites of Sol, which must never be celebrated"; "The Babe of the Abyss has no robe"; and the Magister Templi robe was fitted for "the supernal rites of Luna, and for those rites of Babylon and the Graal. But this robe should be worn by no man, because of that which is written, '*Ecclesia abhorret a sanguine.*'"

The overall look was a cloak with a hood, in red. One was sold at Sotheby's in 1996,[1] and illustrated in the catalogue: it is red, with a Rosicrucian cross embroidered in gold and coloured thread on the chest and the Eye of Osiris in a starry triangle on the hood. More can be seen in Crowley's painting *Four Red Monks Carrying a Black Goat Across the Snows to Nowhere*.

Jean La Fontaine, in her debunking of the 1990s 'Satanic abuse' scares, *Speak of the Devil: Tales of Satanic Abuse in Contemporary England*, makes the point that hooded robe outfits are now associated

---

1   Sotheby's, London, *English Literature and History*, 16-17 December 1996, lot 342. This particular one was taken by Crowley's lawyer when he was unable to pay a legal bill, and survived a stint in a children's dressing-up box.

in popular culture with the Black Mass: "This is the garb of devil worshippers, as described in horror stories by Dennis Wheatley..."

This is largely true, and it is no disrespect to La Fontaine's sound and important study to acknowledge that although such spurious "Dennis Wheatley outfits" are overwhelmingly fictional, they have existed – we need look no further than the Argenteum Astrum.

20

SOUTH AUDLEY STREET: SHOWDOWN WITH GURU PARAMAHAMSA
Child of a pig

Crowley was still searching for teachers and gurus, and a man called T.C. Crawford had recently written a book entitled *A Real Mahatma: A Personal Study*, published in 1906 by the oriental booksellers Luzac, opposite the British Museum. This was about Mahatma Sri Agamya Guru Paramahamsa, then visiting Britain. In November 1906 Crowley sent him a note, "If you are the one I seek this will suffice", and they met. Crowley's first impressions were very favourable, but he became disenchanted, and by the time he read the Mahatma's own book, *Sri Brahma Dara: "Shower from the Highest"* (Luzac, 1905) he noted errors.

The guru held court at 7 Margaret Street and 60 South Audley Street, and it was here that relations worsened, until on Sunday 13 October 1907 they had a row: "a far from silent interview with Mahatma at the weekly meeting" as Crowley called it in his diary ('silent interviews' being part of the guru's practice). The guru was a famously ferocious and angry man, and consequently known as the Tiger Mahatma.

Crowley knew another ferocious man, Captain Fuller, who also had a good working knowledge of yoga – he went on to publish a book on it in 1933, cross referencing it with kabbalistic and magical ideas[1] – and was not impressed by the Mahatma's writings. Crowley asked him to go along to a Sunday meeting, which he did on the 17 November, listening with disdain until the guru shouted "You pig-faced man! You dirty fellow, you come here to take away

---

1   Major-General J.F.C. Fuller, *Yoga: A Study of the Mystical Philosophy of the Brahmins and Buddhists* (Rider and Co, 1933)

my disciples. Crowley send this pig-one, eh?" Fuller walked calmly to the door and let himself out, pausing only to put his head back round the door again and say in Hindi "Shut up! You are the child of a pig!"

"Fuller at 60," Crowley wrote in his diary: "M[ahatma] threatens to murder him." Fuller wrote the episode up in *The Equinox*, with an eye to comic effect, as 'Half Hours with Famous Mahatmas' by "Sam Hardy" ('samadhi'). As for the guru, he came to grief the following year, when he was arrested for indecently assaulting two female disciples at his new headquarters in Goldhurst Road, Hampstead, and sentenced to four months hard labour.

21

BRUTON STREET: AUSTIN OSMAN SPARE
An artist

Also in the autumn of 1907, a young visionary artist named Austin Osman Spare was becoming the *enfant terrible* of the Edwardian art world, and he had a show, 'Black and White Drawings by Austin Osman Spare', at the Bruton Galleries. "His management of line has not been equalled since the days of Aubrey Beardsley," wrote a critic: "his inventive faculty is stupendous and terrifying in its creative flow of impossible horrors." The *Observer* went further: "Mr. Spare's art is abnormal, unhealthy, wildly fantastic and unintelligible, and altogether of a kind which will make the family man hesitate to take his wife or daughter to the gallery."

Crowley sought him out, walking into the gallery at 13 Bruton Street, between Bond Street and Berkeley Square, and announcing himself to Spare as the "Vicegerent of God upon Earth." In due course they became friends, for a while, and Spare joined the fledgling A∴A∴ as a Probationer. He seems to have swapped drawings for his A∴A∴ outfit: "I cannot afford the robe (have nothing) and it's kind of you to pay off on the work. Do you order it or I?"

Spare flunked the academic side of the A∴A∴ curriculum, and never got beyond the grade of Probationer. Crowley failed him and, looking over his Probationer's Oath form a couple of years later, wrote "An artist. Can't understand organisation or he would have passed."

Spare's subsequent recollections of Crowley are not flattering. He remembered seeing Crowley put a dollop of spaghetti on his head in the Café Royal so it ran down his collar, and doing his invisibility routine nearby in Regent Street, wearing a cowl and making the Sign of Harpocrates (for silence). According to his own account, perhaps with the benefit of hindsight, Spare told him "I saw you – so did others!" He also remembered him wearing cosmetics in the Piccadilly area – looking like a male prostitute, he thought – and said "My God, if I had to go to all that effort to attract 'em, I'd give up the ghost."

22

TOOK'S COURT, HOLBORN
The New Age

Took's Court figures in Dickens's *Bleak House* as Cook's Court, and Dickens is believed to have lived at number 15. Crowley knew this 'Court' off Chancery Lane – neither a mews nor an alley – because it housed one of his favourite printer-publishers at number 21, the Chiswick Press (who produced his *Jezebel, Ahab and Other Poems, Rosa Coeli, Rosa Inferni,* and more) and also the journal *The New Age* at numbers 1 and 2.

The New Age was a Modernist magazine that published Ezra Pound, Wyndham Lewis, and short-story writer Katherine Mansfield. It also published Crowley for a while: Crowley was on friendly terms with the editor A.R. Orage, a well-known intellectual of the day with interests in Nietzsche and socialism, who later became absorbed in the work of Gurdjieff. He was from the north of England, where his miscellaneously 'foreign intellectual'-looking name was unceremoniously pronounced Orridge to rhyme with porridge, but in London he came to prefer a French-style pronunciation. In those days references were needed for the British Library, and in March 1908 Crowley used Orage as his referee for a reader's ticket.

23

BRITISH LIBRARY
One thing you can say about Satanists...

Crowley was admitted to the British Library in March 1908. This was the old British Library, or British Museum Reading Room, with its famous blue dome ceiling, in the centre of the British Museum (now somewhat lacking in purpose, preserved at the centre of a hollowed out white space that has been re-consecrated as a temple to tourism).

It was notorious as a place for obsessive research, and when George Gissing wrote *New Grub Street* its distinctive arrangement of desks, radiating out in lines from the concentric circles of bookcases holding the enormous physical catalogue (then in the form of large books) made him think of a web: "the readers who sat here at these radiating lines of desks, what were they but hapless flies caught in a huge web, its nucleus the great circle of the Catalogue? Darker, darker."

In addition to the library's more famous 'ghost' readers such as Karl Marx and Virginia Woolf, it was also a key site for esoteric study. Yeats met Mathers in here, before he adopted the name of MacGregor, and remembered him in his brown velveteen coat, proud but starving, copying magical manuscripts.

There is a beautiful line in one of Crowley's diaries when he writes of "that rich flavour that manuscripts only have in dreams" (which will strike a chord with anyone who has ever dreamt of fabulous tomes and magical second-hand bookshops). There is something definitively bookish about the occult, with the *Sacred Magic of Abramelin*, *The Key of Solomon*, the *Goetia* or *Lemegeton*, *The Enchiridion of Pope Leo*, *The Grimoire of Honorius* and the rest. Or in the immortal words of Robert Irwin, "One thing you can say about Satanists, they are great readers."

24

BRITISH MUSEUM
The Professor from Lhasa

The Museum itself contains many objects of esoteric interest, notably the magic mirror, or scrying stone, said to have belonged to Elizabethan magus Dr John Dee, with which he and his assistant Edward Kelley communicated with angels at Mortlake. In doing so they formulated the 'Enochian' system of magic, as later practised by the Golden Dawn (written up by Meric Casaubon in his 1659 book *A true and faithful relation of what passed for many years between Dr. John Dee and Some Spirits*). Crowley believed himself to be the reincarnation of Kelley. The stone itself is an Aztec obsidian mirror once owned by the 18thC Gothic revivalist Horace Walpole, who loved the idea of its supposed link to the pre-Enlightenment magic of Dee.

In a building packed with the ancient, the alien and the Other, the Egyptian department was of particular interest to Victorian and Edwardian occultists. Among the Bloomsbury objects is the so-called 'Unlucky Mummy',[1] believed to have an aura of evil, which was discussed by Egyptologist Wallis Budge, Madame Blavatsky, and the spiritualist and crusading journalist W.T. Stead. In 1909 it figured on the front cover of *Pearson's Magazine*, in an instance of the popular mystique of Egypt at the time. Crowley had already explored the Cairo Museum, where item 666 was the stele of Ankh-f-n-Khonsu, and in 1930 he thought he had found the sarcophagus of Ankh-f-n-Khonsu in the British Museum ("BM. Discovered sarcophagus of Ankh-F-N-Khonsu!!!"). Unfortunately it turned out to be the wrong one.

Crowley and J.F.C. Fuller were embarked on publishing an occult journal, *The Equinox*. Thoughts of *The Equinox*, in Crowley's account,

[1]   A painted inner sarcophagus lid showing a woman: item 22542.

gave them visions of durability in the face of a coming smash of civilisation and "imminence of world catastrophe": "We saw the New Zealander sitting on the ruined arch of London Bridge quite clearly."

This was the once-famous New Zealander of the future who visited the remains of London and sketched the ruin of St. Paul's Cathedral. Thomas Macaulay had conjured him up in an 1840 review of von Ranke's *History of the Popes*, as an image of the power and endurance of the Roman Catholic Church: an organisation that "may still exist in undiminished vigour when some traveller from New Zealand shall, in the midst of a vast solitude, take his stand on a broken arch of London Bridge to sketch the ruins of St. Paul's".

Like Shelley's ruined statue of Ozymandias, this New Zealander was one of many such images of the sublime vastness of time and the waning fortunes of empires. In the 1770s the same Walpole who owned the Dee scrying stone had already conjured up a "curious traveller from Lima [who] will visit England and give a description of the ruins of St. Paul's." He also suggested a future researcher "from the banks of the Oronooko"² might one day "revive knowledge of the English language and English gardening".

And now Crowley and Fuller had an image of their own, not with the cathedral but the Museum: "We could also see the Professor of Archaeology in the University of Lhasa excavating the ruins of the British Museum." This future Tibetan seems to be particularly excavating the Library, where "He discovered a vast number of volumes of our period purporting to deal with the occult sciences, but there were few indeed of these which had not crumbled into dust. Of those that remained, the vast majority were evidently frivolous. He rejoiced exceedingly to discover one series of volumes, the dignity of whose appearance, the permanence of whose paper, the excellence of whose printing, and the evident care which had been bestowed on their production, showed him at first sight that the people responsible for their production had been at infinite pains to make these volumes testify against the tyranny of time... The first standard work of reference – the key to the wisdom of the buried past."

2   i.e. the Orinoco, in the Amazon jungle.

25

THE ROYAL COURTS OF JUSTICE, STRAND: THE EQUINOX CASE
Keeping it dark

The Equinox contained a magical biography of Crowley, 'The Temple of Solomon the King' (notionally by Fuller, and including Crowley's magical diary, 'John St. John'). This was in instalments and from the first issue, in March 1909, it revealed Golden Dawn rituals to profane readers. Volume I no.II appeared that autumn – they were bi-annual, like the equinoxes – and it revealed more.

Shortly before the following spring equinox, and *Equinox* Vol.I no.III, MacGregor Mathers took legal action; he sought an injunction to stop it, and to prevent publication of what was by now to be the fifth grade of the Golden Dawn system.

Mathers and Crowley had fallen out in the meantime, and Crowley had felt Mathers's magical attacks at Boleskine. Mathers had not been impressed by Aiwass, who – as well as heralding a glorious two-thousand-year period of fire and bloodshed, from 1904 onwards – meant Crowley could now claim a superhuman authority of his own behind him, trumping Westcott with his Fraulein Sprengel and Mathers with his three Secret Chiefs in the Bois de Boulogne.

This was Crowley's first big brush with the Law Courts ("The Royal Courts of Justice"). Located right at the Fleet Street end of The Strand, the Courts are an extraordinary, half-crazed high point of Victorian Gothic, with over a thousand rooms and three-and-a-half miles of corridors, within a powerfully austere, massive, ceiling-vaulted building complex. The style harks back to the thirteenth century, and makes the Houses of Parliament seem almost light and playful in comparison. It was designed by George Edmund Street, who died the year before it was completed – it was popularly thought the magnitude and difficulties of the task had killed him – and opened in 1882 by Crowley's *bête noire*, Queen Victoria.

Justice Bucknill confirmed Mathers's injunction. Bucknill was an eminent Freemason, so Crowley's understanding of what had happened was "though he had no idea what the fuss was about, it seemed to him, on general principles, that nobody ought to be allowed to publish anything which anyone else might wish to keep dark."

Crowley appealed, using the firm of Messrs. Steadman, Van Praagh and Naylor at 4 Suffolk Street, at the National Gallery end of Pall Mall, and consecrated an Abramelin talisman "to acquire the affection of a judge". The case came up before Lord Justices Williams, Moulton and Farwell, and this time Crowley won.

There was much facetious legal banter about letting dead cats out of bags, much laughter in court, and the newspapers enjoyed themselves immensely, foreshadowing the even richer farce to come with the *Looking Glass* court case and then 'The Black Magic Libel Case'.

26

CAXTON HALL: THE RITES OF ELEUSIS
By the power in me vested...

Membership of the A∴A∴ reached over eighty, although it is not clear how many were active members at the same time, or how many were really committed to magic; most of them seem not to have got beyond the Probationer stage, and Crowley later regretted not making more effort to keep the Probationers and higher grades apart socially. In practice it had become a fairly casual and attractive scene for Bohemians, and it was during the A∴A∴ period that Crowley became enthusiastic about magical-theatrical ritual performances with music and drugs. Dance was central, particularly with the involvement of Victor Neuburg, Crowley's magical comrade and apprentice,[1] who would invoke a god by 'dancing it down' and becoming possessed.

Crowley was now involved with Leila Waddell, a violinist from New Zealand, and along with Neuburg they had been to stay in Dorset with Commander Guy Marston of the Royal Navy, another A∴A∴ member. Son of a clergyman, and a friend of the poet Rupert Brooke, Marston was soon to be commander of the cruiser HMS Blanche. He was also a man with an interest in the psychology of sex and particularly the effect of "tom-tom"-style drumming on women, notably respectable married English women, such that the drumming led them to "shameless masturbation or indecent advances." It is an idea of primitive rhythm that runs through into the popular voodoo-and-witchcraft exposés of the 1950s, such as Fabian of the Yard's bestselling 1954 memoir *London After Dark*, where he explains that the police know of a Satanist temple in west London, but it would be too dangerous to raid it: "Not even the London policeman or

---

1   With Neuburg (1883-1940), or Frater Omnia Vincam, Crowley summoned the demon Choronzon in North Africa (1909) and performed the Paris Working (1913).

policewoman can guarantee to be immune, in an atmosphere thick with perfumed ether, throbbing with jungle drums and chants."

While in Dorset they had raised Bartzabel, spirit of Mars, and at a certain point Neuburg had become possessed, dancing and speaking with the voice of the spirit, who prophesied war. But on one level, the most notable thing wasn't Neuburg's channelling, or the prediction, but Marston's suggestion – perhaps half-joking – that the ritual was so good they should perform it for the public and charge admission. "You may be on to something," said Crowley.

One night at no.124 they had improvised for guests, with Crowley reading poetry and Waddell accompanying him on the violin to bring out the mood of the piece. It went exhilaratingly well, and they developed it into a Rite of Artemis, with Swinburne's poem 'When the hounds of spring' and a closing violin performance of Schumann's *Abendlied*, followed by a deliberate period of silence and then Crowley's declaration that "By the power in me vested, I declare the Temple closed." It was first performed for the public at the Victoria Street flat on 23 August, 1910. Incense, dim lighting (with a dull red light shining on an altar) robed figures and a ritual invocation of Artemis made it a heady experience, and it was further enhanced by a 'libation cup' passed around the audience: it has been suggested this contained opium, but it was peyote (mescaline), Crowley's particular drug at the time ("the elixir introduced by me to Europe").

Crowley was excited enough to build the performance up into The Rites of Eleusis, performed at Caxton Hall, Westminster, close to Victoria Street. It was a respectable and moderately grand venue, then associated with suffragette meetings (and later to be the site of, among other things, Churchill's election speech; the assassination of Sir Michael O'Dwyer, in revenge for the Amritsar Massacre; the founding of the National Front; and the wedding of Ringo Starr). The rites ran for seven weekly performances between 19 October and 30 November 1910, and the public were encouraged to buy a ticket for the whole series at the hefty, opera-style price of five guineas; several hundred pounds today. Each ritual was dedicated to a planet, and the audience were encouraged to come in the appropriate planetary colour for each performance.

The idea was not totally new – 'Black Masses' had been staged in Paris, and Mathers had performed 'The Rites of Isis' there for the public at the Theatre La Bodinière, rue Saint-Lazare – but the performance was intoxicating and the Rites were widely noticed in the press. Most papers wrote them up as the work of a weird cult, but it is not far-fetched to see them as an avant-garde psychodrama, and even a forerunner of Sixties 'Happenings'.

27

LOOKING GLASS PUBLISHING COMPANY, FLEET STREET: THE *LOOKING GLASS* CASE
Like Alice in Wonderland

Among the press coverage attracted by the Rites of Eleusis was a piece in an unpleasant paper called *The Looking Glass, or, Things As They Are*, edited by a man named West De Wend Fenton. It was a racing and gossip paper based in an upstairs office at 149 Fleet Street, with the telegram address 'Fentonism', and it seems to have dealt not only in scandal but literal blackmail, whereby someone on the receiving end of an exposé could pay not to have it taken further in subsequent issues. One issue had a cartoon occupying the entire front page, wishing readers a Happy New Year from *The Looking Glass* "or Grave Diggers Journal" and featuring a coffin titled "Reputations" with a bottle of champagne on top of it.

On October 29, 1910, *The Looking Glass* ran a facetious piece about the Rites entitled 'An Amazing Sect', following it up with two further instalments. By the third, the attack had extended to Crowley's friends Allan Bennett ("sham Buddhist monk... there were rumours of unmentionable immoralities which were carried on under their roof") and George Cecil Jones, guilty of nothing more than being a named associate of Crowley. But given the overall drift of the articles that was enough, and Jones sued.

It was back to the Royal Courts of Justice, not far from the paper's office. In April 1911 the case of Jones v The Looking Glass Publishing Co Ltd. was heard before Lord Justice Scrutton. Jones brought the case, but it was Crowley's reputation that was on trial, and two old Golden Dawners – Dr Berridge,[1] and MacGregor Mathers

---

1   Dr Edward Berridge, Frater Resurgam, was one of the GD old guard, having joined in 1889. He qualified in medicine at Bart's, London, and later in homeopathy in America, and he practised in Bayswater until around 1920. Subsequent to this 🖝

– appeared in court to help blacken it. Crowley ("a man of notoriously evil character") was not called, although he lurked in court for the proceedings, nor did he bring any action against *The Looking Glass* himself. Jones lost.

As with Mathers's previous appearance in court, hostile barristers and the press had a field day. Crowley wrote a parody of the courtroom dialogues – only slightly more ridiculous than the real transcripts in *The Times* and elsewhere – entitled 'The Rosicrucian Scandal'. And in reality the judge, Scrutton, found the whole case so bizarre that he said it was "getting very much like the trial in Alice in Wonderland", a little joke chiming with *Alice Through the Looking Glass*. In fact it was more like that than he knew, because Samuel Liddell MacGregor Mathers was a relative of Alice Liddell, Lewis Carroll's original Alice.

Crowley might joke about the case – in his parody he has Mathers say Crowley is "an associate of the notorious Jones" – but the damage was done to his friendships with two of the most impressive men and magical comrades he had ever known, Jones and Fuller (Fuller had also resented receiving an envelope full of dirty postcards from Tangier, as he told Neuburg's biographer Jean Overton Fuller). Fuller considered Crowley a coward for not suing *The Looking Glass* for libel, and not defending himself in order to help Jones. He wrote him a last letter on 2 May, 1911, including the lines:

> If you wish to hoorosh down on a fixed bayonet, like a howling dervish, well good, it really is no business of mine.
> I am extremely sorry that Jones should be the sufferer for your want of pluck.
> Outside the actual cost of the case I do not think he loses much, for modern journalism is so constructed that unless you happen to be Crippen or a Home Secretary, your identity within a week is lost in a Nirvana of senseless sensational headlines.

☛ court case, Crowley described him as a 'vampire' (within his idiosyncratic sexual meaning of the term) in his 1914 treatise *De Arte Magica*.

Looking Glass Publishing Company, Fleet Street: The Looking Glass *Case*

And finally, as a parting shot:

> PS. I said the other day I admired your works. I do: but you have never written so fine a line as this of Blake's
>
> "a little moony night and silence."

28

RALSTON STREET, CHELSEA: SALON OF GWEN OTTER
Curiously unreal

Gwen Otter was "the last of the Chelsea hostesses", part of a Bohemian scene that overlapped with the world of the A∴A∴ members and what Victor Neuburg called "those wonderful days in Chelsea before the War" (the First War). She was said to look like a 'red Indian', and claimed descent from Pocahontas. Otter's salon was in a plain, red brick house at number 1 Ralston Street, on the corner with Tedworth Square. Evelyn Waugh remembered it having black walls with a gold ceiling and "piles of tasselled cushions in the style of the earlier Russian Ballet. She could not bear solitude and her house was always full, spongers mixing indifferently with well-known figures of the stage and arts."

Crowley was a regular guest, and it was here that short story writer Katherine Mansfield tried mescaline. She became upset by a spent match lying not quite straight on the carpet and said she could do up the buttons on her nightgown, "if we talk to them very gently", while repeating every now and then, "Pity that stuff had no effect."

It was also at Gwen Otter's that Viola Bankes found Crowley. Bankes, a thrill-seeking upper-class Englishwoman remembered for her 1934 autobiography *Why Not?*, writes that by around 1930 "For ten years the name of Aleister Crowley had excited me in the fashion that all Europe in the eighteenth century was excited by Cagliostro." And then "One night at a dance my partner and I were discussing flagellation and other ancient and modern habits", when – as if by association – her partner told her Aleister Crowley was in town. "Do we know anyone who knows him?" said Bankes.

And so it was – Otter being a friend of the partner, it turned out – that one Sunday lunchtime Bankes found herself walking up the front steps of No.1: "I trembled with excitement like a schoolgirl going up to receive a prize! Aleister Crowley had stirred in me, as no other man or woman had ever done, the most violent longing to see and speak to him. It always seemed to me that if half the stories concerning him were true he belonged rather to mediæval times than to our own."

Crowley was there, standing in front of the fireplace, "large of figure and inscrutable of face, watching us with glittering green eyes." He was with his current wife, Maria Teresa de Miramar, but Otter had put Bankes next to him at luncheon, and in the dining room Bankes noticed an Augustus John picture of Crowley on the wall: "The drawing, which was in profile, had a mystic look on the upturned face which illustrated yet another side of the poet, magician, and traveller..."[1]

Comparing the portrait to the man, she found Crowley less impressive in the flesh: "He had neither the powerful compelling features of a magician nor the strong and nervous hands of a poet. His hands were unusually small and well-kept, and reminded me of a delicate bird's claws; rapacious, perhaps, but not masterful. His voice, which I had imagined would be sonorous, was light and rather high for a man."

But like Svengali, or the Crowley-derived villain Mocata in Dennis Wheatley's *The Devil Rides Out*, "There was no doubt that this man, with his colossal will-power and deep occult knowledge, could dominate a weaker and untrained will to the extent that is called magnetism, and could, if he wished, obtain absolute mastery over the mind and body of his subject." ; "In repose, the eyes held the sleepy reserve of the Oriental, but when he opened them wide and deliberately fastened them on another person, that person could scarcely fail to feel the thrill of magnetism that emanated from their green depths."

Crowley suddenly turned to Viola and said, "I like you", moving his chair around so he could look into her eyes. "You were born under Aquarius or Sagittarius," he said, "with your peculiar profile. Take your hat off and let me see you better." Crowley then stood up

---

1   This was a lithograph from an issue of *The Equinox* Vol.1 No.7 (Spring 1912).

and slowly walked toward the end of the table so that he could survey her better, finally saying "Yes ... I can see you are an Aquarius."

"How did you guess?" asked Viola; "I didn't guess," said Crowley; "I knew".[2]

The writer Ethel Mannin attended Otter's Sunday gatherings, and she remembered the Aubrey Beardsley prints and the anachronism and the strange atmosphere: "there is a curious quality about those parties, difficult to define. It is not that the people she collects are particularly queer... but everyone else seemed curiously unreal, like people talking and eating in a dream. I had the feeling that we had all somehow got into a land where it was always Sunday afternoon."

She also remembered Crowley, "that high priest of black magic who likes nothing better than to be regarded as His Satanic Majesty the Prince of Darkness, and who would take it as a compliment to be called an arch-devil... Knowing that Crowley is one of Gwen Otter's oldest friends I asked her if she could tell me the truth about him and the dark stories of drugs and black mass circulating about him, but I gathered... that there is no clearly definable truth about him – ; save that he is a poseur who has come to believe in his own poses – so that they are no longer poses – and that having built up this sinister reputation for himself he goes on playing up to it."

Otter remained a good friend to Crowley right from the pre-1914 A∴A∴ days (despite being "expelled"), and writing book reviews for *The Equinox*, through to lunching with him in the 1930s; he still knew her when she moved to 27 Margaretta Terrace – a more atmospheric location, also in Chelsea – in 1932. She figures as Miss Badger in his novel *Moonchild*, where he elevates her address from Ralston Street, with its tenement-like frontage, to Cheyne Walk (Chelsea's best address, home to Pre-Raphaelites and Swinging Sixties Beautiful People). Victor Neuburg observed that their friendship left her unscathed, and she said of course it did: she wasn't in love with him, and she never lent him money.

2   He almost certainly did know, and probably without having to use astrology. He went through the same performance with Charles Cammell (more about him at site 86, in Richmond), also at Otter's.

29

SAVOY HOTEL, STRAND
Exchanging electricity

Opened in 1889, with "electric lighting and artistic furniture throughout", the Savoy is the most opulent venue on the Strand; it was propelled into the first rank by the team of Escoffier as chef and Cesar Ritz as hotelier – before he opened his own hotel[1] – and it had the first hotel restaurant regularly patronised by royalty. In Crowley's day it represented luxury tinged with decadence: Oscar Wilde had stayed there and it was the hotel where his 1895 offences took place (Savoy chambermaids testified in court about sperm stains, one of them famously saying she'd found a stain like a little map of Ireland).

It was punishingly expensive (Wilde told his friend Bosie that it was costing him £49 a week; around £5000 today), and it became associated with transatlantic wealth and Americans in London, partly because it was convenient for the Paris train at Charing Cross. And so it was that on the evening of 11 October 1911, shortly before midnight, Crowley was taken to a party there, being given by the dancer Isadora Duncan for the 40th birthday of her American friend Mary d'Este Sturges: Mary and Crowley sat cross-legged on the floor "exchanging electricity", and within a couple of weeks they had begun a passionate affair conducted mainly on the continent.

---

1   Crowley knew the Ritz all his adult life, recording "A1" lunches there into the 1940s. It figures in a characteristically apocryphal story, in which he picks up a rich, beautiful, aristocratic woman looking into the window of Fortnum and Mason, and they disappear into a suite at the Ritz for the night, or perhaps for several days. He was definitely present at a grand gala dinner on 1 December 1908, the eighth anniversary of the death of Oscar Wilde, held in honour of Robert Ross and celebrating the publication of Wilde's *Collected Works*. Other guests included H.G. Wells and Somerset Maugham, along with Max Beerbohm, William Rothenstein and other Nineties figures.

Born Mary Dempsey, Mary insisted her Irish surname was a corruption of the Italian d'Este (and she had been married to the wealthy Solomon Sturges). She had a gift for magical collusion, and it was through her mediumship, powered by drink and sex, that Crowley encountered the spirit Abuldiz. Mary was involved with some of his best writing in the *anni mirabiles* of 1911-12, including his masterpiece *Book 4* (she is credited as co-author). Outside of sex and magic Crowley and Mary grew to find each other irritating, and Mary escaped unscathed when their relationship burned out naturally around 1912; they remembered each other with respect, and Crowley fictionalises their meeting in *Moonchild*.

She went on to make her fortune with a cosmetics brand; the bona fide Italian aristocratic family of d'Este complained about their name being used, forcing her to change it to Desti. She opened Maison Desti on Bond Street in 1916, at 6-8 Old Bond Street, where she also had a nightclub, where Crowley sometimes went.

Crowley continued to visit the Savoy Grill now and then as late as the 1940s. It grew even grander as time went on (acquiring the metal Art Deco frontage over the entrance in 1927, like the pediment over a Rolls-Royce radiator grille). In 1941, living in Torquay in very reduced circumstances, Crowley tidied up the "morning Sun Room" of his digs, perhaps a breakfast room, and he was so pleased he wrote in his diary "Fixed up the Morning Sun room as a Super-Savoy Super-Grill".

30

SIMPSON'S, STRAND
Boiled toads, Mother

Just down the road from the Savoy, at number 100, Simpson's (originally the Grand Cigar Divan, then Simpson's Divan and Tavern) was the centre for serious chess in Victorian times: Crowley played here frequently, even before his Golden Dawn days. It was also a centre for a certain style of traditional roast-beef dining, with its domed trolley service and wood-panelled walls, and it still is.

Crowley dined at Simpson's through the Twenties and Thirties. One evening in January 1920 he had a "great dinner at Simpson's and went on to Desti's club", and in 1940 he had a bizarre dream that he was going to be hanged in a cupboard at Simpson's (possibly the wood panelling made him think of a courtroom like the Old Bailey, and vice versa).

It was also at Simpson's that he was lunched by novelist Anthony Powell in 1929 in connection with Betty May's autobiography *Tiger Woman*; Powell was working for the book's publisher, Duckworth. Powell thought his shaved skull gave the impression "that he was wearing a false top to his head like a clown's" and that his features seemed "strangely caught together" in the midst of his face, "like those of a horrible baby". Altogether, thought Powell, he was "a sinister if gifted buffoon", with his "ponderous gags", although on a less buffoonish note Powell also remembered him complaining about the unkindness and backbiting of his fellow occultists.[1]

Perhaps Crowley's most characteristic moment at Simpson's was when he dined there around 1912 with his mother (and a friend

---

1   Powell wrote a Crowley-inspired figure, "Dr. Trelawny", into his novel sequence, *A Dance to the Music of Time*. Trelawny is out of fashion for some years after his death, but interest in him revives in the late Sixties.

of Neuburg's called Hayter "Teddy" Preston). The days of his religious mother calling him the Beast 666 were long over, and Preston was taken aback when Crowley snatched the menu from her and said "You can have boiled toads, Mother, or fried Jesus."

31

OLD TIVOLI THEATRE, STRAND: THE RAGGED RAGTIME GIRLS
Taking London by storm

Leila Waddell was a capable musician but she had little work, so in 1912 Crowley came up with the idea of finding some other women – six, remembered in his *Confessions* as three dipsomaniacs and four nymphomaniacs – to form a band, which became a troupe of seven female fiddlers called The Ragged Ragtime Girls.

They played gigs in Edinburgh and Glasgow, and above all Russia in the summer of 1913, where they played at the Moscow Aquarium. Crowley accompanied them there for six weeks, with a burst of creativity that included his best-known poem 'Hymn to Pan' and his Gnostic Mass, perhaps inspired by encountering the high ritual of the Russian Orthodox church. This included his list of Gnostic saints including Pan, Christian Rosencreutz, Gauguin, Nietzsche, Wagner, and Theodor Reuss, through to English figures such as John Dee, Sir Edward Kelley, William Blake,[1] Sir Richard Burton, Swinburne, and Crowley himself.

Meanwhile in March 1913 they appeared at the Tivoli Theatre (also known as the Old Tivoli, or Tivoli Theatre of Varieties) which was at 65-70½ Strand, on the southern side between Durham House Street and Adam Street (it was demolished in 1914, replaced by the Tivoli cinema, and the site is now a featureless modern office block). The Ragged Ragtime Girls were in the Easter programme, on the same bill as George Formby senior, father of the more famous ukulele artist. Crowley's description of them taking London by storm may be an exaggeration.

---

1   Blake lived just off the Strand at Fountain Court; not to be confused with the Fountain Court in Temple, this is now a bleak tiled alley beside the Savoy, by the Coal Hole pub.

32

FLOOD STREET, CHELSEA: DEATH OF IONE DE FOREST
With an astral dagger

There was a tragic postscript to the Rites of Eleusis in August 1912, with the death of the actress-dancer who played the role of The Moon.

Ione de Forest (her stage name; she was born Jeanne Heysel) had already been much praised in a staging of Maeterlinck's *The Blue Bird*, and she was loved by Ezra Pound (she is addressed as "O woman of my dreams" in his poem 'Dance Figure', and mourned in his poem 'Dead Ione'). She was not a member of the A∴A∴, had no interest in magic, and had simply answered an advertisement in *The Stage*, but this brought her in close contact with Crowley's circle, and – despite having recently married engraver Wilfred Meynell, in December 1911 – she had a relationship with Victor Neuburg, distracting him, as Crowley saw it, from magic and from Crowley himself.

Ione was troubled and people noticed her unhappiness, made worse by divorce proceedings. In the summer of 1912 she and Meynell separated; she moved into Flat 1, Rossetti Studios and also acquired a pearl-handled revolver. On 1 August she told her friend Nina Hamnett that she was going away, and that Hamnett could have some clothes if she came round the following day. After letting herself into Ione's studio the next morning, Hamnett found her dead body: she had shot herself through the heart.

Arthur Calder-Marshall shapes this into a polished short-story-like episode, in which Ione shoots herself after Neuburg speaks harshly to her ("If you go out of that door, I shall kill myself!"; "All right – kill yourself then."). Neuburg never forgave himself, and in turn he never forgave Crowley. As Neuburg told it, that night Neuburg had been possessed by the spirit of Mars – he had been violent and aggressive – because Crowley had not "closed the Temple" properly; he had not brought Neuburg down again before letting him out on the street.

Jean Overton Fuller has a completely different version centring on Ione's marriage and her sexual difficulties. Whatever happened, in *Magick in Theory and Practice* (1929), Crowley – writing as The Master Therion – claims magical responsibility:

> An adept known to THE MASTER THERION once found it necessary to slay a Circe who was bewitching brethren. He merely walked to the door of her room, and drew an astral 'T' ('traditore' and the symbol of Saturn)[1] with an astral dagger. Within 48 hours she shot herself.

As a boast for the effectiveness of magic, it reads like something from the fictional pages of *Moonchild*. There is no doubt who this adept is meant to be (and more than one Crowley biographer, perhaps by accident, simply omits the first four words).

---

[1]   *Traditore*: "Traitor".

33

93 REGENT STREET: HEADQUARTERS OF ORDO TEMPLI ORIENTIS
There could hardly be a nicer set of people

One night in 1912 a moustachioed German called Theodor Reuss came calling at 124 Victoria Street, the headquarters of the A∴A∴, and accused Crowley of publishing the central secret of his own organisation the Ordo Templi Orientis, the Order of the Temple of the Orient. Reuss (1855-1923) was a dedicated Freemason, initiated into a German-speaking London lodge in 1876, and Crowley already knew him slightly through Masonic circles. He was a singer by profession (he had performed in Wagner productions in Germany, and sung Mozart in London) as well as a journalist with a shady interest in politics; he had joined the Socialist League, but worked as an informer for the Prussian police.[1]

Reuss picked up a copy of Crowley's *Book of Lies*, and pointed out a passage that could be taken to refer to magical sex, probably the one beginning "Let the adept be armed with his Magick Rood" [i.e. phallus] and "provided with his Mystic Rose" [i.e. vagina]. Crowley said he was unconscious of any such meaning, but conceded that with a sudden shock ("one of the greatest shocks of my life") it all fell into place.

Notionally founded by a German Freemason and industrialist named Carl Kellner, together with a German Rosicrucian and Theosophist named Franz Hartmann, and Reuss, the O.T.O. were exponents of sex magic. This was supposedly from the mystic

---

1   Exposed in a list of German agents published in William Morris's paper *Commonweal*: "Charles Theodor Reuss, formerly theatrical impresario and concert-singer, now Bismarck's political agent on the *Central News* of London... Police spy in London (2 years and six months in pay)." (*Commonweal*, 7 January 1888 p.1)

orient[2] but also drew on the writing of two Americans, the spiritualist and mystic Thomas Lake Harris (1823-1906), whose works were already known and controversial in Golden Dawn circles, and more particularly Paschal Beverly Randolph (1825-1875), whose own work legitimised itself with the idea of the East, this time the Holy Land: "One night – it was in far-off Jerusalem or Bethlehem, I really forget which – I made love to and was loved by, a dusky maiden of Arabic blood. I of her and that experience learned – not directly, but by suggestion – the fundamental principle of the White Magic of Love."

Reuss and Crowley talked, and the upshot was that Reuss, "Supreme and Holy King of Germany", chartered Crowley to become head of the O.T.O. in Britain, and its British offshoot the Mysteria Mystica Maxima. In this capacity Crowley adopted the name of Baphomet, the alleged idol of the original Templars, and was now "Supreme and Holy King of Ireland, Iona, and all the Britains within the Sanctuary of the Gnosis."

To further that Gnosis, Crowley took third-floor offices at 93 Regent Street, an address that pleased him. Within the murky prisms of numerology 93 is the number of Will (as in "Do what thou wilt shall be the whole of the Law", the keynote of his new religion) and Love (as in "Love is the Law, Love Under Will", its companion dictum). In later years he would sign off letters with "93/93".

2   This is not the place to consider the large subject of Crowley and tantra, but – very briefly – he rarely mentions it and tends to distinguish it from sexual magic, as in section XVI of *De Arte Magica*, 'Of Certain Hindu Theories'. He prefers to talk in terms of western science or alchemy, and he is primarily employing sexual forces in pursuit not of spiritual development or consciousness raising but tangible effects in the material world ("BABALON. *Manibus*. Object: $20,000"). Nevertheless Theodor Reuss and his senior colleague Carl Kellner (1851-1905) liked to connect their work with India, where Kellner said he had travelled and studied yoga, in tune with the 'eastward turn' of the esoteric after Theosophy, and Reuss had published a book entitled *Lingam-Yoni* in 1906. Crowley writes in his *Confessions* about the liberating effect that seeing the Shivalingam temple in southern India had on his essentially Victorian and western mind. The larger connections between Crowley and tantra have been explored by Hugh Urban and others.

The office was largely run by a man named George Cowie, Grand Treasurer General of the Mysteria Mystica Maxima, and a woman called Mary Davies, and Cowie has left a cheerful picture of it in his letters to Crowley: "There could hardly be a nicer set of people. All Mary's friends, and all really paying. They are not cranks or even spiritualists, but all sorts..."; "They do love swank! Officers now have Templar cloaks..."

All this went on happily enough until it was raided by the police in June 1917. This was not because they disapproved of magic but because Crowley had been writing pro-German propaganda in America. They found little of interest, but they did manage to arrest Mary Davies (a "motherly old fool" and tea-leaf reader, as Crowley describes her) for fraudulent fortune telling. The whole incident would be farcical but for the distress it caused George Cowie. A deaf-mute from Edinburgh, who worked as picture editor for the publishing firm of Nelson, Cowie had a near-nervous breakdown after the raid.

Cowie and Crowley had already disagreed over Germany and the war (Crowley accused him of being anti-German, and believing allied propaganda), but Cowie tried to keep a rather touching faith for as long as possible. The revelation, after the raid, of what Crowley had been writing in America was "a severe shock" – but "you could not have meant that use to be made of your stuff."

34

PICCADILLY
The mysteries of the IX°

An early entry in Crowley's sex-magical diary, *Rex de Arte Regia* (King of the Royal Art), records that on the 6 September 1914 he had an all-day session with a Piccadilly prostitute, Christine Rosalie Byrne, "a sturdy bitch of 26 or so" who went under the working name of 'Peggy Marchmont' (as in Marchmont Street, then a street of cheap lodgings in Bloomsbury). The "object", since from now on Crowley generally had an object when he had sex, was "Knowledge of the Mysteries of the IX⁰ and power to express same."

Within the Masonic-style language of the O.T.O., the IX⁰ was magically consecrated heterosexual intercourse (with the XI⁰, added by Crowley, being anal sex, and VIII⁰ masturbation – "*manibus*", by hand – also a useful option). The whole procedure – once explained to me as "Have a fuck and make a wish"[1] – involved consecrating a sexual act to a particular purpose (such as money, or healing, or success with a particular project) and maintaining concentration during sex and orgasm, such that visualising a shower of gold during orgasm might (for example) result in a seemingly coincidental lottery win or windfall a week later. Sealing the operation with a further sacramental-alchemical turn, Crowley also liked to consume the combined male and female fluids afterwards, the "elixir".

[1]   By a man at The Secret Chiefs, a series of occult speaker-meetings above the Princess Louise pub in Holborn. It is memorably simple but not quite true; the real idea is to make the wish first, or 'formulate the purpose', and then concentrate on it.

     This was the same man who gave me the neatly worded account of Crowley practising invisibility at the Café Royal [cf p.62]. I also remember him making occult hand gestures under the table towards a friend of mine while talking to him, trying to apply some form of mesmeric-style mind domination (and unaware that he'd been spotted doing it). He died in 2017. I didn't warm to him, but *de mortuis nil nisi bonum*...

Crowley had immense faith in this, and writes that if the secret were understood there is nothing that could not be achieved ("if it were desired to have an element of atomic weight six times that of uranium that element could be produced"). He claimed Cowie was a fool not to cure his deafness with it, and writes of his own work that it had replaced ritual magic: from 1914, although he had known of it earlier,[2] "I made it my principal engine".

On this occasion he reported great success: he was seized with the inspiration and energy to write *De Arte Magica, De Homunculo, De Natura Deorum,* and *De Nuptiis Secretis Deorum cum Hominibus* (Concerning the Magic Art; On the Homunculus; On the Nature of the Gods; Of the Secret Marriages of Gods with Men). At the same time he felt something had gone wrong ("I suppose that I had made some great error") because he developed a thrombosis in his leg, needing a month of rest. Or perhaps, he wondered, "might the ill-health be part of the success, giving me time to write?"

He was back at work in October, this time with chorus-girl Violet Duval, assisted in a threesome by Leila Waddell (now "Grand Secretary General IX⁰ OTO"), and this time the object was "Health".

Piccadilly Circus was already London's focal point, seeming like the centre of the world in the days of the British Empire, and it already had its celebrated advertising hoardings, along with flower sellers around the statue of Eros, and prostitutes. The association with prostitution was strong enough for Crowley – writing about the aphrodisiac properties of hashish – to contrast the purity of his own mind with those sex-obsessed people "who associate nudity with debauchery, and see Piccadilly Circus in [the] Mona Lisa". The whole Piccadilly area continued to be a lifelong Crowley stamping ground. His occasional drinking companion of the 1940s, Collin Brooks, notes that as the twentieth century got under way the pleasure centre of London shifted from the Strand towards Regent

2   At the 1914 start of his magical sex diary, *Rex de Arte Regia*, he writes that the secret was communicated to him by Reuss in 1912. But in his *Confessions*, dictated almost a decade later, perhaps wanting to play down the role of Reuss, he says he had known it since 1911.

Street and Piccadilly, and Crowley's use of the city is largely in accord with this.

In his later years Crowley would walk around Piccadilly raising his hat to courting couples and cursing priests with "Save us from every evil demon" in classical Greek. He only cursed Catholic priests because, as he explained, they are the only real priests.

35

AVENUE STUDIOS, FULHAM ROAD
Rendezvous for spies

After leaving the former A∴A∴ Temple at Victoria Street, Crowley got his version of the O.T.O. under way during 1913-14 at number 2 Avenue Studios, with a courtyard entrance at 76 Fulham Road. The address is usually given as "33" Avenue Studios, which was a Masonic joke. There are only 15 studios, and he notes the real number in his private annotations to *Diary of a Drug Fiend*.

As the Head of the O.T.O. for England, Crowley was now "the Most Holy, Most Illustrious, Most Illuminated, and Most Puissant Baphomet, X degree, Rex Summus Sanctissimus 33 degree, 90 degree, 96 degree, Past Grand Master of the United States of America, Grand Master of Ireland, Iona, etc." and he could be contacted at "33 Avenue Studios, 76 Fulham Road, Kensington, London, SW."

Ellic Howe's study of Reuss's career, and the lack of much real O.T.O. activity within it, suggests that his offer to Crowley was less like a top-down delegation from a working organisation, and in fact more like an invitation to get something up and running. Issuing a manifesto, Crowley explained that 'the M∴ M∴ M∴ (Mysteria Mystica Maxima) is the name of the British section of the O.T.O.... a body of initiates in whose hands are concentrated the wisdom and the knowledge of the following bodies":

1. The Gnostic Catholic Church
2. The Order of the Knights of the Holy Ghost
3. The Order of the Illuminati
4. The Order of the Temple (Knights Templar)
5. The Order of the Knights of St John
6. The Order of the Knights of Malta
7. The Order of the Knights of the Holy Sepulchre

8. The Hidden Church of the Holy Grail
9. The Rosicrucian Order
10. The Holy Order of the Rose Croix of Heredom
11. The Order of the Holy Royal Arch of Enoch
12. The Antient and Primitive Rite of Masonry (33 degrees)
13. The Rite of Memphis (97 degrees)
14. The Rite of Mizraim (90 degrees)
15. The Ancient and Accepted Scottish Rite of Masonry (33 degrees)
16. The Swedenborgian Rite of Masonry
17. The Order of Martinists
18. The Order of the Sat Bhai
19. The Hermetic Brotherhood of Light
20. The Hermetic Order of the Golden Dawn, and many other orders of equal merit, if of less fame.

This would have surprised some of the bodies named, but it was in line with Reuss's declaration in the journal *Oriflamme*: "Our Order possesses the KEY which embraces all masonic and hermetic secrets. It relates to sexual magic and this teaching completely explains all Masonic symbolism and religious teachings."

Like a sequel to the Rites of Eleusis, further "mysteries" for a paying audience of thrill-seekers were conducted at Fulham Road with 'The Mass of the Phoenix', but perhaps more cynically. Poet Trevor Blakemore asked Crowley if he could attend, but Crowley put him off, saying it was just "where he caught the old cats".

There was a ludicrous write-up of this by the once-famous Bohemian Harry Kemp in the *New York World* magazine, entitled 'Weird Rites of Devil Worshippers Revealed by an Eye Witness'. Kemp's revelations involved "a large, high-ceilinged studio the atmosphere of which was coloured a deep blue by the reek of a peculiar smelling incense." There was an altar, and "someone behind a curtain playing a weird Chinese-like air on some sort of stringed instrument." The worshippers were mostly aristocratic women with "costly rings" and "not a few people of noble descent" – the sort of set-up that Dennis Wheatley would make his own a few years later – and all of them were wearing black dominos over their faces. Then the high priest began to chant:

"There is no good. Evil is good. Blessed be the Principle of Evil. All hail, Prince of the World, to whom even God Himself has given dominion." A sound as of evil bleating filled the pauses of these blasphemous utterances...

Evil bleating indeed. Crowley later said he hypnotised Kemp to make him hallucinate all this, which seems a generous explanation.

There was a more serious account given by the popular occult writer Elliott O'Donnell, who had just published his book *The Sorcery Club* (1912). His memories of Crowley's studio were not published until a couple of decades later in his book *Rooms of Mystery* (1931), but he was certainly there, and he found it unimpressive. There was some harp playing; some paying of respects to the busts of deities around the room; Crowley cutting his chest (or pretending to, O'Donnell thought); and some passes made in the air with a dagger. It was "meat only for the most elementary type of thrill-hunter, the very rawest tyro in magic and occultism."

Crowley later claimed "In 1913-14... my studio near Onslow Square was a regular rendezvous for spies. I was always seeing them in the courtyard, skulking behind trees as I went to and from dinner. What they had hoped to find out I cannot imagine."

The courtyard before the Studios is still quiet and atmospheric, like the corridor of the studios: with its tiled floor and large doors, it has the air of a vintage industrial space or perhaps a hospital from the First World War era. John Singer Sargent had a studio here, as did Clifford Bax (where Allan Bennett later gave talks on Buddhism), and number 10 was more recently the premises of the late Oliver Hoare, once known to the newspaper-reading public as the lover of Princess Diana, and better remembered as a dealer in Islamic art and rare objects.

36

OUTRAM ROAD, CROYDON
Count Zeppelin is requested

Crowley went to New York in November 1914 and spent the First World War in America. While there, as well as writing propaganda, he assumed the magical grade of Magus, one step up from Magister Templi, now making him equal to Christ or Mohammed. The great Magi pronounce a word which defines their teaching, as in *agape*, love, in the case of Christ, or *Allah* (God is one) in the case of Mohammed; Crowley's word was *thelema*, will.

He also visited New Orleans, where he wrote *The Green Goddess*, an essay on absinthe with a strikingly 1890s-ish ethos and even style (redolent of the King James Bible, Malory's *Morte d'Arthur*, and Enoch Soames). Absinthe, he writes, can stimulate the truly artistic point of view, "...till you become as gods, knowing good and evil, and that they are not two but one". Understanding this "solves every problem of life and death – which two are also one."

At one point he asks the reader "Do you know that French sonnet 'La legende de l'Absinthe'?" It is unlikely many readers did, because he had written it himself, and published it in the pro-German propaganda paper *The International*. He was a contributing editor and main writer, defending the German execution of British nurse Edith Cavell and comparing Kaiser Bill to Christ.

Much of it is written with a cheery facetiousness, and when the Zeppelin raids took place he wrote

> For some reason or other in their last Zeppelin raid on London the Germans appear to have decided to make the damage as widespread as possible, instead of concentrating it in one

quarter. A house close to my lawyer's office in Chancery Lane[1] was entirely destroyed... A great deal of damage was done at Croydon, especially at its suburb Addiscombe, where my aunt lives. Unfortunately her house was not hit... Count Zeppelin is respectfully requested to try again. The exact address is Eton Lodge, Outram Road.

Or to be really exact, Eton Lodge, 55 Outram Road.[2] It was fortunate number 55 escaped because, returning from America with no money and nowhere to stay, he lived there on his aunt's Christmas hospitality though December 1919 and January 1920. "Not only has the war changed nothing," he noticed, "but they haven't altered the position of a piece of furniture since Queen Victoria came to the throne."

1   His family solicitors Todd, Dennes and Lamb, 22 Chancery Lane (later Dennes and Co.), who administered a small trust fund.

2   There was a snobbery about houses in the suburbs and country ordinary enough to have numbers; it was the sort of thing that might get you ridiculed at boarding school.

37

WELLINGTON SQUARE, KING'S ROAD: LEAH HIRSIG & *DIARY OF A DRUG FIEND*
Spirit soothing oasis

In 1920 Crowley went to Sicily and established the Abbey of Thelema at Cefalu with the current Scarlet Woman: a woman named Leah Hirsig, whom he had met in America. It was hand-to-mouth communal living with a fluctuating crew of about half a dozen, including children and visiting disciples.

While in Sicily Crowley became an Ipsissimus,[1] an old Golden Dawn word preserved in popular culture in Dennis Wheatley's occult thrillers *The Devil Rides Out* and *To The Devil – A Daughter*. It is the highest grade in the Golden Dawn/A∴A∴ system. Having left Christ and Mohammed behind at the Magus stage, he was now "wholly free from all limitations soever... The Ipsissimus is pre-eminently the Master of all modes of existence... [with] no relation as such with any Being... and no consciousness of any kind involving duality."

Crowley seems to be the only human being who has ever officially attained this grade, albeit self-conferred. He had also lucked in with Leah Hirsig ("Alostrael"), an extraordinary woman in her own right, but whom a High Court judge might describe as depraved: she was happy to shit on him, have sex with a goat, and sexually abuse her children. Crowley's prolix, cocaine-fuelled paeans to her in his Magickal Record crank *fin-de-siècle* decadence up to a rarely seen voltage: she is "the fiend, Satan-Alostrael", with "Her Satan-secret Asp-brew in Her Cup's Blood (Filth, Madness, Poison, Inchantment, Putrefaction)"; "She's of sound Satan-stock... the stuff of my ideal, fiend-whore...".

---

1   From the Latin "*ipse*", an intensified pronoun: not just I, or you, or he, but emphatically myself, yourself or himself, further intensified to an exalted or supreme degree by the suffix "*-issimus*".

And I the Worm have trailed my slug-slow slime across Her Breasts; so that Her mother-mood is turned and Her breasts itch with lust of Incest. She hath given Her two-year bastard boy to Her lewd lover's whim of sodomy, hath taught him speech and act, things infinitely abhorred, with Her own beastly carcass. She hath tongued Her five-month girl, and asked its father to deflower it... Then Her blood's grown icy hard and cold with hate; and her eyes gleam as Her ears ring with a chime of wedding bells, dirty words, or vibrate, cat-gut fashion, to the thin shrieks of a young child that Her Beast-God-Slave-Mate is torturing for Her pleasure – ay! and his own, since of Her Cup he drank, and of Her soul he breathed.

He loved it all. He rolled each drop of filth around His tongue. All this because He loved Her. He loved Her as nor God nor Man nor Beast nor Devil has loved. All this because She loved him as he Her; because She was of his bone marrow, and his flesh nerve, and of his blood the spirochaetes...[2]

Sounds romantic, I hear you say. But at the same time "there She lies, the lazy lump of nastiness, no more to me than my cut toenails... I don't love Her; it's her lust for evil, for our Lord, for me..."

Remembering her in Paris, he wrote "I have made my Scarlet Woman, perfect beyond all praise, from a dull ugly school-teacher, ignorant, tired, old and common. Only three years and three months – behold a peerless Proctophile,[3] a Priestess of Passion, prehensile to the Phallus of Pan... her faith, her courage, her candour unmatched in the world... No deed but we dared it and did it! No sorrow but we suffered it. No filth and no venom but we made it our meat and drink..."

Trying to have sex with a goat (after which Crowley cut its throat) seems innocuous enough compared to other activity in the paean above, which doesn't sound either allegorical or pure fantasy.

2   Spirochaetes: the bacteria of syphilis.
3   Literally 'anus lover', coined from Greek.

The "lewd lover" with the whim of sodomy is Crowley himself, and the two-year bastard boy is Leah's son Hans ("Hansi") from a previous relationship, whom he describes elsewhere as "my darling little brother and concubine Dionysus Ganymede"; Ganymede is a reference to the Greek myth of Zeus, in the form of an eagle, carrying off the boy Ganymede to be his catamite, as in the slightly queasy painting by Rembrandt. The five-month girl is their daughter Anne Lea ("Poupée"), who was about six months old at the time of Crowley writing.

Whatever happened, it wasn't all fiendish exultation at the Abbey. Both parents were devastated a couple of months later when Poupée died. She was always a sickly child, and as her health worsened – two or three months before the screed above – Crowley had been distraught, "howling like a mad creature all day. I want my epitaph to be 'Half a woman made with half a god.'"[4]

In 1922 Crowley returned from Cefalu, and after almost lodging in Russell Square (not an area he liked; he mentions staying in "a horrible hotel in Russell Square thronged with hustling hooligans of the middle classes") Gwen Otter encouraged him to look down the King's Road, where he found new digs at 31 Wellington Square.

Crowley was now out of money and tried to sell some journalistic pieces such as 'The Crisis in Freemasonry' and 'The Jewish Problem Re-Stated', but he hit a more saleable subject with drugs. Writing as an expert in curing drug addiction – which was ironic, because it was in Cefalu that his own use of cocaine and heroin had become uncontrollable – he wrote 'The Drug Panic' as "A London Physician" and 'The Great Drug Delusion' as "A New York Specialist".

Crowley failed to sell a book idea to the literary publisher Grant Richards, creator of the World's Classics series, who didn't want either his autobiography or a book on drugs, but recommended he try the more popular firms of Hutchinson or Collins. And so it was that Crowley went to Collins, then at 48 Pall Mall, where J.D. Beresford gave him a £60 advance for the book which became *Diary of a Drug Fiend*.

---

4   A striking self-formula for Crowley, although not original: it is a quotation from Swinburne's *Phaedra* (1886).

Over four weeks, at 31 Wellington Square, Crowley dictated the 121,000 word book to Leah – taking longhand dictation, a feat in itself – at well over four thousand words a day. Characteristically high-minded in tone, it presents the Abbey of Thelema as a radical clinic where drug addicts can be cured by the book's Crowley figure 'King Lamus'.

Beresford was surprised to see Crowley reappear so soon, manuscript in hand, but he was impressed and gave him a further £120 advance for an autobiography.

As for Wellington Square, Crowley was drawn to 31 for numerological reasons (31 is the "secret key" to *The Book of the Law*) and it is very pleasant: he took "a large front room on the first floor, with French windows opening upon a balcony which overlooked the spirit-soothing oasis of the square: the small green oblong with its ancient trees." Still addicted to heroin, he writes to disciple Jane Wolfe in Cefalu that he has taken a room in "a nice quiet house where I shall be able to work", asking her to send on his white flannel trousers and striped flannel jacket, and to "sew up 10 grammes of the Hero's Bride in small flat packets" into the jacket lining.

Wellington Square was also an address of James Bond, where it appears as the plane-tree-filled square in *Moonraker*.

38

CLEVELAND GARDENS, BAYSWATER: HOUSE OF BETTY BICKERS
Perfectly evil

With *Diary of a Drug Fiend* finished, Leah went back to Cefalu and Crowley moved to stay with Betty Bickers and her daughter Sheila at 21 Cleveland Gardens (their name is changed to Dartnell in the *Confessions*). Originally a working-class girl from Leicestershire, Betty had been the second wife of Horace Sheridan-Bickers, who was part of the old A∴A∴ circle from before the First War; his magical name was 'Superabo', and Crowley later noted on his Probationer's Oath form "Sex maniac. Moved to British Columbia."[1]

As Crowley tells it, Betty "begged me to stay in her house... Finally I consented... I went with my eyes open, saying to myself, 'Whatever mischief may come of this, it is none the less my duty to save this woman's soul.'" (It was important, if possible, that she should come to Cefalu, "and develop her spiritual and moral self beyond reach of the constant temptation of London to drown her aspiration in drink and debauchery".)

Convinced that Betty was nevertheless in "genuine communication with intelligences of a very high order of initiation", it was at this address that he showed her how to "invoke the gods, and to banish evil and malignant entities that had hitherto deceived her by impersonating them. The very first experiment succeeded. She brought back information of great value."

Betty hosted Crowley's lectures on Thelema at Cleveland Gardens and invited her friends, to promote the cause and raise money for the Abbey at Cefalu. Along with the lectures, Crowley

---

1   He had some success as a screenwriter in Hollywood, but was increasingly given to fraudulent claims, later presenting himself as a philosopher with a heroic record in both world wars.

remembered, she "brought a number of friends to seek my assistance." One of the people who would come along was Raoul Loveday, soon to die in unfortunate circumstances.

Betty's teenage daughter Sheila also lived with her. Always alert to the presence of evil, particularly in tradesmen, creditors and former associates, Crowley spotted it at once in Sheila:

> I went round to Cleveland Gardens. Betty was out. Sheila, whom I had not seen since she was a baby, gave me tea. She fascinated and horrified me. I had never seen a girl so perfectly evil. She had no trace of heart. Such callous cynicism would have been abominable in a rake of sixty. A sinister malice lurked in her most casual remarks. Her deceitfulness was overpoweringly evident in her looks, no less than her words. Her eyes gleamed with ghastly glee. It suggested that she imagined herself as a sort of scourge to inflict obscene suffering upon anyone she might meet.

After Crowley returned to Cefalu, Betty spoke to the press (this was when the sensational papers were beginning to step up their attacks on him, notably the gutter press Sundays and *John Bull*) and mentioned that he had left owing her money. Crowley blamed this on the malevolent influence of Sheila.

39

THE HARLEQUIN CLUB, SOHO: BETTY MAY
Sordid and filthy drinking den

Just off Regent Street at 55 Beak Street, the Harlequin Club was a key Bohemian site in 1920s Soho, and it was frequented by friends Betty May and Nina Hamnett. May, "Tiger Woman", born in the East End, was a model, singer, and hardcore Bohemian who claimed to have been an Apache in Paris, and Hamnett was a former member of the A∴A∴ who had been introduced to Crowley by Ione de Forest. Daughter of an army officer, she studied art at the Slade and was an artist's model for Epstein, Augustus John and others; "Modigliani said I had the best tits in Europe".

Both women had already been prominent, 'life and soul' members of an earlier Soho club known to Crowley, the Crab Tree club on Greek Street, which was started by Augustus John and ran from 1912-1914. Both wrote memoirs, and both were to play a role in Crowley's long downfall between the wars.

Betty May had recently married Raoul Loveday, a bright young man just down from Oxford, and she was a friend of Betty Bickers, who was another Harlequin regular. Learning of Raoul's interest in Crowley, Bickers introduced them, and May was disturbed when Raoul came home after three days smelling of ether and talking about his travels on the astral plane. Crowley was a bad influence, and May attempted to keep them apart. At one stage May and Loveday lived in a room above the Harlequin, and she writes of him coming home in a terrible state and knocking on their window ("We were in the third floor of one of those tall houses in Beak Street") having climbed up a drainpipe.

Hoping to keep Loveday and Crowley apart, May found "another room whose address should not be known", in Fitzroy Street. This worked for a while until one day there was a knock at the door, and she opened it to find "a ponderous man attired in a Highland kilt... on one of his very small hands was a curious ring." He was also carrying a wand with a snake on it, and wearing cosmetics and a black glossy wig. Announcing "Do what thou wilt shall be the whole of the Law", he invited himself to dinner and produced a bottle of hock from his sporran.

In Crowley's version of events, Raoul had committed "the fatal folly of marrying a girl whom he had met in a sordid and filthy drinking den in Soho, called the Harlequin, which was frequented by self-styled artists and their female parasites. One of these went by the name of Betty May. Born in a slum in the East End, she had become an artist's model of the most vicious kind"; subsequently they lived "in one filthy room in Fitzroy Street, a foul, frowsty, verminous den". Crowley was appalled when Loveday took him to the Harlequin, where he saw Betty May singing, "three parts drunk, on the knees of a dirty-faced loafer, pawed by a swarm of lewd hogs, breathless with lust... Her only idea of life was this wallowing in the hog trough nuzzled by the snouts of the swine of Soho."

When Crowley returned to Cefalu, Loveday followed (followed in turn by Betty, who disliked it intensely). In 1923 Loveday caught typhoid and died, either from drinking the blood of a sacrificed cat or – more likely – drinking the local water, which Crowley had warned him not to do.

This stimulated a campaign of vilification in the press, where Crowley – already noticed for the Rites of Eleusis, his German propaganda activities, and *Diary of a Drug Fiend* – became "A Man We'd Like To Hang", "The King of Depravity", and "The Wickedest Man in the World". May was a major source for this, and later published her sensational ghost-written autobiography, *Tiger Woman* (1929). Three years later Hamnett published *Laughing Torso* (1932), a minor classic memoir: it has only a relatively brief mention of Crowley, but led to the 'Black Magic Libel Case'.

As for the Harlequin, it came to a sad end. It was run by a former Café Royal waiter named Yannis ("Johnny") Papani, who enlarged the premises by taking the cellar walls out, not realising they were structural. He came back after a short prison sentence, opened the door, and was killed when the building collapsed.

40

EIFFEL TOWER RESTAURANT, FITZROVIA
The most criminal street in London

Just north of Soho, the area along Fitzroy Street and Charlotte Street has become known since the 1940s as Fitzrovia, another Bohemian area that takes its name from the Fitzroy Tavern on Charlotte Street: a pub Crowley knew well, along with the Eiffel Tower restaurant further down the road at number 1 Percy Street. This was a more expensive Bohemian-Modernist haunt, particularly associated with Wyndham Lewis and the Vorticist painting group. It was started around 1914 by Rudolf Stulik, who had been chef to Emperor Franz Joseph and Lord Kitchener.

Meanwhile there was a young man named Arthur Calder-Marshall – later to become a writer – at Oxford University, who was a friend of Victor Neuburg, and he wanted to meet Crowley. He was fascinated by the scene at the Fitzroy Tavern, where he would often see Betty May and Nina Hamnett (Hamnett was so much a regular that she used the pub as her c/o address). In autumn 1929 Betty May told him that Crowley had returned to London and was staying at the Eiffel Tower (it was also a hotel), just fifty yards from the Fitzroy. "I begged her to introduce me, but she refused. 'We're not on speaking terms,' she said, 'but if we were, I still wouldn't introduce you. That man is utterly evil.'"

Calder-Marshall found someone else to introduce him, an unnamed poet ("He'll see anyone who'll see him," said the poet, "but watch out he doesn't land you with the bill") and he met Crowley for an evening drink in the Eiffel Tower dining room. Crowley had – just by chance, he said – been looking in *Who's Who* and found his surname; was Arthur related to the Robert Calder-Marshall of Shanghai? Young Arthur saw that Crowley was looking for money in his family, but despite this unpromising start he invited Crowley to speak at the Oxford University Poetry Society.[1]

In his all-or-nothing, hot-or-cold, permanently extreme way Crowley later described Charlotte Street as the "most criminal street in London", and he complained in his diary that his friend Gerald Yorke, who was acting as his manager, had let Crowley's German partner Bertha Busch "stew in the stinking slum of Charlotte Street all this time". This later attracted Yorke's incredulous annotation "At the Eiffel Tower!"

Crowley continued to go to the Eiffel Tower occasionally, brushing up against Modernism without quite being part of it. The same is true of the Cave of the Golden Calf, another venue remembered for avant-garde artists and decorated by Wyndham Lewis, which was in Heddon Street off Regent Street (Heddon Street is now better known as the site of David Bowie's telephone box). Crowley gives a caricature mention to Wyndham Lewis and The Golden Calf (as The Smoking Dog) in *Diary of a Drug Fiend*, but by now he was not only a notorious figure but an unfashionable one (D.H. Lawrence told publisher P.R. Stephensen "I feel his day is rather over") and successful artists and writers were not interested in his company. Augustus John – not much older than Lewis, but a different generation artistically – was an amiable exception.

Rudolf Stulik, the Eiffel Tower's proprietor, took to drink, and the business failed in the later Thirties. Crowley gave a series of lectures on yoga there in the spring of 1937, in the restaurant's final days. One Friday night, in September 1937, he noted "Goodbye to Stulik and the Eiffel Tower for ever. The last bottle of Burgundy. Only Monty[2] and I and two others to sit with Rudolph at the end."

It limped on into the following week before closing altogether, but re-opened in 1938 as the White Tower, to which Crowley went quite often. It is currently the upmarket Vietnamese restaurant House of Ho.

---

1 The lecture, on Gilles de Rais, the fifteenth-century mass-murderer of children, was cancelled by the university authorities and published by P.R. Stephensen as *The Banned Lecture* (Mandrake Press, 1930).

2 His friend Montgomery Evans, also a friend of Arthur Machen.

4 1

DUKE'S HOTEL, ST. JAMES'S PLACE
Mr Bishop checks in

Crowley was expelled from Cefalu in 1923, having meanwhile dictated his extraordinarily prolix memoirs, his *Confessions*, to Leah Hirsig. Subtitled an autohagiography, the autobiography of a saint, it has flashes of great richness, insight and fascination amid a general tone of airy self-satisfaction, in which Crowley constantly insists on his innocence, purity of mind, and continual surprise at the shabbiness of the world.

After Cefalu, Crowley spent much of the 1920s in Tunisia, France, and Germany, returning to London occasionally and staying in hotels and short-term apartments: around 1928-30 these included Oddenino's Hotel near the Café Royal, Yeoman House on Haymarket, and the Georgian House at 10 Bury Street, just south of Jermyn Street. On at least one of these returns he stayed at the Duke's Hotel, in its secluded location (convenient for the Mayfair / Piccadilly area) just off St.James's Place, one of London's discreetly plutocratic little corners tucked away towards the foot of St.James's Street.

Mindful of his notoriety, and perhaps foreseeing trouble over the bill, he checked in here under the resonant name of "Mr Bishop".

42

MANSFIELD STREET: HOUSE OF GERALD YORKE
Unspeakably treacherous swine

Gerald Yorke (1901-1983) was much on Crowley's mind through the early Thirties. Born in 1901 into a well-to-do family, he was educated at Eton and Trinity Cambridge, Crowley's old college, and was the brother of the novelist Henry Yorke, better known by his pen-name Henry Green. He had been an army officer and he was a serious cricketer, playing county cricket for Gloucestershire.

Yorke had a strange bereavement during his schooldays, as bizarre as it was tragic, when two other Eton boys put a curse on his much-loved elder brother Philip using a wax effigy, and Philip died (one of the boys was Eric Blair, later to write as George Orwell).

In his early twenties Yorke became interested in Crowley's work. At this point he was still based at the family's townhouse[1] at 9 Mansfield Street (moving to 5 Montagu Square in 1938). Number 9 is a handsome, late 18thC neo-classical building in a terrace designed by the Adam brothers. Radio producer Lance Sieveking was brought here by Crowley in the Thirties, and (no doubt thinking of the pillared doorway, the fanlight above the door, and the railings in front of the house) he remembered it as "a perfect setting for anything to do with the great Black Magician. Number 9 was indeed just such a house as Dr Jekyll must have lived in, and, from time to time, Mr. Hyde."[2]

After reading Crowley, Yorke had contacted him, met him in Paris, and in 1928 joined the A∴A∴ as Frater Volo Intelligere. The upshot was that he became Crowley's business manager, agent, and

---

1   They also had a country house in Gloucestershire, Forthampton Court.

2   Like the black-and-white, vintage Hollywood ideal of Victorian London in the 1931 *Dr. Jekyll and Mr. Hyde* film.

trustee, overhauling the chaos of Crowley's affairs and getting him regularly funded with an allowance of ten pounds a week (far more than it sounds now).

For this he was soon rewarded with endless abuse in Crowley's diaries ("rat", "skunk", "utter shit", "heartless cad", "unspeakably treacherous swine" and so on) and an attempt to sue him for £40,000 (about three million today). This figure was optimistically calculated as the money Crowley would have made, around 1930, without Yorke's interference.

Yorke stopped managing Crowley in 1932 to travel in China and Tibet, and after studying Buddhism he briefly became the agent for the Thirteenth Dalai Lama, Thubten Gyatso. But by the time he left for the East he had studied with Crowley for several years and had a good working knowledge of magic. In later life he knew the Rolling Stones, who came to his country house for tea. Politely declining Mick Jagger's offer of a tea-time joint, he said he had bad memories of being on a 'magical retirement' in Tunisia, in his old Crowley days: "Forced to smoke that beastly stuff for nearly a month".

Remarkably, Yorke and Crowley remained friends. Yorke bore no grudge, keeping up an intelligent and unfazed interest in Crowley's work and collecting books, manuscripts and ephemera. The Yorke Collection is now in London's Warburg Institute. He has a further memorial in the superb volume edited by Keith Richmond, *Aleister Crowley, The Golden Dawn and Buddhism: Reminiscences and Writing of Gerald Yorke*.[3]

3   (York Beach, Maine, Teitan Press, 2011). He is more unexpectedly remembered on the Vincent Price LP *Witchcraft-Magic: An Adventure in Demonology*, where – about 59 minutes in – Price briefly tells an apocryphal story of Yorke invoking Thoth while at Cambridge.

43

MANDRAKE PRESS, MUSEUM STREET
The man who saw the point

Crowley went through a remarkable period of publishing in 1929-30, consolidating his life's work with *Magick in Theory and Practice* (Paris, 1929) and his monumental *Confessions* (Mandrake Press, 1930; it had been cancelled by Collins) as well as his novel *Moonchild* (Mandrake, 1929).

Mandrake press was at number 41 Museum Street. It had been started by an Australian, Edward "Teddy" Goldston, who had an oriental book and print shop at number 25, but was soon in the energetic hands of Percy Reginald ("Inky") Stephensen, another Australian, together with Gerald Yorke (*Magick in Theory and Practice* was printed in Paris by this same team of Stephensen and Yorke). Mandrake had come to the attention of the police for publishing a book of D.H. Lawrence's erotic paintings, and Stephensen – a young Communist sympathiser who had been a Rhodes Scholar at Oxford – had strong feelings about the need to defy censorship.

He also sympathised with Crowley as a man misunderstood and unjustly vilified – *John Bull*, for example, had accused him of being a cannibal and eating two of his mountaineering sherpas – so he published his own book of Crowley's outrageous and often ludicrous press coverage, *The Legend of Aleister Crowley* (Mandrake, 1930), in which he also notes the "'ninetyish romantic bravado" of the younger, Edwardian Crowley's attitude.

Stephensen returned to Australia after the Mandrake Press venture. From being a Communist at Oxford he moved to the far-right, and in 1936 he was running a magazine called *The Publicist*, which advocated not only monarchy – not universally popular in Australia – but also fascism and anti-Semitism. He later founded the 'Australia First' political party, and in the Second World War he was interned for supporting Germany and Japan.

Stephensen is one of three living dedicatees of Crowley's Confessions ("P.R. STEPHENSEN, who saw the point"), the others being Augustus John and J.W.N. Sullivan. Augustus John remained on cordial terms with Crowley all their lives, and he was such an eminent artist in their day that citing him as a friend is almost an endorsement or testimonial. Crowley credits him with "practical assistance", and John had rallied, in fairly general terms, on Crowley's side against hostile press coverage. Sullivan was an eminent mathematician, introduced to Crowley by Nina Hamnett, and it was for Sullivan that Crowley produced the memorable opinion that "every phenomenon should be an orgasm of its kind."

44

ATLANTIS BOOKSHOP, BURY PLACE AND MUSEUM STREET
At the Sign of the Beast 666

The idea of Bloomsbury now has a rather refined and genteel ring to it, largely due to Virginia Woolf and the Bloomsbury Group, but this was not always the case. It once had a more ambiguous character, where cheap lodgings[1] and sometimes down-at-heel scholarship met the slumminess of St. Giles, where Centre Point is now. This had long been notorious – it is the setting of Hogarth's *Gin Lane*, with the distinctive antique-pagan spire of Hawksmoor's St. George's Bloomsbury in the background, modelled on the mausoleum at Halicarnassus – and in more recent times it was home to Madeline Montalban, "the witch of St Giles". Writing to a friend from Marseilles in 1930, the artist Edward Burra says "I am surrounded by so many negroes and dwarfs that I can hardly believe I am not in the heart of old Bloomsbury." Add the proximity of the British Museum and the bookishness of the area, and it adds up to the kind of richly marginal area that suits occult business ventures.

One of London's best known occult bookshops (now at 49A Museum Street, along the road from the former site of Mandrake Press), Atlantis was an important venue for Crowley to sell books in the 1930s and 1940s. Founded by Michael Houghton in 1922, it was originally round the corner at 14 Bury Street (now the London Review of Books shop, in the renamed Bury Place; Houghton moved

---

[1] Austin Osman Spare, for example, lodged in Gilbert Place during one of the more impoverished periods of his life, between Museum Street and Bury Place. For more on the character and background of the area see Thomas Burke's authentic if rose-tinted account, *Living in Bloomsbury* (1939). Famous in his day as a writer of horror stories and potboilers about Limehouse Chinatown, Burke knew Crowley, who wrote in his diary on the 22 September 1945 "Tommy Burke is dead, alas."

to Museum Street around 1940). Crowley had plans for a small press there in the Thirties, variously imagined as the "Brazen Head Publishers, 14 Bury Street", the "Banyan Press, c/o Atlantis Bookshop 14 Bury Street", along with "The Apocalypse Bookshop 41a Museum Street", adjoining Mandrake Press. His plans have a nice ring to them: "At the Sign of the Beast 666 / Magickal and Occult Booksellers / New and Secondhand / The Trade Supplied".

Timothy d'Arch Smith knew Houghton slightly and remembers him as "almost a dwarf, his demeanour exactly comparable with that of Grumpy in *Snow White*." Atlantis sometimes figures in Crowley's diary just as "Mike" or "Mike's", with notes of how many books taken, although Crowley was never over-fond of him. In 1934 he wrote a limerick

Atlantis book shop.

A dwarf kike, who called himself Houghton!
– His balls, in his boyhood, were caught on
His mother's false teeth
In a foul slum in Leith
She stewed them with truffles and Corton.

Corton is a Burgundy, and a kike is someone who is Jewish. He notes "This was impromptu, a challenge by Tom Driberg, C.K. Ogden, and McGregor Reid. Line 1 was 'given' me. Idea all right, but Corton is a bad rime. I don't know if the incident described is authentic." It is a bad rhyme if Corton is given its proper French pronunciation. It doesn't reflect well on Driberg – later to be a prominent Labour politician – if he really gave Crowley that first line.

Houghton, whose original name seems to have been Hurvitz or Hurwitz, always tended to bring out Crowley's casual anti-Semitism: "These low Jew thieves justify *Der Sturmer*"[2] he wrote to German disciple Karl Germer in May 1937, and as late as June 1944, after more dealings with Houghton, he wrote in his diary "Oh God! Send us a Hitler!'"

2   Rabidly anti-Semitic Nazi propaganda paper (1923-1945). More about Germer shortly, at site 46.

There was a loose occult scene around Atlantis, and Crowley met people there including Jean Michaud, a musician with an interest in Rosicrucianism. Based at 40 Langham Street, Fitzrovia, he also headed a London group called The Order of the Hidden Masters, and went off with Houghton's wife. In the late Thirties, years after his disastrous relationship with Crowley had ended, Victor Neuburg was in the shop with his partner Runia Tharp, looking at secondhand books, when he suddenly moved closer to her. As quietly as possible he said "Let's leave", and when they got outside she saw he'd gone white. He'd just seen Crowley: "He was standing looking at books. Almost next to us. I don't think he saw me." It was the last time Neuburg ever saw him.

Crowley already had a history with the Bury Place shop even before Houghton, because it had been the Bury Street Buddhist Bookshop, a pioneering venture established by Lieut.-Colonel Ernest Rost, R.J. Jackson, and Col. J.R. Pain, where Crowley had a run-in of some kind with the management; possibly over money, or perhaps a reluctance to stock his books. Bury Place was the Atlantis Crowley knew best, but he knew Houghton had moved and in February 1943 he writes to a friend, Noel Fitzgerald "Mike still thieving in Museum Street, I believe."

Crowley also knew the Oriental booksellers that were once a feature of the area – Arthur Calder-Marshall writes of "the Oriental bookshops by the British Museum with their latent mystery as if they were the beginning of a story by Algernon Blackwood" – and along with Goldston's there was Luzac's, which was at number 46 Great Russell Street (now Jarndyce bookshop) from 1890 to 1986, and Probsthain's, still there at number 41. In 1910 Probsthain's distributed Crowley's Richard Burton-influenced, homo-erotic, Persian-style verses *Bagh-i-Muattar* (The Scented Garden).

Also in the area, along with the Mandrake Press and the bookshops, is the Plough pub, which Crowley drank in (it is mentioned very occasionally in the diaries). It was a moderately Bohemian pub between the wars, sometimes known as the Plug, for obvious reasons, or the Baby's Bottom, perhaps because the outside was painted a fleshy pink.

45

LANGHAM HOTEL, PORTLAND PLACE
Colonel Carter

Crowley's early Thirties time in Germany, initially as an artist exhibiting his paintings, involved numerous women, two of whom achieved Scarlet Woman status: Hanni Jaeger ("Anu", held office autumn 1930), and Bertha Busch ("Bill", held office autumn 1931 to autumn 1932). It also involved two rather more unexpected players: Gerald Hamilton, the original for "Mr. Norris" in Christopher Isherwood's novel *Mr. Norris Changes Trains*, and Lieut.-Colonel John Fillis Carre Carter, C.B.E., of the Special Branch.

After Crowley's expulsion from France there were popular and journalistic calls for him to be charged with various crimes, including murder. This inspired Colonel Carter – who knew Gerald Yorke – to find out how bad he really was (and whether he could be useful). Yorke insisted Crowley wasn't so bad when you knew him, so Carter gave him money to bring Crowley over from Belgium.

One night in June 1929 they had dinner at the Langham Hotel on Portland Place, a grandly Victorian building in 'Florentine Palace' style: it is mentioned in several Sherlock Holmes stories, and Conan Doyle and Oscar Wilde dined there together with their publisher. Crowley stayed at the Langham occasionally, and this end of Regent Street is another nexus he knew well in the Thirties. Along with the Langham Hotel he frequented the Bolivar restaurant attached to it; two or three of his many dentists were in the area, including Watson Turner at 50 Wimpole Street and Bywaters and Piper at 3 Portland Place, and he was for a while very involved with the Aquila Press at 2&3 Langham Chambers, All Souls Place, run by his associate James Cleugh. Crowley used it as c/o postal address, and around 1930 hoped to take it over, less for its publishing activities than for its premises, to use as a base.

Crowley and Carter got on like the proverbial house on fire, all the way through to brandy and cigars. Crowley was apparently much amused by Carter advising his son to masturbate on Saturday nights, so as to get it out of the way and not interfere with his studies (he evidently thought once was enough, like the bygone practice of having a bath on Sunday night to get clean for the week).

Carter's responsibilities included keeping an eye on 'secret societies', and he wanted Crowley to infiltrate the Theosophical Society (not as bizarre as it sounds; Theosophy was associated with anti-colonial tendencies threatening British rule in India). In the event Crowley was too famous for this, but they sent his secretary Israel Regardie[1] along, with a subscription paid for by the Special Branch. Carter also wanted to know what was going on in Germany, and here they struck gold with the notoriously corrupt Gerald Hamilton, who was well connected with the Comintern in Berlin.

A physically rather ugly, or at least grotesque, man, with a bald head and lips so full and blubbery they were almost indecent (a friend said he should cover his mouth with a fig-leaf), Gerald Hamilton had a fruity charm and the rare distinction of being interned in both world wars as a German sympathiser. When Crowley first met him he was working for Communism in Germany, but he later drifted to the far-right. He was also well-connected in the European gay underground,

1   Born Israel Regudy in the East End in 1907, Regardie grew up largely in America after his family emigrated, and became Crowley's secretary in 1928 after reading Crowley on yoga. This lasted for a couple of years, after which he became secretary to once-bestselling author Thomas Burke. Crowley and Regardie fell out in 1937 after Crowley ridiculed him for being an East End Jew ("Israel Regudy was born in the neighbourhood of Mile End Road, in one of the vilest slums in London. Of this fact he was morbidly conscious, and his racial and social shame embittered his life from the start.") Regardie hit back ridiculing Crowley for homosexual tendencies ("Darling Alice, You really are a contemptible bitch!").

Influenced by Jung and particularly Wilhelm Reich, Regardie later had a successful career in the States as a chiropractor and occult writer: he eventually forgave and appreciated Crowley enough to write *The Eye in the Triangle: An Interpretation of Aleister Crowley* (1970). This and other esoteric books brought him a large correspondence from the unfortunate and unhinged, which towards the end of his life he was collecting into a private book, 'Liber Nuts'. There is a biography by Gerald Suster.

with friends in the Vatican. Hamilton was introduced to Crowley by Jean Ross, the original for Isherwood's "Sally Bowles" in *Goodbye to Berlin*.[2] After a while Hamilton moved in as Crowley's Berlin lodger, in a profitable arrangement where Crowley seems to have received money from Colonel Carter for informing on Hamilton's Communist activities, while Hamilton seems to have received money from the German authorities for informing on Crowley, so their flat-share helped pay for itself.

2   Whom Crowley was later surprised to bump into in the London restaurant Hatchett's, at the corner of Dover Street and Piccadilly, one day in July 1932.

46

PARK MANSIONS, KNIGHTSBRIDGE
Wife of the Beast

In November 1928 Crowley had met the woman who would become not only the new Scarlet Woman but his second wife; this was Maria Teresa Ferrari de Miramar ("Marie"), a Nicaraguan. She claimed to practise voodoo, and Crowley liked to think of her as "The High Priestess of Voodoo." She also said she had raised the Devil when younger, and in Paris (without Crowley) she attempted to do this again in a ritual with Yorke and Israel Regardie. This involved her dancing, with a burning fire in an otherwise dark room and a heavy use of Abramelin incense, while all three chanted a mantra. Both men felt a strong presence of some kind, and in Yorke's case, by the end "I was on the verge of some sort of hysteria. My muscles were rigid, jaws champing and face working"; "I sensed a Being, Presence, or Force... something alive and apart from myself, with an atmosphere or will power stronger than mine and alien to me."

Crowley was refused leave to stay in France in 1929 and returned to England, marrying Maria (partly to overcome immigration difficulties) in Leipzig on 16 August 1929: this was reported in the *Times* ("ALEISTER CROWLEY MARRIED. CEREMONY IN LEIPZIG AFTER BEING BANNED FROM FRANCE") as the wedding of "Mr. Edward Alexander (Aleister) Crowley, the English mystic writer...". The marriage certificate describes him as an author, living at Georgian House, Bury Street. They lived for a few months in Kent, but Crowley had already met her nineteen-year-old replacement Hanni Jaeger (Anu) in Germany before they even moved into apartment 89, Park Mansions, Knightsbridge (SLOane 8534) in the summer of 1930. Crowley seems to have discovered the address through Colonel Carter, who had been living at apartment 8 in 1929.

Park Mansions is a large, ornate red-brick edifice in Knightsbridge, at the corner by Hyde Park where Knightsbridge itself – the road – meets Brompton Road, not far from Harvey Nichols (and Harrods a little further along). The building now houses Burberry, its huge wooden front doors now replaced with plate glass (and that same Knightsbridge/Brompton spur now houses Mr. Chow's, and a spectacular sculpture of a rhino hoist in a sling, along with jewellers and sports-car dealers). In Crowley's day it had tailors, an embroiderer, a gown shop and a "court furrier".

While they were here Crowley employed a cleaner from Mrs Stuart's Domestic Agency and "Servants Registry Office" at 550-552 Fulham Road (FULham 2123, with the rather nice telegram address "Royalize"). Karl Germer[1] was now largely supporting Crowley, and he queried why Crowley and Maria couldn't clean their own flat. Crowley was incensed, writing back "Your letter of June 20th is, I think, the most nauseating thing I have ever read... in your second paragraph you are even more psychopathic." Lecturing Germer on dirt, disorder, slaves, and kings, he had to insist a few days later that "a properly educated person expects a bath to be clean."

Knightsbridge was never Crowley's territory in the way that Piccadilly was, and although Harrods was just down the road he never patronised it to the extent that he patronised Fortnum's, which was much more his shop. He did, however, have some dealings a few years later with a small eccentric church just behind it on Basil Street. This was The Sanctuary, at number 23, run by a "Bishop James" (an irregularly ordained 'Wandering Bishop'[2]) who belonged to the so-called 'Old Catholic Church': his small congregation

---

1   Germer (1885-1962) was an honourable man who been awarded the Iron Cross in the First World War, was interned in a concentration camp before the Second, and was the only man prepared to testify to Crowley's good character in a London courtroom in 1934. Like Yorke, he is rewarded with endless vituperation in Crowley's diary: "insane swine", "unclean masturbating pimp", "really an utterly unimaginable shit." Nevertheless their friendship endured. He emigrated to America, and became Crowley's successor as head of the O.T.O.

2   For more on the often very peculiar world of Wandering Bishops or *Episcopi Vagantes* see Peter Anson's classic *Bishops At Large* (Faber, 1964).

included several wealthy women and he was known as "The Bishop of Harrods". Crowley attended a number of times in the second half of 1937, noting the similarities between James's teaching and his own, and seems to have wondered if it might be ripe for takeover. Long gone, the setting of this church is thought to have been one of the inspirations for Ngaio Marsh's 1936 thriller *Death in Ecstasy*.

Maria, meanwhile, was volatile and paranoid and believed Crowley was trying to poison her. He was in fact buying arsenic and strychnine from a chemist in St.James's Street called Pope Roach (he would have known it from his Jermyn Street days) but they were used as tonics in small doses, and popular with the Victorians.

Maria drank – shades of Rose – and Crowley was quite dispassionate about dumping her ("I gave you a great chance in life, and you threw it away. *Tant pis!*"). Her later life was a sad business: she lodged for a while at 7 Buckland Crescent, Swiss Cottage (from where she wrote "AC is died for me, he have not a drop of honneur"), then at Lower Marsh, Waterloo, and then at the Wandsworth "casual ward" for homeless women, the former workhouse at Swaffield Road. Finally she ended up in what was then the great London lunatic asylum at Colney Hatch.

Crowley saw a parallel with Rose, noting that when one Scarlet Woman goes to the "Bug House", another one comes along. He wrote in his diary "Hear Marie is in Colney Hatch", wondering a few days later if it was a case of mistaken identity (he later alleged the real Maria had died in an earthquake in Managua). As he wrote, lots of loonies (with moon symbol) thought they were his wife or mistress. Annotating this in 1950, Yorke noted that in fact she was still there; she died in Colney Hatch, forgotten, in 1955.

Yorke appealed to Crowley to treat her decently and at least let her know how things stood, but he was uninterested in visiting. Among her symptoms was a belief that she was related to the British Royal family, and that she was married to the Beast 666. When Yorke visited her he showed the psychiatric staff Crowley's calling card, and managed to clear up a misunderstanding she must have found intensely frustrating. She really was married to the Beast 666.

47

FRIBOURG AND TREYER, HAYMARKET
Perique By Appointment

Hamilton had no interest in magic, and Crowley didn't waste his time trying to explain it. Instead Hamilton saw Crowley as "a typical *bon bourgeois*", fond of "good eating, rare wines, ladies and fine cigars."

Whenever Hamilton returned to London from their flat in Berlin, Crowley would give him a shopping list. This included a particular tea available only from Fortnum and Mason on Piccadilly, a shop Crowley knew well, and a Pure Perique Medium Cut Pipe tobacco purveyed by Fribourg and Treyer, tobacconists by Royal Appointment, nearby at 34 Haymarket. The firm had been established in 1720.

Crowley was very particular about his smoking, and other tobacconists he used included Dunhill's on Duke Street, by Fortnum's, Philip Morris at 22 New Bond Street, and Van Raalte at 2 Glasshouse Street behind Piccadilly Circus, where he bought Latakia tobacco and cashed cheques.

In 1942 a complete stranger in Oddenino's restaurant told Crowley that he looked like Winston Churchill, and he liked this idea so much that he went in search of a hat and cigar as 'props' to complete the likeness. Having looked without luck ("tried vainly all probable places") for such a cigar, he was walking across from Watkins bookshop, Cecil Court, to a bus-stop in Lower Regent Street when he saw exactly what he needed in the window of the tobacconist Galata at 36 Leicester Square, and was astonished to find that the man selling it was a Turk named Joseph Zitelli, "Churchill's own Cigar Merchant!!! So I got the actual thing I was looking for in the most fraternal spirit!"

Zitelli was, quite literally, Churchill's own cigar merchant, but Crowley was fascinated by him in a way that went beyond that. He saw the whole business as auspicious and perhaps of great import, and it struck him that the name was rather like Zanoni in Bulwer-Lytton's once famous occult novel.[1]

Fribourg and Treyer's former premises is still there on Haymarket, with its classically 18th century double bow windows. And next door at number 35 was Heppell's, a branch of the chemist Crowley relied on for heroin in his later London years.

---

1   Edward Bulwer-Lytton, *Zanoni* (Saunders and Otley, 1842). Crowley put it on the A∴A∴ reading list as "Valuable for its facts and suggestions about Mysticism." He also took the obscure word Augoeides (a kind of neo-Platonic higher self, important in Crowley's thinking) largely from *Zanoni*: "Soul of mine, the luminous, the Augoeides".

48

L'ESCARGOT, SOHO, AND OTHER RESTAURANTS:
Truffles in Hell

"Admirable", "magnificent", "A1" and "excellent" are among the adjectives Crowley lavishes on this classic French restaurant in Soho where he often went with Yorke and others in the late thirties. The picturesque figure of a man riding a snail outside (now coloured; it was plain white in Crowley's day) shows the original owner Monsieur Gaudin, who farmed his own snails in the basement.

Food was very important to Crowley, especially as he grew older. Back in 1906 he'd assured Gerald Kelly "They live on old brandy, caviar and truffles in Hell"[1] and by the Thirties he was something of a gourmand: "Nothing to eat all these two days but oysters, caviar, foie gras" he writes one day in 1932, and on another occasion he wonders "Could one not stuff a chicken with oysters?". When the *I Ching* says "IX – Hsiao Khu. Small restraint", he interprets this as lunch from 1.30 until 5.00: "Caviar, lobster, foie gras, white Burgundy, brandy &c. All out!"

It was a matter of faith to live like a king, even in poverty. Money was a constant issue with Germer ("Once get me on my feet and I will repay royally", Crowley wrote to him, "But kings in exile are always beggars"). Germer complained that the money he was sending was all going on cigars and fine dining.

Crowley dined regularly at Chez Victor, another French restaurant at the south end of Wardour Street, on one occasion starting his lunch with four absinthes. Run by Victor, former head waiter at L'Escargot, it was associated with a gay clientele in the

---

1   Not in a context with any disapproval or disenchantment. It is more like an expression of good cheer, possibly related to an imminent trip to Paris.

Thirties and survived into recent times.[2] He also remained a loyal regular at the Café Royal, on the Piccadilly/Regent Street hub, together with Oddenino's, along with occasional visits to other establishments including the White Tower, Simpson's, the Savoy, the Ritz, Claridges, the Berkeley Grill, Czarda's, Hatchett's on Piccadilly, the German restaurant Kempinski (underground below Veeraswamy's at the start of Swallow Street; he had known the more famous Berlin original), Verrey's on Regent Street, and the Ivy.

Temperamentally more suited to restaurants than cafes, he nevertheless spent plenty of time in Colombo's at 51 Greek Street (the Soho branch of Joseph Colombo's longer-established café in Fitzrovia, at 35 Great Portland Street, which he also knew), and he sometimes went to Santini's at 17 Frith Street, run by Mario Santini (now Ceviche). At Christmas 1936 – he didn't, of course, celebrate Christmas, although he did send "Anti-Christmas cards" to a few close friends – he noted Soho was dead and almost empty but for "that robber Santi Romani" (a virtual anagram; he loved word games and would have made a good crossword compiler). There is something memorable in the image of Crowley prowling around Soho on his own on Christmas Day.

He knew Soho well, for prostitutes as well as restaurants, and even lived there briefly. He stayed at the Astoria Hotel at 11-13 Greek Street, which became an Italian convent shortly afterwards, where he met shipping heiress Nancy Cunard. She became a friend, although she had no time for what she called "hoolie-goolie" stuff, and he never bothered her with it. Her first impression was a sound like bats squeaking, coming from his room, which turned out to be his rubber soles on the floor. He also seems to have lived briefly at 14 Edward Street (now the stretch of Broadwick Street between Wardour Street and Berwick Street, and no longer separately named); he wrote to Germer using that address in November 1936, and the addition of a phone number, GERrard 1223, suggests it was more than a *poste restante* service.

2   Michael Caine, Peter Cook, and Diana Rigg all ate there; it finally closed in 2007.

Foreign cuisine other than high French was still a cosmopolitan novelty in Britain, and Crowley – nothing if not cosmopolitan – ate regularly at a Greek restaurant called Demos, which was at 166 Shaftesbury Avenue, and a smart Spanish restaurant Majorca ("Soho with a Mayfair accent," says a guide, "chic and the waiters wear the sort of well-cut coats you associate with first-class expensive restaurants in the West End"); that was at 66 Brewer Street. Italian restaurants were more common, and Crowley went occasionally to Frascati's at the Bloomsbury end of Oxford Street, Pagani's on Great Portland Street (both magnificent buildings and now gone), Monico's on Piccadilly Circus, and Leoni's Quo Vadis, still there on Dean Street but no longer Italian.

Along with L'Escargot and Chez Victor he was particularly fond of Bentley's (still there in Swallow Street), where he might have lobster and where his favourite waitress told him one day in January 1942 that he was looking like hell.

Another favourite haunt was the long-gone Casa Prada, a Spanish restaurant on the Euston Road: one evening he met his friend Louis Fox at El Vino's, then they went on to "White's Oysters Euston Road. Casa Prada ditto for best steak in London." Casa Prada was at number 292, and was associated with musicians; Crowley would occasionally bump into the composer Constant Lambert there, and it was also frequented by other friends such as Charles Cammell and Tom Driberg.

Most of this dining was dependent on the generosity of friends. When Crowley notes that he met Bruce Blunt (friend of the composer Philip Heseltine, or 'Peter Warlock') one lunchtime and it was "A perfect steak and excellent brandy after a struggle. The Clos Vougeot A.1.", it is not clear if the struggle was with the kitchen or Blunt.

When Crowley entertained it was more likely to be at home, and he was an accomplished cook of steaks. He did sometimes dream up Western-style dishes,[3] like his "Canape Talisman" or his "Biftek Crapaudine" – for which you had to pound together "olives, anchovies, capers, onions, garlic: smear minute steak, bake in batter" and preferably serve with asparagus – but his signature dishes were good plain steak and more especially curry.

---

3   See also Chester Terrace.

49

SHANGHAI, SOHO, AND OTHER RESTAURANTS:
Ordeal by Curry

Down at the far end of Greek Street from L'Escargot, Crowley's favourite Chinese restaurant was the Shanghai at number 8 (now the Japanese Knife Centre) next to the former Pillars of Hercules pub. Founded in 1924, this was a fairly Spartan establishment but with an extensive menu, and decorated with Chinese characters on scrolls. He also went occasionally to Ley-On's at the corner of Gerrard Street and Wardour Street, in those days the most popular and best-known Chinese in the area, and he liked Young's, then at 178 Wardour Street, where he sometimes went with his last partner Alice.

Crowley had a strong taste for Asian food in general. Indian restaurants were still not common in Britain. Crowley went to Shafi's at 18 Gerrard Street (one of the earliest, founded in 1920) and to Dilkush at 4 Windmill Street in Fitzrovia, opposite the Fitzroy Tavern. Veeraswamy's was a high-class pioneer in the field (and still there on Regent Street). Churchill, Gandhi and Charlie Chaplin all ate there, but Crowley was not impressed. In 1941 he recorded that he had tried it again after a seven-year absence and found it "coarse and bad as ever". The following year he accused them of serving rabbit as chicken.

Although Crowley had real, down-to-earth experience of the Far East, his taste for Asian food involved strong elements of exoticism and orientalism. This was true of his taste for curry, which was part of a more general taste for extremes ("I want blasphemy, murder, rape, revolution, anything, bad or good, but strong"). In a very British fashion this had elements of the comic ordeal (long part of the British attitude, with people boasting about eating "the Brick Lane ring stinger" and so on) and even of the practical joke: entertaining a friend in 1936 he writes "Bracewell put through Ordeal by Curry."

Dylan Thomas gives this attitude a further surreal twist, writing to a friend in 1937:

> Last week, a man called Mulk Raj Anand[1] made a big curry for everybody... The first course was beans, little ones. I ate two and couldn't speak. A little man called Wallace B. Nichols... took a whole mouthful and was assisted out... After the main dish, which was so unbelievably hot that everyone, except the Indian, was crying like Shirley Temple, a woman, Mrs Henderson, looked down onto her plate and saw, lying at one corner of it, a curious rubbery thing that looked like a red, discarded French letter. In interest, she picked it up and found it was the entire skin from her tongue.

Anand had written to Crowley a few years earlier (from Sunningfields Road, Hendon, north west London) on this very subject of extreme curry, wanting to cite Crowley in his own forthcoming book.[2] On his first page he quotes the *Confessions* on Singapore curries: "They sting like serpents, stimulate like strychnine; they are subtle and sensual like Chinese courtesans, sublime and sacred, inscrutably inspiring and unintelligibly illuminating, like Cambodian carvings."

Dining at Crowley's, another friend remembered

> at the first mouthful I thought I had burned my tongue with caustic acid... Crowley, however, shovelled an enormous plateful away... fortifying it as he went with chillies and other spices... sweat pouring down his face... He explained that he had learnt about real curry in India, Burma and Ceylon, that its object was to

---

1   Mulk Raj Anand (1905-2004), a distinguished Indian writer and novelist who knew the Bloomsbury Group. He was also interested in tantra and the unconscious, looking back on the inter-wars period in his memoir, *Conversations in Bloomsbury*: "Romanticism led to the unconscious as in the new vital works of D.H. Lawrence... I wanted to liberate the unconscious via the Shakti-Shakta Tantric thought and dig down to the depths."

2   *Curries and Other Indian Dishes* (Harmsworth, 1932)

produce sweating, hence a cooling process... He pointed out that this was only one of many cooling processes he was familiar with in these lands and that one of the great points of hospitality was to have one's *partes viriles* lifted up by a maiden attendant, and fanned from below with an exquisitely painted fan... He assured me that I would soon get to enjoy such things, as well as curry, once I got out there, to say nothing of the delights of opium, hashish and heroin.

Louis Umfreville Wilkinson,[3] whom Crowley said was his best friend in later life, remembered Crowley curries as "astounding", but "rather too moving for me" (possibly a euphemism) "though I ate them with joy for their very excessiveness."

Crowley's interest in food and drink inspired him to think of opening restaurants. In the Thirties he was floating the idea of a Black Magic Restaurant or Bar 666, with a "unique aesthetic": there would be goats' heads and skulls, and lights that would "come on automatically when certain objects are approached." Another plan outlines atmospheric ideas including situation ("Obscure ill-famed quarter, but not too inaccessible. Narrow dark alley") and furnishing ("Furniture. No chairs or tables, but mattresses, armchairs, bolsters... dyed to appear dirty.") In addition to these ideas of ghost-train engineering and psychological decor, he also planned to open an "Exotic Restaurant", and here he was probably more sincere about the food. In 1936 he even got as far as investigating a possible site for it at 16 Clay Street, Marylebone, a fairly bleak back street (more than an alley, but not a mews) between Crawford Street and Dorset Street. Now largely redeveloped, it had no real 'walk-by' for casual customers but it could have worked for a deliberate 'destination' restaurant, as it could for a brothel.

Crowley's diaries frequently record dishes at home such as "Zambar of Lobster: Iced". That was one hot day in the summer of 1936 (zambar was ready-made spiced lentil powder he bought in tins,

3   Louis Umfreville Wilkinson (1881-1966), writer and novelist who wrote as Louis Marlow, was certainly Crowley's most literary friend. His works include the novel *Swan's Milk* (1934), a memoir of Crowley in *Seven Friends* (1953) and an inspired parody of Henry James, 'The Better End'.

along with tins of Madras curry powder and jars of vindaloo paste; and eating curry chilled seems to have been a once popular practice). Sometimes the boat was really pushed out: "Altogether my lunch was memorably exotic: cooked by host himself in a Bloomsbury flat".

chilli con carne – Mexican dish so hot that it makes strong men weep. With it were four "side-dishes" – concoctions based on (a) red macassar fish & poppy-seed (b) tamarind-fish (c) Burmese balichow made from rotten prawns (bottled, very Spilsburyesque) (d) Kasoondee – minced mango in spiced oil.

"Spilsburyesque" is nice: Sir Bernard Spilsbury was a leading forensic pathologist, and his famous cases included identifying Dr Crippen's wife from her remains.

He was always devising new dishes, typically with chillies and cayenne pepper:

Pot au feu Ang-Kor...[4] Cocotte: bed of bhindi with chillis. Middle layer: prawns and chillis in vindalu; top, chillis and Chinese onions.

My new savoury. Fried rye bread smear with Chinese chili sauce grilled sardines top with egg fried in olive oil.

My savoury. Fried bread smeared with tamarind fish paste. On this grill anchovies and sardines alternate. Over this yolk of egg scrambled with cayenne.

Gold fish toast. Brown bread and dripping nearly toasted. Add stripes of red chilli and anchovies: finish.

My Almond Chicken. Steep cold chicken in red & green (or bird's eye) chillis. Add Bamboo pickle (in oil), Col. Skinner's Chutney,[5] & lots of almonds. Stew it all up. Oh boy!

4   As in Angkor Wat.
5   A Fortnum's preparation; they still sell it.

50

WESTMINSTER ABBEY
A past life

While they were living in Berlin, Bertha Busch stabbed Crowley with a carving knife just below the shoulder. He lost a good deal of blood, and it made him sufficiently aware of his own mortality to draw up a will on 22 December 1931, in which he wanted his body to be embalmed in Egyptian fashion or, failing that, his ashes interred in an urn placed either at Boleskine, or Cefalu, or Westminster Abbey. The Abbey – a joke, since burial there is not at the wish of the deceased – is about a desire to be recognised as a truly great poet, interred in Poets' Corner with the likes of Shakespeare.

Westminster Abbey had already figured in his longer story. When he recovered his previous incarnations, he remembered being Eliphas Levi (1810-1875), the French occultist who played a major role in the 19thC occult revival. Levi visited London in 1854, where he met with Bulwer-Lytton and other students of the esoteric, and one day he found a note at his lodgings. It contained half of a card cut in two, with half of the Seal of Solomon, and a scrap of paper which read "Tomorrow, at three o'clock, before Westminster Abbey, the other half of this card will be presented you".

Levi stood there holding his half card as nonchalantly as possible, and saw a carriage standing before the Abbey. A servant beckoned him to the carriage, where he met a woman in black, with a veil, who showed him the other half. Unveiling, she told him ("with a very strong English accent" – she was evidently speaking French) that she knew he had been asked for magical demonstrations before, and had declined. "Perhaps you have not the necessary things," she said; "I will show you a complete magic cabinet." Swearing him to secrecy, she showed him a collection of magical instruments and robes, "even lent me some curious books that I needed" and wanted him to carry out a full necromantic evocation of a dead spirit. They agreed to evoke Apollonius of Tyana, a first-century Greek, and ask him two questions, "of which one concerned myself and the other interested this lady."

The 'cabinet' for the evocation was in a small tower of her house, with four concave mirrors. There was a sort of altar with a marble slab, on which was a little brazier, and there was another brazier on a tripod in front of Levi, who held a sword and a ritual to be read. Levi felt he had invoked the clear shade of a man, larger than life-size and not looking as Levi had expected, before he passed out. The shade had not spoken, "but it seemed that the questions which I wished to ask it answered themselves in my mind. To that of the lady an interior voice replied in me, "Dead!" (it concerned a man of whom she wished to have some intelligence). As to myself I wished to know if reconciliation and pardon would be possible between two persons, of whom I thought, and the same interior echo answered pitilessly, "Dead!"

The effect of all this made a deep impression on Levi, who writes that after it, "I was no longer the same man..."

✝

There is a coda to Crowley and Westminster Abbey in the 1940s, during the war, by which time he was a slightly comic figure in Britain. William Joyce, "Lord Haw-Haw", regularly broadcast wireless propaganda at England from Berlin. In his distinctive hectoring tones, he said that prayers and church services were clearly failing to help the British cause – so perhaps Crowley should be invited to celebrate a Black Mass at Westminster Abbey.

51

ALBEMARLE STREET, MAYFAIR
Magick

After a couple of years largely in Berlin, Crowley returned to London with Bertha "Bill" Busch in July 1932. Before settling in they had to visit Colney Hatch (more of that later) and they also spent eight days at the celebrated and rather louche Cavendish Hotel on Duke Street, just south of Jermyn Street, popular with 'fast' members of the upper classes and run by the formidable Rosa Lewis. She figures as "Lottie Crump" in Evelyn Waugh's novel *Vile Bodies*, and Crowley writes in his diary "Shifted our Vile Bodies to the Cavendish hotel."

Lewis was not a woman to be trifled with, and she embarrassed Cyril Connolly at a wedding by shouting "Ere's the man wot owes me money!" After Crowley's stay ended with an unpaid bill, he and Bertha then took a flat in Albemarle Court, service flats at 27 Albemarle Street, off Piccadilly. This was near Crowley's old Mayfair haunts, joined to Bond Street by the Royal Arcade and just round the corner from Stafford Street and memories of Whineray. They were opposite the Royal Institution ("for the diffusion of mechanical and scientific knowledge") with its impressively-pillared classical façade modelled on a Roman temple. It was here that Faraday had first demonstrated electromagnetism. A century earlier Bishop Berkeley, the idealist philosopher who believed the apparently material world existed only in the mind (and therefore figures in Crowley's A∴A∴ reading list – "The classic of subjective idealism" – and in *Magick*) had also lived on Albemarle Street.

While Crowley was here, on 17 August 1932, the bookshop Foyle's asked him to come and give a talk on 'Magick' in September, so on 2 September he consecrated a magical fuck to the task: "Opus 140. Success to 15 Sept. speech."[1]

1   Opus 140 because it was the 140th such opus, dedicated to a purpose, that year.

52

GROSVENOR HOUSE HOTEL, PARK LANE: FOYLE'S LITERARY LUNCHEON
An herd of many swine

Crowley had a good business-like relationship with the well-known London bookshop Foyle's, which was then in its enormous flagship premises opposite the Phoenix Theatre on Charing Cross Road, abutting Manette Street (now moved to slightly smaller premises next door at 107 Charing Cross Road). In Crowley's day, and until recently, Charing Cross Road was the centre of London's secondhand book trade – a couple of shops still survive, valiantly hanging on – and when Crowley was looking for a book, Thomson's *City of Dreadful Night*, he told a friend he was going to "ransack Charing X Road".

As for Foyle's, he was on almost social terms with Christina Foyle, and was a familiar face in the occult department, buying as well as selling, although selling was important: after being asked to speak, he manage to sell them 200 copies of *Magick* on account at 5/- each.

Foyles Literary Luncheons were something of an institution: they were held at the Grosvenor House Hotel on Park Lane, and sometimes attended by several hundred people. "Where are 'literary lunches' mentioned in the Gospels?" Crowley asks in his diary. And the answer is "An herd of many swine feeding."[1]

And so it came to pass that on 15 September 1932 Crowley gave his talk about 'The Philosophy of Magick', and was able to record in his diary "Made a good speech!!!!!!".

---

1   King James Version, Matthew 8:30 and Luke 8:32.

53

PRAED STREET, PADDINGTON: THE MODERN BOOK COMPANY
Libel discovered

After a couple of stormy months in Albemarle Street, Crowley and Bill started moving to shorter-term addresses: towards the end of September 1932 Crowley moved to the Queen's House Hotel at 20 Leicester Square, and after more moves they checked in to the Park Lane Hotel on Thursday 5 January 1933, by which time things were coming to an end.

Bill's health was bad, physical as well as mental – she had to go to the Grosvenor Hospital For Women in Vincent Square, Westminster – and on Saturday 7 January Crowley packed her off to Brighton to convalesce and found himself in the Paddington area. Like several of London's railway termini, including Victoria and Marylebone, the Paddington area was by now an equivocal zone where faded Victorian gentility met transience and vice. A man called A.G. Macdonell, writing in 1933, discusses what we would now call psychogeography, with his protagonist walking the streets and trying to understand the lines where the qualities of one district give way to another, like the elusive "exact spot where the influence of Nude Picture Post Cards in Praed Street wanes before the empurpled major-generals of Petersburg Square."[1]

Crowley was walking along Praed Street, possibly looking out for prostitutes, when he looked in the window of a bookshop at number 23 called The Modern Book Company. The nondescript but progressive name would suit a miscellaneously sensational-sleazy bookshop – perhaps like yesterday's 'Read and Return' book and adult magazine shops – but in fact it specialised in books on popular

---

1   A.G. Macdonell, *England Their England* (Macmillan, 1933)

science and wireless technology, for radio enthusiasts, with just a few spicier and more interesting items. One of these was Crowley's novel *Moonchild*, in the window with a display placard that said "Aleister Crowley's first novel, *Diary of a Drug Fiend*, was withdrawn after an attack in the sensational press."

"Discovered libel," Crowley wrote in his diary. Clearly the bookseller, Mr Gray, was trying to sensationalise his work: Crowley went to his solicitor to sue, and the case came to court on 10 May. Fortunately the judge had recently arrived from another planet, and declared "There was not the smallest ground for suggesting that any book Mr. Crowley had written was indecent or improper."

He decided the case in Crowley's favour, awarding him £50 damages.

54

CUMBERLAND TERRACE: PEARL BROOKSMITH
The flame of fornication

In July 1933, during a run of short-term addresses, Crowley met Pearl Brooksmith, 34-year-old widow of an older naval officer, Captain Eldred Stuart Brooksmith, who had died in 1931. She drank heavily, as Crowley noticed, and not long after their meeting he wrote an imaginary epitaph:

> Here lies a Pearl of a woman
> Who lived in open sin.
> One end collected semen,
> The other guzzled gin.

She lived at number 40 Cumberland Terrace, just near the western edge of Regent's Park. He called to see her on 9 August, and before too long they began having sex: on the 15th he records Opus 1, "i.m.d." (*in manu dominae*; in the hand of the mistress) and that it was "A.1", a favourite Crowley expression. Next day Opus 2 took place, and on the 19th he moved in with her.

Further works were consecrated to 'Success', 'Lust' and 'Love', and it was business as usual with Opus 7: "Sell Magic to Selfridge at a good price". Pearl was an intense sexual partner, and their bouts included shouting, screaming and clairvoyance on both sides, while Crowley's notes include "marvellous lust".

It was Pearl who produced the memorable line "I feel the flame of fornication creeping up my body."

55

CARLOS PLACE, MAYFAIR: OFFICE OF ISIDORE KERMAN
Abominable libels

Readers of Crowley's *Magick* found a flyer inserted, telling them "Your interest in Magick should be the dawn of a new life," and concluding "To assist the Master Therion in his Great Work, the Establishment of the Law of Thelema, Your first step will be to write to Aleister Crowley, 9 Carlos Place, London W1." This was not Crowley's address but discreetly 'care of' his solicitor, Isidore Kerman, and number 9 Carlos Place was a door that Crowley saw far too much of for his own good, leading to eventual bankruptcy.

Crowley felt ill-used in memoirs by old friends, and in particular by Nina Hamnett's 1932 autobiography *Laughing Torso*, published by Constable. This had recollections both tragic and light. She recalled how desolate Crowley and Hirsig had been over the death of their daughter Poupée. And she recalled Crowley in Paris, wanting to sleep with a particular woman; when he succeeded, Hamnett had seen him next morning at the Dome café when someone said "Hullo A.C., what was it like?" and he said glumly "It was rather like waving a flag in space."

Crowley saw a copy of *Laughing Torso* in September 1932 and he was not amused – "abominable libels," he wrote in his diary. Next morning he was at Carlos Place. The passage he particularly objected to was about Cefalu: "He was supposed to practice Black Magic there, and one day a baby was said to have disappeared mysteriously."

The case of Crowley vs Constable publishers finally came to court in April 1934, and included Betty "Tiger Woman" May as a witness on the side of Constable. As ever, the press had a field day with the "Black Magic libel case", as it became known, and Crowley seems to have been one of the last men in Britain to wear a top hat in court. He writes in his diary as if he'd won, with the "collapse" of the opposing side, and "General joy – the consternation of Constable & Co.", but he had in fact lost. He made an appeal, and in November 1934 he lost that as well.

Meanwhile he had lost another case against the writer Ethel Mannin. In her *Confessions and Impressions* she had described Crowley at Gwen Otter's as a man "who likes nothing better than to be regarded as His Satanic Majesty the Prince of Darkness". He sought an injunction, which came to court in July 1933 and failed, on the grounds that the book had come out in 1930 and he had made no objection earlier.

When it came to legal action, Crowley never seemed to learn from experience (his victory over the Praed St bookshop may have given him a misplaced confidence). In 1935 he wrote an article called 'My Wanderings in Search of the Absolute' for a paper called *The Sunday Referee*. When they declined to publish any more in the series he was hoping for he sued for breach of contract, and once again he lost.

All this had to be paid for, and when Crowley was unable to pay his legal fees he had to give Kerman books, manuscripts, magical regalia and jewellery, some of which finally surfaced at Sotheby's in 1996.[1] On at least one occasion he managed to buy his property back: in 1939 he bought back a piece of tribal art, his "old South Sea stick", an Easter Island staff, at the auction house of Miller, Paxton and Fairminer at 34 Chancery Lane. It figures in photographs of Crowley and ended up in the Yorke collection catalogued as a "Maori walking stick."

Like Crowley, Kerman was a character. He had charm, good looks and chutzpah. He had started up in business as "Forsyte and Kerman", but there was no Forsyte: he'd taken the name from *The Forsyte Saga*. The firm's cable address, "Kybo, London" has the generic look of such addresses, but in fact stood for "Keep your bowels open". And where Crowley went bankrupt, his lawyer died (in 1998) worth £14 million.

1   See Henrietta Street.

56

UPPER MONTAGU STREET
Explorer Granted Bail

Crowley and Pearl left Cumberland Terrace just before Christmas 1933, and Crowley checked in to the Cumberland Hotel on 20 December. He didn't like it, and although he seems to have been with Pearl he wrote "Oh so bloody lonely! I cannot stand the Cumberland any more." In slightly higher spirits, he thought the hotel was geared towards a 'sales rep' lifestyle. Quoting Shelley's *Prometheus Unbound*, he wrote that it was "run on the assumption that every 'traveller from the cradle to the grave through the dim night of this immortal day' is a Commercial Traveller."

This was the beginning a welter of short-term addresses largely in the Marylebone area, including the Grand Central Hotel.[1] On 11 June he took considerably less grand digs at 21 Upper Montagu Street, Marylebone, near Montagu Square. There is a side door by the corner with Crawford Street, behind the Victorian chemist's shop of Meacher, Thomas and Higgins, still there with its beautiful Victorian wall-lamp just by Crowley's door.

He was with Pearl, who wrote from this address to an American disciple "The money question is the very devil, isn't it?". They weren't here long, but it was the address given in widely syndicated reportage of his arrest for receiving stolen letters ("Explorer Granted Bail").

1   On Friday 22 December 1933 he took lodgings at 11 Cavendish Court, Wigmore Street, and on 22 February 1934 he left London, spending time in Brighton and elsewhere before returning in April to stay at the Waldorf Hotel (now the Waldorf Hilton) on Aldwych. Still in April he moved to 5 Nottingham Place, and then in May to 44 Upper Gloucester Place, not long before going to Marylebone's Grand Central Hotel (now the Landmark Hotel).

> Edward Alexander Crowley (58), who was described on the charge sheet as an explorer, of Upper Montagu Street, London, was accused at Marylebone Police Court, to-day, of feloniously receiving five letters, the property of Betty Sedgwick. He was remanded until Thursday, bail being allowed in the sum of £10.

Crowley had been arrested in Kerman's office at Carlos Place, after buying some stolen letters for five pounds from a Captain Eddie Cruze. These letters were the property of Betty May, from whose flat at 1 Seymour Street, Marylebone, Cruze had stolen them (he seems to have lived in the same building). They contained accounts of Cefalu that Crowley thought would help his forthcoming appeal against Nina Hamnett and the firm of Constable, in which May was likely to be called again as a witness.

57

THE OLD BAILEY
Thank you, My Lord

The stolen letters case went from Marylebone Police Court to the more intimidating Old Bailey, site of many famous cases: Dr Crippen had been tried there, and hanged. Crowley was tried before judge Cecil Whiteley on 24 and 25 July 1934. Whiteley had been to Crowley's old university, Cambridge, graduating with a third-class degree in Classics, and before becoming a judge he had been a barrister, unsuccessfully defending Edith Thompson in the Thompson and Bywaters case. Widely felt to have been innocent, she was also hanged.

The nub of the letters case was that Crowley had the letters from Captain Cruze, and Cruze (who could no longer be found) had them from Betty May. Crowley's defence claimed she had given Cruze the letters as security for a loan, and so they were his to dispose of as he wished. Considering letters to be valueless, and not suitable as security, the jury refused to believe this and decided that Crowley was guilty.

It could have been a custodial sentence, but Whiteley let him off with two years' probation and 50 guineas costs. Crowley knew he should have been acquitted, at least according to his diary ("Attack of asthma stopped me spilling the beans in the witness box") but he nevertheless mustered his dignity to say "Thank you, My Lord."

58

HUNGARIA, LOWER REGENT STREET
Babe of the Abyss

In May 1934 the popular novelist Dennis Wheatley was researching his black magic thriller *The Devil Rides Out*, so he contacted Crowley and invited him to lunch at the Hungaria Restaurant. The go-between was their mutual friend Tom Driberg, discreetly referred to in Wheatley's accounts as "Member of Parliament Z". Wheatley used aspects of Crowley to create his villain Mocata, a Satanic but oddly precious occultist with a shaven head and hypnotic eyes, as well as borrowing magical jargon such as "Ipsissimus".

The Hungaria was at 16 Lower Regent Street, just south of Piccadilly Circus, and the site later became the Japanese department store Mitsukoshi. When Mitsukoshi itself went the way of all flesh, around 2015, and the site was refurbished again, the old Hungaria lettering was suddenly back from the dead and briefly exposed as a ghost frontage.

Soon after their meeting Crowley gave Wheatley a customised copy of *Magick in Theory and Practice*. Where the title page read "Published for Subscribers Only 1929", Crowley altered it to "This unique copy... Published for Dennis Wheatley only 1934 e.v." [era vulgaris], added a photograph of himself captioned "The Beast 666" and inscribed the book to Wheatley "in memory of that sublime Hungarian banquet."

At the back he drew a diagram of the Kabbalah, with a squiggle representing the Babe of the Abyss,[1] and wrote in the inside cover "Recommendations to the Intelligent Reader humbly proffered."

---

1   The squiggle is foetus-like, with the abyss to be crossed as a horizontal line towards the top of the Tree of Life, just below the emanations Binah and Chokmah.

Read introduction very thoroughly indeed.

Skate lightly at first reading over chapters (e.g. like Chap V) which go off the deep end over the Holy Qabalah. But go back to them studiously after getting Appendix V by heart.

Study – early in the process – Appendix II, to get our Aim and Method.

He then advised the intelligent reader to "Study Liber XV pp.345 etc" – those pages are his 'Gnostic Catholic Mass' – "with a view to putting on this ritual in London as it is done in Hollywood. Amen" and "Read 'Hymn to Pan' aloud at midnight when alone with INTENTION to get HIM."

59

HOTEL WASHINGTON, CURZON STREET
The Adorable Tanith

Crowley was always on the lookout for disciples and associates with money or journalistic influence, and he would have liked to continue his acquaintance with Dennis Wheatley ("Public Thriller Writer No.1", as he was known in the Thirties). They had several friends in common, including Tom Driberg and Lord Donegall, an aristocratic journalist and radio personality ("wonderful time at Punch's club with Donegall", Crowley wrote of a night in October 1932; Punch's was at 5 Waverton Street, Mayfair, now demolished, and figures in Wheatley's thriller *Three Inquisitive People*).

But Wheatley was less keen to see Crowley again, and seems to have used pressure of work as an excuse, after which Crowley's communications take on an increasingly jibing quality. "Most ingenious," he wrote at one point, "but really a little Ely Culbertson, to advertise your love of rare editions in a thriller blurb!" (Ely Culbertson was an American bridge player, whom Crowley evidently found vulgar).

Crashing through short-term addresses as usual, in October-November 1934 Crowley was staying at the Milestone Hotel, Kensington Court (opposite Kensington Gardens). He had been abrasive ("Rumpus at Tombstone," he wrote in his diary like the title of a cowboy novel: "Farewell speech – very loud and clear in main lounge. 'I think everyone in this hotel should know that there is a spy to listen in to telephone conversations. And I warn you all to beware of blackmailers.'"). That was 29 October. He then seems to have moved to the Hotel Washington on Curzon Street (now the Washington Mayfair). But on 9 November, the day after he lost his appeal against Nina Hamnett and Constable publishers, he had to write "Hotel chucks me out!!"

Wheatley's novel, *The Devil Rides Out*, went on to become the greatest popular occult novel of the twentieth century, as *Dracula* is of the nineteenth. In it, his hero the Duke de Richleau – who leads a thoroughly Mayfair life, with a Rolls-Royce, a smoking jacket, and coincidentally a flat on Curzon Street – saves a girl called Tanith from Satanists, and prevents a war with Nazi Germany.

On Halloween, 31 October 1934, the first serialised instalment of *The Devil Rides Out* appeared in the *Daily Mail*, and Crowley wrote Wheatley a note on Hotel Washington letterhead: "Dear Dennis Wheatley," it said, "Did you elope with the adorable Tanith? Or did the witches get you Hallowe'en?"

60

MAYFAIR HOTEL, DOWN STREET: ALEXANDER CANNON
Levitator bowled out

Early in *The Devil Rides Out*, the Duke de Richleau has to convince his friend Rex of the reality of the occult, starting with hypnotism, then the will to good or evil, and then "the invisible influence which is all about us": "A very eminent mental specialist who holds a high position in our asylums wrote a book with that title [i.e. *The Invisible Influence*] and I have not yet asked you to believe a tenth of what he vouches for."

This man was Dr Alexander Cannon, and Crowley had met him in unexpected circumstances. When he returned from Berlin in July 1932, one of his first calls was Colney Hatch, the gigantic mental hospital up at Friern Barnet, to see Maria de Miramar. Colney Hatch had 2,500 patients and the longest corridor in Britain, and for many years it was a London byword for lunacy ("Eccentric?", says Bertie Wooster, in one of P.G. Wodehouse's comic novels, "She could step straight into Colney Hatch, and no questions asked.")[1]

Not otherwise interested in visiting, Crowley seems to have needed Maria to sign something, perhaps a statement admitting adultery. He took Billie (Bertha Busch) along. Bill had a habit of making scenes and shouting obscenities in public: "So showed her two other ladies doing it," he writes. "One specialized in 'fucking old piss-hole' the other 'fucking old shit-bag.' Edifying."

The psychiatrist they met there was none other than Cannon. Crowley found him "very nice", although he noted a "bee in his bonnet about hypnosis". Hypnosis was just the tip of the iceberg: Cannon also had a bee in his bonnet about levitation, which he claimed to practise, levitating himself and his native porters across a chasm

---

1   *The Code of the Woosters* (Herbert Jenkins, 1938), p.273.

in Tibet. He had already published *Hypnotism, Suggestion and Faith Healing* (Heinemann 1932) but with *The Invisible Influence: A Story of the Mystic Orient With Great Truths Which Can Never Die* (Rider, 1934) he went too far for his employers. He was asked to resign, later developing a lucrative private practice on Harley Street and being consulted by Edward VIII. He proceeded to publish other books including *Sleeping Through Space: Revealing the Amazing Secrets of How to Get What You Want and Keep Well* (1938) and he cultivated an impressive personal manner: he liked to be known as "His Excellency Doctor Sir Alexander Cannon" (among other things; he was also "Fifth Master of the Great White Lodge of the Himalayas"). He later lived in a castle-like mansion, on the Isle of Man, and affected a cloak with high wing-collars.

Cannon held magical teas, where he would lecture and demonstrate hypnosis, at what was then the Mayfair Hotel; this was at number 7 Down Street, not far from what is now Down Street's 'ghost' tube station. Crowley – who had meanwhile decided Cannon was a charlatan – went along to one of these teas on Sunday 13 May 1934. Cannon tried to levitate a girl named Kyra (a daughter of Nijinsky) by hypnotising her with a light in her eyes. She failed to rise but went into a trance where she was clearly distressed, with spasms and convulsions, and members of the audience shouted at Cannon to stop.

Along with Crowley, who heckled Cannon about something unrelated, another member of the audience was West Indian occultist Rollo Ahmed, who became the star of the afternoon: he said he would levitate himself instead of Kyra (this also failed, but he had stolen the show). Crowley wrote in his diary "Rollo Ahmed... V. good"; Cannon was "bowled out... completely."

61

REDBURN STREET, CHELSEA
The unfortunate Norman Mudd

Crowley always attracted lost souls, and one of the saddest was Norman Mudd. Mudd came from modest origins in Manchester, where his father was a teacher; he won a scholarship to study mathematics at Cambridge, and was for a while a university lecturer in South Africa. Tom Driberg remembers him as a dim, grey figure who would come up at parties and say "You won't remember me – my name is Mudd." Unlucky in name, unprepossessing in appearance, Mudd had also lost an eye to a gonorrhoeal infection, making Crowley think he might be one of the four deformed men foretold in a vision during the Paris Working.

Mudd (as Omnia Pro Veritate) was one of Crowley's most ardent disciples, Renfield to Crowley's Count. Encountering Crowley and Thelema, he "understood for the first time what life was or might be", threw up his career, and went to Cefalu, where he presented Crowley with his savings and fell in love with Leah Hirsig. For a while Crowley held him in high esteem, listening to his mathematical insights into *The Book of the Law*. He also gave him the task of being his PR man and challenging the Beaverbrook Press.[1]

Returning from Cefalu to do this, Mudd found lodgings at number 27 Redburn Street, not far from Gwen Otter, back in the days when Chelsea was a cheap, Bohemian, and slightly off-the-beaten-track district. It is now hard to imagine Chelsea as shabby and disregarded, but in 1945 Graham Greene wrote in a letter "I should hate to live in Chelsea. So dirty and the real fume of creepy evil."

---

1   This later gave rise to the 1933 pamphlet *An Open Letter to Lord Beaverbrook*, largely written by Crowley but signed by Mudd from 37a Tressillian Road, Brockley SE4. This was the house of J.G. Bayley, a longstanding student of Crowley: he had joined the A∴A∴ in March 1910.

Sadly, Crowley tired of Mudd, writing to Germer "to me he is just a religious maniac." Mudd went from being an esteemed magical comrade to "the basest and grossest of all types of men I have ever seen... It's the horribly amorphous mollusc quality in Mudd which gives him the nightmare quality which appals so irresistibly. 'Hoglike abortion'[2] is rather rough on hogs and their abortions. They have organic form at their worst. Mudd is 'a nearly liquid mass of loathsome – of detestable putrescence'..."[3]

Meanwhile Leah Hirsig, a highly intelligent and in some respects phenomenal woman, was growing disenchanted with Crowley. For a while she remained loyal to the cause, if not the man, and as the twenties went on she endured absolute poverty (she had to sell the dead Raoul Loveday's shoes for bread); drudgery as a restaurant washer-up and coal-heaver; possibly prostitution (biographers differ on this); and a relationship with Norman Mudd. They were having sex when she asked him what his name was, and he answered "Omnia Pro Veritate". She recorded in her diary that she'd had sex "with a man who does not know who he is but is commonly called Norman Mudd."

Hirsig's attempts to break free of Crowley's influence – not 'morally', but just in terms of breaking out of the force field of someone who is always right and always has the last word – make extraordinary reading. Long after Crowley had lost interest, in the autumn of 1930 she was driven to revoke all former bonds, oaths and loyalties in occult-legalistic terms with a ceremony and symbol Ẍ, combined with "lygs". Lygs were seemingly a form of sarcasm or transcendental irony ("I define the term Lyg to be a common noun meaning a proposition which I offer to the cognizance of another – some supposed intelligence other than myself – as if I believed the proposition whereas in fact I disbelieve it"). Mudd helped her draft this, and the final letter was in his handwriting.

---

2   Crowley had written a limerick about Mudd: "A hog-eyed abortion named Mudd / Was like a one-eyed rotten spud. / His one chance to clean / His person obscene / Is to wash himself out in his blood."

3   A quotation from Edgar Allan Poe's short story, 'The Facts in the Case of M. Valdemar'.

Mudd, as well, eventually wanted nothing more to do with Crowley. In 1934, now in his mid-forties, he moved from the Rowton House hostel for homeless men at 220 Arlington Road, Camden, and went to the Channel Islands, lodging briefly at a hotel in Guernsey. While there he went down to the beach, fastened his trouser ankles with bicycle clips, and then filled his trousers with stones before walking into the sea to die.

His body was found on 16 June 1934. Crowley's quip on Mudd's suicide was "I feel sure he must have left a long, elaborate, mathematical proof as to why he had to do this."

62

CAREY STREET: BANKRUPTCY COURT
On Queer Street

The publicity surrounding the Black Magic Libel Case had a disastrous side effect; many of Crowley's creditors were reminded of his existence, and now had routes to find him.

The first creditor to weigh in was a moneylender, B.S. Rhodes Ltd of 13-14 New Bond Street. Crowley had borrowed £126 from them at a surprisingly reasonable rate of 5% annual interest, and with no repayment it had grown to £140.[1] A bankruptcy notice was issued in December 1934, and on 14 February 1935 the case came to the Bankruptcy Court in Carey Street.

"Carey Street", Crowley says, "is well-known to prosperous Hebrews and poor Englishmen, as the seat of the Bankruptcy buildings." Today it is a pleasant old street off Chancery Lane with a good public house, The Seven Stars. The bankruptcy court that Crowley knew, built in the 1890s, was a long building that stretched along the western side of Carey Street reaching to the Strand, and it was bombed during the Second World War. Being "on Carey Street" (bankrupt) came to merge in the public mind with another more popular expression, "on Queer Street" (also bankrupt, before acquiring sexual associations; a corruption of Carey Street has often been given as the origin of the phrase, but it seems to pre-date the move of bankruptcy business to Carey Street in the 1840s).

Rhodes was the start of what turned out to be a flood of claims. Crowley, "author and psychiatrist", owed legal fees to Kerman; legal costs to Constable publishers; £500 to another moneylender; personal debts to Pearl Brooksmith and Count Lewenhaupt (a

---

1   Almost £10,000 at today's values. These debts are far worse than they sound: £500, for example, is somewhere between £30,000 and £35,000 today.

friend who lived at 72 Ladbroke Grove); money to shirtmakers, bootmakers and tailors (including Rogers and Co., military tailors of New Burlington Street, who were due £535); wine merchants Block, Grey and Block (£170); several tobacconists; opticians Dollond and Aitchison; hotels including Rosa Lewis's Cavendish, the Waldorf, and the Savoy; and many others. There were 48 creditors. Crowley pointed out that as the author of some of the noblest prose in the English language, he could hardly be expected to have the talents of an accountant as well.

With no significant income, Crowley had relied on his gentlemanly air to keep spending, and not with any sense of fraudulence; he felt it was a right. He was affronted that Philip Morris tobacconists wouldn't sell him any more cigars just because he owed them £60: "Do they think they are doing me a favour in selling me cigars?".

Taking the old Victorian-style disdain for tradesmen and their bills one stage further, he decided during the Second World War that "the refusal to count money" was laudable as "Naysaying to the spirit of the Jew, which has rotted the soul of mankind."

Crowley's creditors eventually got 2d in the pound, some years later.[2] He had been on and off Queer Street for a long time; effectively since his inheritance ran out. But from now on, and officially, to borrow a characteristically nice line from his later diaries,

> I am what St. Francis of Assisi used to call "fucked on the financial front."

2   Or 1/120th, at 240 old pennies to the twenty-shilling pound.

63

GREAT ORMOND STREET, BLOOMSBURY: LIFE WITH PEARL
The Eye of God

Crowley continued to go through plenty of short-term addresses in the Thirties; the bankruptcy proceedings had described him as an Englishman and an author, but beyond that he was a man "whose present address or place of business the petitioning creditors are unable to ascertain."

He travelled light, and most of the few possessions he still had were in storage with Whiteley's. The great firm of Whiteley's, on Queensway near Bayswater station, had been one of the first large transatlantic-style department stores (and there was a celebrated trial after the millionaire Whiteley was shot dead, in his office, by his illegitimate son). Whiteley's had storage facilities out in West Kensington and Hammersmith (their enormous 'Furniture Depository', still visible from passing trains), and from time to time Crowley would go out to Avonmore Road W14, just by Olympia, when he needed to consult his books and manuscripts.

In April 1936 Crowley and Pearl moved to 59 Great Ormond Street, on the Bloomsbury edge of Holborn. They had just been thrown out of a flat at 23 Albert Road NW1 ("the house on the corner of Primrose Hill," Crowley wrote to a student, "exactly facing the North Gate entrance of the Zoo"). It was quite a grand house, now replaced by a block of flats, where the landlord – a retired Indian Army officer named Wilfrid Nicholas – had put their belongings on the pavement.

Crowley had already lived in Great Ormond Street, and nearby Coram Street, before the First World War, and in April 1935 he seems to have been briefly nearby at Flat 8, York House, on the junction of Southampton Row and Theobalds Road (a couple of letters survive). Now, in the words of a visitor named Bernard Bromage, he was in "the ground floor flat of an old and rather dilapidated house" – still there, opposite Great Ormond Street Hospital, at the Queen's Square end – and Bromage has left a vivid picture of Crowley and Pearl at home in a room "of the 'furnished' variety". It might usually suggest nothing more than "a faded history of the shabby genteel", says Bromage, but in this case things were a little more outré: an estate agent told him he had found the pair of them in the communal basement, "stark-naked putting on a 'Rite of Pan' act", and sought legal advice.

Pearl ("pale, neurotic" and "chlorotic-looking") told him about their woes in Albert Road, while Crowley, in his plus-fours, walked around Bromage inspecting him from all angles. As they proceeded to talk, Bromage saw a certain pathos in the Beast down on his luck: "a battered, weary, yet strangely courageous figure." Crowley had been fashionably infamous in the 1920s ("No neurotic undergraduate was complete without the whispered hint, 'One of the Crowley set!'") but now he was out of fashion, morally and financially disreputable, and people "laughed at his misery and ignored his perverse and unmistakable courage."

Bromage continued to see Crowley around town, on one occasion running into him at the entrance to the National Gallery: Crowley grabbed his arm and they went in to look at the Wilton Diptych, the late 14thC altarpiece with the Virgin and Child, where Bromage was impressed with Crowley's grasp of painting. He also saw him a few times around Piccadilly like a Victorian dinosaur: "wandering about Piccadilly wearing the same suit of brown plus-fours with the silver buckles at the knees... An ageing, disillusioned magician, crossing from pavement to pavement like some antediluvian monster, lost in a world of superficial irrelevancies and transitory values."

After nearly three years with Pearl, meanwhile, the honeymoon was over. She was volatile, and she had already hit Crowley for his failure to get a job or earn money: "Because I can't (however gladly, for her sake, I would) prostitute myself, Pearl struck me." At least he managed to take a paying student at this address, a French occultist named André Pigné, and like a psychoanalyst he noted "There is much resistance to analysis in André, now that it is taking hold: so broken appointments must be charged for."

Pearl meanwhile suffered from shouting, kicking nightmares. Crowley had misgivings about her right from the start – "SW [Scarlet Woman] goes on prolonged wild visions, very uncontrolled, & is near the border-line. I don't like it too well." The standard occult line is that such women were useful as seers, because of their aptitude for getting on the astral plane, but Crowley himself was more judgmental: at this address he noted constant hallucinations and that she was "showing serious symptoms of insanity." Someone called Oke, possibly a doctor, had already said – in Crowley's paraphrase – "Pearl to Bat Club", which probably means that he advised a spell in a mental hospital, following Rose and Maria to the "Bug House".

These were not good days, exacerbated by poverty and Pearl's drinking, but Crowley was not defeated: "Not all the filth of London is thick enough to hide me from the Eye of God," he wrote in July, "and by that Ray I live." He still cheered himself by cooking and inventing new dishes. As for Pearl, rather endearingly, she told Bromage she loved him ("poor thing") because, she said, he "needs someone to mother him," – he was "only a child".

64

WELBECK STREET, MARYLEBONE
Pig's trotters and incense

Among the people present when Crowley and Rollo Ahmed challenged Dr Cannon at the Mayfair Hotel was a young man named Alan Burnett-Rae. Burnett-Rae didn't know who the character in the brown tweed plus-fours was, and Cannon told him afterwards it was Aleister Crowley. A couple of years later Burnett-Rae found himself, at the age of twenty-five, in possession of a large house at number 56 Welbeck Street, near Harley Street in Marylebone, which he divided into eight or nine small flats with a Belgian steward and his family looking after it. He'd meanwhile got to know Ahmed, and one day Ahmed rang and said he had a friend looking for accommodation: "a very highly evolved personality."

Burnett-Rae recognised Crowley at once from the hotel confrontation, still wearing the same knickerbocker suit, and on 30 August 1936 Crowley rented room 6, on the third floor. Burnett-Rae wrote a vivid memoir of his stay, during which Crowley made "rather a nuisance of himself", initially by burning strong incense. He also sent the steward's son out on errands for "strange foods and drinks"; Burnett-Rae particularly remembered pig's trotters, which Crowley liked to prepare Chinese-style.

Crowley seemed to have few possessions except for an incense burner, the famous tweed suit, a few books, and a machine which helped him breathe when he had asthma attacks (this was quite a contraption: it had a drive belt and took cartridges). Burnett-Rae was struck by how unfit he was, and that he had to be abstemious with drink; after a couple of glasses of brandy he fell on the floor "as if unconscious". Pearl, "the middle-aged widow of a naval officer" as Burnett-Rae describes her, helped him back into his chair and explained he shouldn't drink spirits, due to malaria and other afflictions. This is considerably at odds with other accounts of Crowley's drinking, so unless it was a practical joke it may be that drink was interacting with medication, or the flare-up of some condition.

Crowley suffered from ill-health all his life, and by the Thirties he was trying to take more care of himself. He had long been concerned about his weight and distended abdomen, for which he took a German product called Uricedin. Crowley had also visited masseurs for his weight and general health, including a course of abdominal colon massage from Archibald Cockren at 146 Great Portland Street; Cockren is now remembered for his writing on alchemy, notably *Alchemy Rediscovered and Restored* (1941). They briefly collaborated in a scheme to market rejuvenation treatment, with Crowley hoping to sell courses of his Amrita rejuvenation pills, featuring his own semen, for 25 guineas a week (about £2000 today), but it foundered and Cockren became one of Crowley's creditors in his bankruptcy proceedings.

He must also have feared that ageing would affect his ability to attract women, and around this time he began visiting not only masseurs but beauticians. At Welbeck Street he went for wrinkle treatment by a Mrs Grant and Mme Arnsohn of Gee Bee Université de Beauté, "complexion specialists" nearby at 7 Mandeville Place, and he later went to Amie McClymont, "beauty specialist", at 158 Brompton Road.

Along with the incense burning, one night Burnett-Rae heard there was "infernal screaming, shouting and general commotion" as if Crowley was attacking Pearl. Burnett-Rae banged on the door and Pearl appeared, saying Crowley had been having a nightmare. Next morning the steward's son Adolph – he changed his name to Jack a while later – was surprised, as Crowley records it, when he brought Pearl her morning tea and was greeted with "'Go and shit yourself!' for a genial 'Good morrow, fair sir.'"

Calling on Burnett-Rae downstairs, "They appeared perfectly amicable with each other and deeply contrite" about Crowley's alleged nightmare ("an obvious fabrication"), but it was becoming clear Pearl had to go, which she did after settling Crowley's overdue rent (they were living largely on her money), although she still came back to visit.

Burnett-Rae also met Nina Hamnett and Betty May at the Fitzroy Tavern. Hamnett was still on cordial terms with Crowley, but May said one day she would kill him, and added that she was a witch herself. She was drunk, and her companion told Burnett-Rae not to let her know Crowley was in his house, lest she come round and attack him.

Finally, with the incense and the rent, Crowley himself had to go, but he remained friendly with Burnett-Rae. He cooked him curry, and tried to interest him in business ventures such as printing buttons in support of Edward VIII (saying "We want our king!") during his 1936 abdication crisis. In some respects Crowley had met his match in Burnett-Rae, who once asked him why he didn't seek fame rather than notoriety. Crowley had no use for ordinary fame, he said: he had once thought of the Diplomatic Service as a career, "but can you tell me now who was our representative at the Sublime Porte,[1] say, eighty years ago?"

"Stratford de Redcliffe," said Burnett-Rae.

[1]   i.e. our Ambassador to Ottoman Turkey.

65

WARREN DRIVE, SURBITON
Amazing treachery

Crowley had to leave Welbeck Street at the end of October 1936. "Evacuated the Doomed Bastion with flying colours", he wrote; he often referred to the 'doomed bastion' when being forced to leave lodgings. He went to stay with his friend and magical student Arthur Richardson, at number 68 Warren Drive, Surbiton. "Queen of the Suburbs", just to the south-west of London, Surbiton has a reputation for quintessentially suburban blandness that makes Crowley seem a very incongruous resident.

It was a short-term expedient and Crowley also stayed elsewhere during these weeks, including the Imperial Hotel by Russell Square, which he didn't like. Nevertheless he joined quite a domestic set-up in Warren Drive and even helped Richardson's son with his homework, although he never quite won Mrs Richardson over.

Arthur Richardson had been a member of the A∴A∴ since the 1920s, and he was serious in his studies. He also helped Crowley financially, and guaranteed the rent on his next flat at Redcliffe Gardens. It was probably money that caused a falling out, and Crowley's diary records "Richardson's amazing treachery". In revenge Crowley seems to have attacked Mrs Richardson's morals by slipping notes under the neighbours' doors – not his finest moment – and in December 1936 Richardson quit his A∴A∴ membership.

66

REDCLIFFE GARDENS, CHELSEA
Entrenched

On 16 December 1936 Crowley "entrenched" at 66 Redcliffe Gardens, a pillared Victorian house in what was then the rather depressing, run-down region of Chelsea digs and lodgings past World's End, down at the Fulham end of the King's Road towards Brompton Cemetery and the old gasworks at Sands End (Samuel Beckett, who had lodged in nearby Gertrude Street a couple of years earlier, puts the district into his 1937 novel *Murphy*). Redcliffe Gardens becomes Edith Grove as it continues across Fulham Road, and Crowley had long been aware of the area: a list of early sexual partners includes "biting girl in Edith Grove."

Crowley and Pearl were still companionably attached, but he was sexually involved with several other women, and Pearl's misery and jealousy came to focus on her inability to bear him a son: in January 1936 she'd had a hysterectomy at West London Hospital, Hammersmith (and while she was in hospital Crowley performed magical sex with a woman named Jane Warrilow).[1] Another woman named Elsie Morris had turned up at Cumberland Terrace in June 1936 claiming that Crowley had made her pregnant after entertaining her to dinner that same January ("Possible," Crowley wrote in his diary, "but I paid 5/- at the time.")

There had been even worse, for Pearl, in the wake of the 1935 bankruptcy case. A nineteen-year-old woman named Deirdre Patricia "Pat" Doherty, a former debutante, had been staying with Lord Justice Slesser, and he suggested she might find it interesting to watch a court case. She also happened to be the mistress of a Major Robert Thynne, who was involved with the Mandrake Press and knew

---

[1]   "Opus for Eve benefit". It would be good to think Eve was Pearl, and it probably was: she was Pearl Evelyn Brookesmith.

Crowley, and he introduced them. Contrary to popular myth, she didn't rush up to Crowley offering to bear his child, but they became friendly and, when he asked if she would try to have a child with him, she agreed.

Pearl caused a scene at the Eiffel Tower Restaurant, at one of Crowley's yoga lectures, when Pat turned up heavily pregnant (their son, Aleister Ataturk Crowley, was born in May 1937; Pat maintained friendly relations with Crowley but brought the boy up on her own). Not surprisingly, this all increased Pearl's jealousy and drunken rages in the Redcliffe Gardens period, especially since Crowley had Pat to dinner in her presence. With an unbearable domestic life, peaceful only when Pearl was away in Eastbourne, 1937 was the year Crowley turned increasingly to prostitutes and other women, beginning with a Mrs Meg Usher at this flat; Crowley cooked her a curry here while Pearl was in Eastbourne, and a number of 'works' followed.

67

FAIRHAZEL GARDENS, HAMPSTEAD
On the Astral Plane

On Wednesday 17 March 1937, at 8.30pm, Crowley gave a talk on astral projection a number 32 Fairhazel Gardens, NW6. It was billed as "Travelling on the Astral Plane... The Master Therion will give a practical demonstration."

This was the flat of Maurice Skipsey, better known as Victor Dane, "The White Yogi". He and Crowley shared an interest in sun-ray lamps, and he wrote a number of books including *The Sunlight Cure* (1929), *Naked Ascetic* (1933), *The Gateway to Prosperity* (1937), *Modern Fitness* (1934) and *Amazing Secrets of the Yogi* (1937). Some of his ideas were unorthodox (physical exercise could be done entirely in the mind, and adenoids could be cured by not eating for several weeks) but he had a popular fame in the Thirties: the *Daily Mirror* described him as "the only fully initiated white Yogi in the West".[1]

Astral travel, a much-loved staple of western occultism, is a technique of imagination that Crowley had been taught in his Golden Dawn days and earlier, after meeting Jones and Baker. For his Fairhazel Gardens talk he encouraged the audience to attempt it themselves; it was what a later generation might have called a 'workshop'. Although it was a public talk, people he knew seem to have predominated in the small audience, including Pearl Brooksmith. She had "good visions", as did F.W. Hylton, Eve Brackenbury, and someone called Hugh, possibly Hugh Austin, while Eileen Curtis couldn't do it at all, and never got beyond her vision of a gate.

Crowley judged the night "a great success", and on the same day he moved to Duke Street.

---

1 *Daily Mirror*, March 9 1936, p.11. He emigrated to America in 1938.

68

DUKE STREET
A little bi-location

On the same day as his astral talk in Hampstead, Crowley moved into a garret at number 41 Duke Street for about a week, during a spell of near-homelessness. There are two Duke Streets likely, one in SW1 and one in W1, and he knew both of them well.

The case for Duke Street W1, or Duke Street St. James's as it is now often called, is that it is totally on Crowley's stamping ground, intersecting with Jermyn Street. Number 41 is on the slope running down southwards from Jermyn Street, with Fortnum's, the Cavendish Hotel, and Dunhill's all just a stone's throw up the road, and on one of Germer's visits to London Crowley arranged for him to stay further down this same slope. Of less interest to Crowley, next door at number 43 was the Godfrey Phillips Gallery, where Austin Spare had his last West End show in 1930 (and a few doors down across the road is Dalmeny Court, where William Burroughs lived in the late Sixties, as did Eric Burdon of The Animals).

The Duke Street in Mayfair is not quite so much on Crowley's territory, between Oxford Street and Grosvenor Square, but he was in Duke Street with Pearl, and she then took lodgings at the Grosvenor Hotel, on Duke Street towards Grosvenor Square (and in later life he had a regular doctor for heroin on this street) [cf site 87].

The building in St. James' (where the lodging would have been above a jewellers, whereas the Mayfair one would have been above a large, department-store-sized haberdasher) seems slightly more likely for a garret, but perhaps proximity to the Grosvenor Hotel makes Mayfair more likely. In the absence of more evidence it is impossible to decide, so at this point – at least for the purposes of this book – Crowley bilocates, like the more slippery sort of old school Catholic saint.

Crowley also stayed all night in the "Turker" (Turkish bath; he used one on Jermyn Street, and particularly the one attached to the Imperial Hotel by Russell Square). People such as soldiers on leave would sometimes stay all night in Turkish baths if they missed the last train. In February he had written to Germer, using his Chancery Lane solicitors Dennes as a c/o address, "I am at present living in a Turkish bath. And I simply do not know what to do about anything."

He records "Turker at night, down to 6d", and another night he has to stay in a hotel, the Imperial, because he has "no money for bath". The Turkish bath was in the Imperial's arcade (the signage is still in the pavement on the corner with Guilford Street, just outside what is now Pret a Manger) but it sounds as if the Turker, although ultimately cheaper, needed money up front, whereas you could just check into a hotel and hope for the best.

He also stayed the night with friends, and at the Grosvenor Hotel and the Eiffel Tower, before landing in Paddington Green, in May.

69

MANOR PLACE, PADDINGTON GREEN
A remote slum

Crowley moved to number 11 Manor Place, Paddington Green, where his landlady was a Miss Catherine Stanton ("apartments"). Louis Umfreville Wilkinson remembered that Crowley always managed to give the impression of careless wealth, "Except once, when I found him living in Paddington Green in some frightful lodging." And even there, says Wilkinson, he brought his own atmosphere with him: "There was incense burning... that may have helped."

Crowley found himself here because he stayed for a few nights next door at number 10 with an acquaintance named Colin Evans. Evans was a medium who specialised in levitation, and there is a rather eerie and uncanny 1937 photograph of him in mid-air. He achieved a brief fame with this before being debunked as a fraud by investigator Harry Price among others: he was simply jumping, and audience members demanded their money back.[1] On a different level to the people Crowley had known in his Golden Dawn days, Evans belonged with the more hucksterish supernaturalism of men like Rollo Ahmed and Victor Dane.

Crowley had lived in Paddington before: in 1933 he had lodged briefly at 40 Cambridge Terrace, towards Bayswater (now called Sussex Gardens) as a lodger of Miss G. Brown ("furnished chambers") and he had liked it. More than that, Manor Place – now

---

1   Born Ivan Julius Collins in 1894, Evans was briefly so famous that he was featured in *Life* magazine (July 1938). The notorious photograph continued to have some currency in Fortean circles and was still being given away in the 1980s by PG Tips tea as a card in their *Unexplained Mysteries of the World* series. After his career as a medium and levitator collapsed, Evans then put his energies into astrology. He continued to live in Paddington Green and later converted to Islam.

completely demolished – was parallel to St. Mary's Terrace where he had lived with Rose, just on the other side of the old burial ground (still there). But a block away and thirty years later, this was Paddington in a very different key. He moved in on 22 May 1937, "for the next few days, I fear."

Paddington had come down in the world: like adjoining Bayswater it was one of those genteel areas gone to seed. Bayswater is a wealthy and respectable district for millionaires in John Galsworthy's *Forsyte Saga* (published 1922, but flashing back to the 1870s) but by Anthony Powell's mid-twentieth-century novel *The Acceptance World*, set in the early 1930s, it has developed an air of fortune-telling and fish-paste sandwiches in 'private hotels'. The narrator's Uncle Giles stays in a seedy private hotel called the Ufford, where he is a regular client of the psychic Mrs Erdleigh, an associate of Powell's Crowleyish character, Dr Trelawny.

Victorian Paddington developed into slums, giving the area "an unsavoury reputation", says the *London Encyclopaedia*, so by the mid-twentieth century "Paddington became a byword for overcrowding, poverty and vice", with counter-attempts at redevelopment from the 30s and earlier. In the words of John Betjeman

> Through those broad streets to Whiteley's once
> The carriages would pass,
> When ever-weeping Paddington
> Was safely middle-class.
> That silent land of stable smells,
> High walls and flowering trees,
> Is now rack-rented into flats
> For busy refugees.

Crowley hated Manor Place: "The stench is ghastly", he told Germer, in this "remote slum". Not that remote in distance – it is still relatively central – it must have felt remote psychologically, and for an educated and formerly well-off man like Crowley the depressing aspects of a room in Manor Place were his deepest encounter with what would shortly be known as 'bedsit-land'. A touch of faded gentility gave areas like Paddington, Notting Hill, Bayswater and Pimlico more social nuance than a straightforward slum, and "bedsit land" gained its character from individuals in single rooms rather than poor families. The novelist William Plomer gives a particularly seedy and atmospheric picture of Bayswater between the wars: a "fluid margin in which sank or swam the small-time spiv, the deserter, the failed commercial artist turned receiver,[2] the tubercular middle-aged harlot, the lost homosexual, or the sex maniac".

With the railway station, the proximity of Edgware Road, and Praed Street (with its dirty postcards and radio manuals) Paddington was one of those equivocal "ambiguous or transitional districts" that William Burroughs identifies in *Junky*: "Stores selling artificial limbs, wig makers, dental mechanics, loft manufacturers of perfumes, pomades, novelties, essential oils. A point where dubious business enterprises touches Skid Row."

It was becoming a cosmopolitan interzone, where the remains of pie-and-mash working class culture met Jewish business and increasingly the Middle East (much of Edgware Road has now consolidated into London's upmarket Arab quarter, good for Lebanese food and oud scent). This was underway in Crowley's day, and in September 1937 he notes "Met Camille Comer. French-Arab from Alger. 149 Edgware Road."

It is not always easy to tell which of the numerous women noted in Crowley's diaries (with just bare names, addresses and sometimes phone numbers) are sexual contacts, paid or otherwise. Crowley had been a user of prostitutes all his life, catching gonorrhoea in his teens. The idea of the whore was part of his ethos, and in his writing on sex magic he suggests it is better if your sexual partner doesn't know what you are up to, or the job she is playing a role in; she "should be in ignorance of the sacred character of the Office."

Some women are unambiguously noted with a sign for an "opus" and its details, like "Lola Breton, 32 King Street, Portman Square" (objective "156", i.e. the number of Our Lady of Babalon); or Hilda Goodwin, 7 Old

---

2   'Receiver', i.e. of stolen goods: a fence.

Gloucester Street; or Pat Harvey, 11 Sinclair Gardens (Olympia, near Blythe Road) with three works for "health". Crowley had clear sexual hopes with Camille Comer (who was probably above a furrier's at 149, unless she worked in it) because he tried to interpret his possible relations with her in terms of his daily *I Ching* reading, noting it should mean "great pleasure – perhaps flagellation". Early in 1933 Crowley was visiting a Central European woman named Marie or Marianne in Room 2, 35 Gower St (telephone MUS8598)[3], whom he declared was "the most marvellous fuckstress alive." But others shade into ambiguity. No doubt some are potential landladies, masseurs and other therapists, or people who have expressed interest in buying a book, and some are genuinely just social.

Sometimes districts are suggestive, such as Soho, and areas near railway termini have long been associated with prostitution, be it Paddington itself, or Waterloo; or Pimlico near Victoria; or King's Cross and Euston, shading down into north Bloomsbury and Fitzrovia from the Euston Road. North Fitzrovia was once very seedy, and "Miss Cooper 11 Howland St. T[ottenham] C[ourt] Rd. Prettiest [indeterminate Greek word] I've seen" sounds suggestive, but what of "Lilian Williams 41 Howland St"? Who knows? Some are only obvious when something has gone wrong:

> Late: dashed out: met nurse Lily Parker W. Middlesex. P.S. One of the "self-respect" class. Thought she was dishonoured under 5/-.

"Marta Allen (Russian) 39a Cremorne Road ground floor bus 22 World's End FLA3658" is neutral enough, down at the end of Edith Grove, but next day "Marta here: wanted... to be treated as a lady and paid as a prostitute." Many more remain inscrutable:

> Paula Fyffe 25 Lancaster Terrace PADdington3522.
> Hilda 4 Park Lane Flat F MAYfair 0339 Probable. Rita Douglas 3057 May (King's Court). Isabel do (blond) 91 Morshead Mans. ABER 4349.

3   The phone number identifies it as "Madame Augusta Faillie's boarding house, 35 Gower Street".

What does "Probable" mean? And who was "Susie King PAD 34287"? Or "Gipsy Rae 8 Cambridge Court [on Edgware Road] PAD 6104?" (who was "Astonishingly like de Miramar!").

Also in the Paddington area Crowley met a woman called Violet who was living at the Jamaica International Hotel, Eastbourne Terrace:[4] she may be the Violet Davidson he decided was "interesting but psychologically stupid beyond words", who rang up from police custody a couple of months later expecting him to stand bail. He arranged to meet a more cordial woman called Evelyn Harley (EDGware4469)[5] in the Paddington Station Hotel, and the Paddington Station lounge a couple of days later, and managed several works in late 1937 and 1938.

Not far from Manor Place (just off St. Mary's Terrace, going towards the more salubrious Little Venice) he met a Joan Dobson ("11 Porteous Rd. We stayed playing outside her door – no reason at all for not going in! – for half an hour!!!") and consummated things next day with an opus consecrated to success with publication – and then a while later he ran into her again, now moved to 62 Argyle Street, just on the once-notorious Argyle Square, King's Cross.

As for Manor Place, Crowley was there for over a year before moving to Chelsea, and although it horrified him it was a fertile time for writing and publishing, including the 1937 edition of *The Equinox of the Gods*. Finally his landlady, Miss Stanton, had to write to his financial minders Gerald Yorke and George Cecil Jones (his old mentor from the Golden Dawn days, and still the trustee of a small trust fund set up by Crowley's mother) to complain that Crowley owed her £43 and she had caught him sneaking his clothes and possessions off the premises, evidently doing a flit, or "shooting the moon" as it was once known.

---

4   Untraced. Eastbourne Terrace was filled with 'private hotels', with at least thirty of them in 1937.

5   She lived at 16 Manor Park Crescent, up in Edgware.

70

RAC CLUB, PALL MALL
Frieda Harris and the Great Work

Crowley had a friend named Clifford Bax, who had also known Allan Bennett and Austin Osman Spare. They had met at St. Moritz three decades earlier, and played chess: Bax remembered Crowley's "black magnetic eyes", and also felt that "to play chess with a man is to realise the voltage of his intellect. A strong and imaginative mind directed the pieces that opposed me."

Bax had a flat in Albany, the celebrated bachelor apartment complex on Piccadilly, opposite Fortnum and Mason, where other tenants have included Lord Byron and Aldous Huxley. He also belonged to a couple of clubs, including the RAC (Royal Automobile) Club a block or two south on Pall Mall; not as socially exclusive as some clubs, it is materially one of the best in terms of premises, built by the same architects as the Ritz. Crowley had asked him if he could introduce him to a woman who could help him in his work, so Bax brought three to lunch at 89 Pall Mall on 9 June 1937. Along with writer Lesley Blanch and actress Meum Stewart, he brought Lady Frieda Harris, an artist who was married to Liberal MP Sir Percy Harris.

Lady Frieda was only two years younger than Crowley – 60 to his 62 – and rather plain, with a beaky nose giving her a somewhat Edith Sitwell appearance. Fortunately they never became lovers, but they did become friends. Harris had always had a sense of the spiritual and esoteric, and had been through Christian Science and Rudolf Steiner's Anthroposophy, as well as Co-Masonry (an offshoot branch of Masonry that admitted women; British Co-Masonry was headed by Annie Besant, more widely remembered as a Theosophist).

When Crowley took Frieda on as a student he felt she was "seriously on the Path", and she told him of an experience of Dhyana she'd had as a child, outdoors in a field of gorse. A while later he gave her an unusually good explanation of the Great Work – far clearer than those in *Magick in Theory in Practice* – in terms that combine the oath of the Magister Templi with the alchemical Great Work or Magnum Opus, the transmutation of base matter (or ordinary life) into gold by the Philosopher's Stone. She had to "'interpret every phenomenon as a particular dealing of God with your soul'... then, having embraced and loved the fact (however repugnant) you thereby transform it into holiness and beauty. This is the Great Work."[1]

Frieda's husband Sir Percy Harris ("the foul Jew she married") was Liberal MP for Bethnal Green. He worked for the underdog and the disadvantaged, and in that respect he was the polar opposite of *The Book of the Law*, as Crowley seems to have noticed; in 1943 he suggested Frieda should stand against him as the Thelemite candidate for Bethnal Green.

Sir Percy was extremely busy and rather boring: Tom Driberg remembers he was nicknamed 'The Housemaid', because he emptied the chamber.[2] Lady Frieda was far more unconventional, verging on eccentric: she had exhibited her paintings, at the New English Art Club in 1929, under the name of "Jesus Chutney". She had already had a lover, but with the lover gone – he died – she was glad of Crowley's company. They dined together regularly, and between them they came up with the idea that she should illustrate his innovative Tarot deck, *The Book of Thoth*, a complex, Modernist and austerely disturbing deck very different from the almost fairytale comfort of the Rider deck, probably the twentieth century's best-loved popular tarot, designed by A.E. Waite and illustrated by Pamela Colman Smith.

Harris took Crowley under her wing, giving him £2 a week (which sounds like his pocket money, but it was a useful allowance of well

---

1   A different emphasis from the old Golden Dawn definition: "the Great Work – which is, to purify and exalt my Spiritual Nature so that with Divine Aid I may at length attain to be more than human, and thus gradually raise and unite myself to my higher and Divine Genius..."

2   i.e. because his boring speeches emptied the chamber of the House of Commons, playing on chamber-pot. It was funny once.

over £100 today). Like Yorke and Karl Germer she gets her share of vituperation in Crowley's diaries and letters – "a dangerous lunatic, the most treacherous and deceitful person that I know, or have ever known"; "constant thieving from me"; "Frieda's latest disloyal but imbecile intrigue"; "really ill from Frieda's savage ravings" – but she was perhaps Crowley's main friend in later life.

When she first met Crowley she gave her address as Percy's flat, 15 North Court, Wood St, Westminster (convenient for Parliament) but the Harrises' larger and more long-term house, which Crowley came to know well, was Morton House, The Mall, Chiswick. She was an executor of his will at his death in 1947, using the address of her studio at 3 Devonshire Terrace, Marylebone, and she put together and published the Order of Service from his funeral, *The Last Ritual*.

7I

SANDWICH STREET, SAINT PANCRAS
Bobby Barfoot

In June 1937 Crowley met another casual magical partner, Agnes "Bobby" Barfoot, or Barefoot, who lived in what was then a multi-tenanted Victorian house at 8 Sandwich Street, just south of King's Cross. It is difficult to know if Barfoot was a sex worker and whether the magic sum of five shillings ever changed hands (the price Crowley mentions a couple of times elsewhere; it is probably about £15 today).

This is true of a number of the women Crowley consorted with, and he probably wasn't many women's idea of a casual sex partner or what might now be called a "friend with benefits" (nor was that a popular arrangement in the days before reliable contraception and social independence). He was already rather old for his age, an effect exacerbated by eccentric old-fashioned clothing like the tweed knickerbockers, and he had bad teeth, strange parchment-like skin, a heavy paunch and a ponderous, wheezing manner that some people found sinister or off-putting. But at the same time he had a confident, direct approach, an air of intelligence, and he could occasionally be very funny. And he smeared himself with Ruthvah, a scent which was supposed to make him irresistible.[1]

Sex with Bobby seems to happen now and then throughout the year, with little other contact, as if going back to a masseur or some other service, while meanwhile having sex with several other women on a similar basis. It is not quite a romantic relationship, although friendly: they have drinks and meals, and he runs into her socially now and then in the Fitzroy Tavern. She sometimes

---

1 Musk and civet on a base of ambergris, which Crowley rubbed on his skin and into his eyebrows. It gave him a sweetish smell and made horses whinny after him in the street.

went to Manor Place, and he may have gone to Sandwich Street.

We don't know much about her, but when Crowley first met her he noted the *I Ching*'s advice to "bear with the uncultivated". Born in 1892, she was in her mid-forties when he knew her; she came from Portsmouth, had been abandoned by her husband, and had an illegitimate child. She lived until 1985.

Crowley performed works with her about ten times in 1937, and slightly more in 1938, but often several months apart. Aims included "power over men", "money", "health and strength" and "health especially for Pearl". It is interesting, since Crowley had earlier noted that he preferred partners not to know what he was doing, that in December 1937 (the aim on this occasion being "money") he "told her how" and "she tried too."

72

CHEPSTOW VILLAS, NOTTING HILL
Educating Phyllis

On 17 September 1937, still in his Paddington Green days, Crowley struck up a relationship with Phyllis Wakeford. She lived in a respectable boarding house run by a Lucy Whitby at 35 Chepstow Villas, in what was meanwhile becoming the run-down area of "Rotting Hill": an area of large Victorian houses subsiding into bedsitters, furnished rooms, and cheap lettings generally, soon to be associated with serial murderer Christie and notorious landlord Rachman.

Phyllis Wakeford was Anglo-Indian, born in Bengal, where her father had a responsible job with the Bengal Nagpur Railway, and in Britain she had a family connection with the Delhi Indian restaurant at 117 Tottenham Court Road, where her mother Amy Wakeford lived.

Crowley had sex with Phyllis on the 17th and 19th, and again a couple of times the following month, before subjecting her to jaw-dropping insults. He writes with a rather arch unkindness in his diary, "Educated... Phyllis. The poor zebu has been choked with lies: quite upset when I pointed out that her chief charm was her musky nigger stench." (A zebu is a type of humped cattle; he also refers to her as a Brahmin cow, a related type of cattle but punning on the Indian caste). Nevertheless their relationship continued on and off, including drinks and meals, until on 31 October he writes "Phyllis has disappeared!"[1]

---

1 She went through a bad time around this period, marrying a man called Frank Davison-Light in 1938; described as a managing director, he went bankrupt, was arrested for passing dud cheques, and they tramped the country in poverty – at one point attempting to get to Liverpool on foot – before his suicide in 1939. She is described at the inquest as well-dressed and dignified, wearing a veil. She remarried in 1957 and again in 1966.

John Symonds asserts that Phyllis Wakeford is the woman Charles Cammell later remembers in Richmond: a woman who comes through Cammell's slightly cringe-inducing description as a rather charming person (or at least one with a smiling disposition). He writes that he visited Crowley in Richmond, and there in the hallway, "The girl who stood before me, smiling with big red lips and the whitest of teeth, was black! Ah, what a girl was that! A real fuzzy-wuzzy with a shock of sable curls, with eyes of jet and diamond, and a figure as light and lithe as a gazelle's and much more undulating... there were gold rings about her round, almost-ebony arms..."

Aside from the fact that this woman doesn't sound Anglo-Indian, the main problem is that the Richmond flat is a couple of years later. I believe this woman is an embroidered caricature of Beryl Drayton, from the Caribbean,[2] whom Crowley picked up in Hyde Park in September 1939; Cammell writes discreetly that in addition to having a very sweet voice, she "bore the name of a jewel that has magical attributes". As well as being a sexual partner she acted as housekeeper for a couple of weeks while he was living in Petersham Road, before they fell out.

It is noticeable how many of the women Crowley consorts with are black or other ethnic minority; and this is before large-scale Caribbean migration began with *Windrush* in 1948. Along with Phyllis and Beryl, the list includes a "coloured girl" in Windmill Street, "Marie Johnson 11 St. Peter's Sq. Hammersmith. Mulatto", and the slightly mysterious "black-bumbed Blowzabella", at 5 Florence Court Maida Vale W9.

Florence Court was a fairly recent inter-wars apartment block with porterage, redolent – like all such blocks – of discreet vice, and Blowzabella refers to an 18thC song, where a man and a prostitute are arguing about money in alternate verses ("Blowzabella I'd have you to know, / Though you fancy my Stock is so low, / I've more Rhino[3] than always I show"). There is a further mystery because this was the

---

2   Crowley thought she was half-Jamaican; she was Barbadian.

3   Puzzling but rather nice eighteenth-century slang for money.

3

address of an unpleasant man with a history of violence, supposedly living there alone; he may instead have been a pimp.

Black women had been 'over-represented' in British prostitution since at least the 18thC, compared to the percentage of black women in the population as a whole. Along with what must often have been disadvantaged starts in life, with a high incidence of illegitimacy, children's homes, and the stigma of being "half-caste", they must also have appealed to an 'exotic' taste in clients. This was certainly true in Crowley's case. After a 1933 gathering in Trafalgar Square to demonstrate against the Scottsboro Boys verdict (which he attended through his friendship with Nancy Cunard) he reports "turned to African Rally 8 P.M... I danced with many whores – all colours." On another occasion he had a dream of a "superb young jet-black nigger whore", and in his Magical Record of Ankh-F-N-Khonsu, a 1929 diary, he resolves in harmony with his *I Ching* to "Fuck negress, or other very low woman."

The year 1939 started with "Began by kissing nigger, hoping for the best. Took home alleged Maisie Wilson 15 Buckingham Gate???". She is one of several Maisies and Wilsons, and seems to be a different woman to Mary Wilson, also in the Victoria area, a little later in the year: "Mary Wilson – no, no! VICo628 80 Belgrave Road. Beautiful, voluptuous, vicious – I think touch of black blood. Refrained..."

73

THE OBELISK, EMBANKMENT
Charter of universal freedom

Crowley was publishing industriously in the Paddington Green period, including *The Equinox of the Gods*; this contained *The Book of the Law*, with supplementary material, and it was handsomely produced, with a facsimile of the Cairo manuscript in a pocket at the back.

He had published *The Equinox of the Gods* already in September 1936, in the Welbeck Street days, with a celebratory dinner for Pearl and Karl Germer at which Pearl became unpleasantly drunk. Now he published a second edition with all the fanfare that should have accompanied the first, and with a dramatic prospectus asserting that publication of The Book of the Law caused wars by supernatural means. "THE FIRST PUBLICATION" was "nine months before the outbreak of the Balkan War, which broke up the Near East." "THE SECOND PUBLICATION", in September, 1913, was "was nine months before the outbreak of the World War, which broke up the West" (when "the might of this magick burst out and caused a catastrophe to civilisation"). "THE THIRD PUBLICATION", the one in 1936, was nine months before the Sino-Japanese War (July 1937) and now "THE FOURTH PUBLICATION", in December 1937, was to be the big one, with the world clearly heading for a smash. This publication would bring on another massive war, after which Thelema would triumph.

Crowley had some trouble with Simpkin & Marshall, over at Stationers Hall Court in the City. They were supposed to distribute the book, but he took charge of it himself, publishing from a box address BCM/ANKH at British Monomarks (today in Old Gloucester Street, but then at 188 High Holborn). He wanted the ritual launch to include the giving of a copy to a representative of each of the world's races, so the night before the Winter Solstice, with a representative white man (Gerald Yorke), Crowley went on an extended pub crawl. They were also accompanied by his politician-journalist friend Tom Driberg, who came along as an observer and wrote the whole thing up rather drily in his *Daily Express* gossip column. They picked up the full complement of a "An Englishman, a Jew, an Indian, a Negro, [and] a Malayan", the Malayan representing the "yellow race" since they couldn't find any Chinese or Japanese people. Perhaps surprisingly, Rollo Ahmed doesn't seem to have been roped in (possibly they had to be strangers, new to the business: civilians, as it were). Instead they found a black "dancing-girl". The Indian was a Bengali Muslim who spoke no English, and "seemed rather puzzled by the whole business".

It was an ordeal keeping the party together until 6.22 in the morning, helped by drinking whisky and going to the room of "one Erskine" ("a terribly dull party", Crowley wrote in his diary; either the gathering or Erskine himself). Finally, at the obelisk, it was time, and Crowley made a brief speech: "I, Ankh-f-n-Khonsu, the Priest of Princes, present you, as a representative of your race, with *The Book of the Law*. It is the charter of universal freedom for every man and woman in the world." Then everyone could go home, and he went to bed.

Meanwhile daily life continued. It was a couple of nights before this that he'd had his dalliance with Joan Dobson in the street outside her flat on Porteous Road, and then the day after that he'd managed an opus with her (dedicated to "Publication," but "premature – too much excitement"). After the Obelisk party he had a hangover ("v. bad") and finally roused himself to go up to Euston Road and meet Joan for dinner at Casa Prada, but she didn't turn up.

74

ALDERNEY STREET: MATTIE PICKETT
The women of Pimlico

Crowley was still close to Pearl, despite her drinking and madness. She helped to fund *The Equinox of the Gods*, but her "flame of fornication" days were over: she was visiting 11 Manor Place in September 1937 when she got stranded there for the night, and Crowley let her have the bed while he slept on a chair in his clothes.

There were no more official Scarlet Women, but in the Spring of 1938 a significant partner came along in the shape of Mattie Pickett. Just before her came Joan Gibbons, in her early forties, and a "Marvellous pick-up... Opus A.1.": next day Crowley had to work on book business, "But I have savoured Joan all day. I hope she comes back". She didn't, quite, but he did run into her again towards the end of the month and made a date for Demos restaurant that went off well: "Joan Gibbons alias Brooks. Kissed her all wrong but she was A.1. No hint of failure. Opus." (the object this time being success to Crowley's play *Mortadello*: "Mortadello to go big"). But after that she fades from the scene; he noted in his diary that he didn't want to "compete", possibly with other men.

On the same evening he wrote that, he found another woman; not on the street but at a drinks party. This was Mattie Pickett, who lived in a basement flat at 139 Alderney Street, Pimlico (Alderney Street itself has more recently been in the news due to the unsolved 'spy in the bag' case, with a dead MI6 employee in the top-floor flat at number 36). Born Marguerite Razzal in Texas in 1904, Mattie was a nurse with experience of both ambulance and psychiatric work, and she already knew about Thelema. Crowley wrote excitedly to Karl Germer from Manor Place, as if his own faith had been wavering, that she was "pure Thelemite" and "has been living for 10 years by 'Do what thou wilt' told her by a journalist! So, you see, it does work! a staggerer to have a stranger start to convert me."

The journalist was a man named John Fitzgerald-Hanrahan (1892-1951; originally from Manchester, he was living on Stanwick Road, West Kensington, near Crowley's storage unit). He was imprisoned for cheque fraud in 1939, with a relatively lenient ten-week sentence, after blaming psychiatric problems from a head wound in the First War.[1]

Altogether Mattie was an exciting find, "the first truly sympathetic woman I have had for years", with whom he carried out magickal sex for "health – power &c"; "health and energy", "health and au." [i.e. *aurum*, gold: money], and "money for new lodgings". She was "the best yet – a superb artist", and at times they were "both completely entranced."

As with Bobby Barfoot, he told Mattie what he was doing and how to do it; on 14 May 1938 he met her at lunchtime in the Shakespeare pub, still there on the corner by Victoria station, and "taught her the IX°". This meant she could do it herself, so on one occasion, when he was concentrating on "health – power", he suspected she was not in tune: "I think she was doing au." (money).

He took her back to Manor Place, where his landlady disapproved of her ("Letter from Miss Stanton libelling Mrs. Pickett by innuendo") and to West End restaurants such as Demos and Chez Victor, and he nicknamed her Maat, the Egyptian goddess of truth and justice. But he fell in love with her, and it ended unhappily. She sent him a letter he felt was rude (who knows? – it might simply have said he wanted more of a relationship than she felt able to have) and he sent one back, which no doubt was: "Rude letter from Mattie: my reply ditto."

After the break-up he even felt he had a kind of succubitic visit from her (or a heart-rendingly acute and transparent wish-fulfilment dream): "Maat came astrally to caress me in sleep, or half-sleep; the most nearly real experience of the kind that I remember." Next day Frieda took him to Regent's Park Zoo, and he told her everything. He was suffering: "Sudden spasm of sheer misery: took whiskey and *The*

1   'Mental Torture From Cheque Frauds: Relief To Be Arrested', *The Times*, 29 August 1939 p.6.

Author of Trixie to bed early" (a 1924 comic novel by William Caine, about an archbishop who writes a novel anonymously).[2]

A year later, looking for women in Hammersmith, he ran into her again at Hammersmith tube station, by which time she had moved (luckily: the Alderney Street house was destroyed by a bomb the following year).[3] "I go into station and who but Mattie?!! Nurse M. Pickett. Basement flat (W. Ken) [i.e. West Kensington was the nearest tube] 62a Castletown Road W14."

A beautiful and strangely quiet district, Belgravia's more modest sister, Pimlico was run-down between the wars and associated with rented accommodation and lodgings. Anthony Powell describes it atmospherically in his novel *Casanova's Chinese Restaurant*, with reference to two men Crowley knew, both composers. The character of Moreland is closely based on Constant Lambert, and Maclintick is inspired by Philip Heseltine ('Peter Warlock'), the composer who committed suicide, allegedly after dabbling with Abramelin:

> We took a bus to Victoria, then passed on foot into a vast, desolate region of stucco streets and squares upon which a doom seemed to have fallen. The gloom was cosmic. We traversed these pavements for some distance, proceeding from haunts of seedy, grudging gentility into an area of indeterminate, but on the whole increasingly unsavoury complexion.
>
> 'Maclintick is devoted to this part of London,' Moreland said. 'I am not sure that I agree with him. He says his mood is for ever Pimlico.[...] Maclintick is always to be found in this neighbourhood, though never for long in the same place.'
> 'He never seems very cheerful when I meet him.'
> [...]
> 'He is a very melancholy man,' Moreland agreed. 'Maclintick is very melancholy.'

2   Oddly Caine's book figures in Vladimir Nabokov's novel *The Real Life of Sebastian Knight*, which has saved it from oblivion.

3   The location is now Russell House, a large red-brick apartment block at the Lupus Street end of Alderney Street.

It was also strongly associated with prostitution, probably due to the proximity of Victoria Station. During the split with Mattie, Crowley consoled himself, somewhat vengefully, with another woman on the same street. This was Ethel Donley, at number 113: "another Alderney (street) cow" – Alderney is a type of cattle – and "dreadfully well-meaning", and moreover "one in the eye for Maat", as he thought of it, although he was "three parts drunk, agonizing for Maat."

Other women in the area included Peggy Young, in the basement at 87 Gloucester St SW1, and Rose Wilson, at 46 Lillington St SW1 ("Fat toothless hag – & superb!").[4]

Crowley also had frequent sex with a woman named Maisie Clarke, overlapping with Mattie. She worked a regular beat in Hyde Park but her bed was on the Victoria edge of Pimlico at 1 Gillingham Street (at the corner with Vauxhall Bridge Road, currently a sushi bar).

Crowley had a number of 'works' or 'operations' with Maisie in 1938 specifically directed to bringing on the likely war, hoping for an "A1 War" and putting their mixed fluids on a dagger. He was not only a regular client – he records having sex with her about 25 times – but they grew to know each other socially and ate together, although he continued to seek her out in Hyde Park. Sadly and rather touchingly, she cried when she felt excluded from his more middle-class circle.

When things were good with Maisie they were very good ("Opus... Superb opn."), but they didn't always run smoothly. Nonetheless he thought of taking her on as his housekeeper, and at best found her pleasant company: he even wondered if another woman, Mary Wilcox ("amusing"), might be a "possible Maisie." It seems to have petered out in boredom and bitterness after a couple of years, but at his most affectionate Crowley invented a dish in her honour. This was along the lines of Peche Melba (invented in the 1890s by Escoffier at the Savoy, in honour of the great soprano Nellie Melba) and it was

---

4   46 Lillington Street is long gone, now under the Lillington Gardens Estate, but the flats of Ethel Donley and Peggy Young are still there. When I went to see them there was a bit of Harry Potter merchandising on a windowsill, a faux-vintage wooden box proclaiming "English wand makers". You don't know the half of it, I thought.

Peche Maisie: "Steep peaches in cream with sugar whipped up with Kirsch & Benedictine. Ice some hours."

+

Crowley had also had what might briefly have seemed a classier and more exotic option with Lady Edmee Owen, a French woman and former actress around twenty years his junior. She lived about a mile down the Vauxhall Bridge Road at 1 Drake House, Dolphin Square, a newly built (1937) Pimlico apartment complex associated with single men working unsociable hours (members of parliament and waiters, for example) which would develop a strange reputation for spies and scandals of one sort and another. "I am getting really keen on her", Crowley noted in July 1937.

Born Edmee Nodot, at the age of 16 she had married a wealthy, 60-year-old Englishman – tea and rubber trader Theodore Owen – and used his money to finance a career as an actress. They separated due to her adulteries, but were still technically married when he was knighted in 1926, making her Lady Owen. Better yet, his death in the same year now made her fabulously rich. Edmee continued to have affairs, the most fateful with Dr Gastaud, a doctor-beautician helping her with her weight. Becoming jealous of Gastaud's wife, Lady Owen bought a gun and shot her four times.

Madame Gastaud survived, and Lady Owen received a five-year sentence, serving three. In 1934 she published her autobiography, *Flaming Sex,*[5] and she also colluded with sensational magazine accounts with extraordinary illustrations, notably a photograph of her jewellery-covered hand holding a gun and captioned "Ma main, la main qui cajolait les enfants, la main qui caressait les animaux" (My hand, the hand that used to pet children and animals).

---

5   (John Long, 1934). John Long was a downmarket publisher of sensationalistic books who also published Rollo Ahmed's *The Black Art* (1936). Lady Owen followed *Flaming Sex* with *The Sleepless Underworld* (John Long, 1935), a spectacularly unconvincing memoir of her time as "queen of the Paris underworld".

Lady Owen developed a passion for gambling and in 1936, perhaps unknown to Crowley, she had gone bankrupt for the catastrophic sum of a million pounds. Their fledgling relationship soon petered out – he may have had a lucky escape.

✝

Not least of the women Crowley knew in Pimlico was Bertha 'Bill' Busch, the eighth of the official Scarlet Women. Having moved to London with him, they had drifted apart but she had stayed. In 1935 Crowley told Gerald Yorke that she was living with a boxer he knew, who forced her into prostitution and beat her face black and blue, but this is a typical Crowley retrospect on the unlucky fate of former friends and may not be true; he also alleged Mathers had put his wife Moina on the street.

Towards the end of the 1930s she was living at 82 Warwick Way, and then in 1939 at 3 Cornwall Street (a demolished street at the back of Dolphin Square, now under Pimlico Academy sports area) with an older man, retired Royal Artillery captain Harry Frowd St. George Caulfield. She was described as a saleswoman of household machinery (possibly sewing machines or vacuum cleaners). She knew Crowley's then girlfriend Margot Cripps, and she still had sex with him occasionally, a couple of works being dedicated to the success of an invention he was trying to patent, his 'Memodial' for phone numbers.

At the beginning of the war Bertha was judged not to need internment, and opted not to be repatriated. But then, bizarrely, in September 1944 she was sent back to Germany (it is hard even to imagine how civilians were safely conveyed to Germany, only a couple of months after the D-Day landings; possibly it took Red Cross help, and might have been on compassionate grounds). It was the worst possible moment to go home, with Germany falling and Russian invasion imminent, and the rest of her story is presently unknown.[6]

6   If anyone with access to German records cares enough to look into it further, she was born Bertha or Berta Kruger on 6 March 1895 in Crussow, north-east of Berlin, and at some point married a Herr Busch (she was divorced). Her middle initials appear in adult life as E.A., and she also used the name Anna.

75

HASKER STREET, CHELSEA: LIFE WITH PEGGY
Most accidents happen at home

In May 1938 a man called John Jameson wrote to Crowley, and they had lunch. He was a young actor who suffered from stage fright, and Crowley took him on as a student. Jameson had money, and Crowley saw him as a possible financial backer for various projects including rejuvenation pills and a stage production of *Mortadello*. In the summer of 1938 he went on tour and sublet his flat at number 6 Hasker Street to Crowley, precipitating a discreet flit from Manor Place.

Crowley had bad dreams at Hasker Street, and blamed them on the *Book of Abramelin*: "Two or three really bad nightmares. I am a fool to sleep with Abramelin in the room, as I have for some 4 or 5 days." The following night was no better: "Another terrific nightmare. Removed Abramelin. (This was a 'double-decker' dream: i.e. one in which one dreams that one wakes & checks up on the dream, & finds it true!)"[1]

Frieda brought Sir Percy here to meet Crowley and talk about politics, and Pearl was still visiting as a friend, but meanwhile Crowley had met a new woman, housekeeper Peggy Wetton, who became his primary partner and moved in with him. This had all fallen apart in drink, madness and jealousy by the time they moved out. It was like Pearl all over again (and it was the same horrible formula, living with a highly strung woman who drinks and then making her jealous).

---

1   This was not his Abramelin notebook of talismans, as I would have imagined, but the published Watkins edition of 1898; he had a more relaxed attitude to the notebook. I am indebted to William Breeze for this information.

"Kempinski A.1 wild duck with Louis Wilkinson; back to 6 [Hasker Street] to enjoy 1827 Brandy & Peggy's ravings"

"Peggy hopelessly drunk again"

"Peggy raving all P.M."

"An admirable dinner: my prawns now perfect. Peggy raving & weeping most of P.M."

Peggy was unlucky with accidents. One evening in November, Crowley asked her to fetch the *Evening Standard* so he could find the time of the news on the wireless, and she went out only to smell something burning. Opening the stove, it exploded into a fat fire, and as she got the dish out with a wet cloth she was badly burned on her right arm and hand (and, Crowley noted, "utterly heroic and unselfish").

After a Dr Cosgrove said they should wait 24 hours and see how it developed, she was taken into Charing Cross Hospital for what turned out to be ten days; she made a violent scene about being kept in. "The day was curiously peaceful," Crowley noted that Saturday at Hasker Street: "*One must not have women about.*" After ten days she was discharged, but then admitted a couple of days later to St. Lukes, Muswell Hill; this was a psychiatric hospital ("a positive paradise for Peggy") where Charing Cross may have recommended assessment.

Meanwhile Crowley was involved with several other women, including a Norah Knott ("She has a complex or fixation, but is as nymphomaniac as Peggy") who did some secretarial work for him. This is almost certainly the Norah Knott who had been secretary to the Reverend Harold Davidson, disgraced for his relations with prostitutes, who ended up as a circus performer and met his end after being mauled by a lion. Like Crowley he was an extrovert public figure (in his performances he acted out being roasted on a spit by the devil) and he had recently died, in June 1937.

Crowley also had a couple of works with Pat Harvey and, most notably, on the day Peggy went into hospital, a woman called Josephine Blackley (more about her shortly): this was "*Wunderschon!*"

[wonderful] and it was done with the intention of healing Peggy's arm, to which end he put some elixir (mingled fluids) on the right arm of Peggy's dressing gown.

There has been a widely noted 'psychologization' of twentieth-century magic, which Crowley spearheaded with 'The Initiated Interpretation of Ceremonial Magic' back in 1904. In it, he argues that when an old magical grimoire talks of evoking a demon who finds money, this really means stimulating the part of the brain that governs business ability. In line with this, much of his sex-magical activity (for his own health, or for a creative endeavour, or for giving a good talk) is within the realm of motivation, confidence, and inspiration, along with more nebulously causal but still partly self-determined areas such as 'luck' or 'prosperity' or success with another woman. But, like his works with Maisie to bring on the Second World War, his opus with Josephine Blackley and the arm of Peggy's dressing gown is notable not only for its generosity – although it might not be a generosity Peggy would have appreciated – but for its fully supernatural expectations.

There was more love interest during the Hasker Street period with Marie-Louise Draghici, a sometime dressmaker (at one point she had or was involved with a lingerie business at 77 Baker Street) who lived at 48 Chepstow Villas, not far from Phyllis Wakeford: Crowley performed a couple of works with Maisie Clarke intended to "get" Marie-Louise,[2] but their relationship petered out in social engagements and lunches, including lunch with Peggy, who fell down the steps at number 48 as they were leaving.

Crowley was well dug in at Hasker Street for about eight months, and he had a letterhead printed there with "666". But eventually young Jameson wanted his flat back. In February 1939 he wanted Crowley and Peggy out, and it came to conflict:

2   Similarly, he performed works with Maisie, Jessie Moran and Rose Wilson all dedicated to success with an Angela Considine, or Constadine, (although when he finally succeeded he found he didn't like her – "quite unthinkably stupid. Simply not there to any intelligent remark." – and was keen to get rid of her in the morning).

John Jameson shows heroic rage
Against sick men of thrice his age.
Against sick women in his care,
Nothing John Jameson does not dare
Yet opposition soon dries up
The frenzy of the Pansy Pup.

Frieda Harris helped Crowley look for new lodgings, and in the last
week of February 1939 he moved out.

76

WEST HAMPSTEAD
Love in Hampstead

In June 1937 Crowley wrote what might have been "If able, live in Hampstead" in his diary. The original diary is no longer extant, surviving only in slightly unreliable Chinese-whisper transcriptions, and the transcription is unequivocally "If able, love in Hampstead". If he really did write that, then it is certainly more aphoristic.

Crowley's comings and goings in Hampstead – leafy, prosperous, supposedly intellectual, historically quite Jewish, famously pleasant – and north London generally, are slightly mysterious. He had chess business up there, and book business,[1] and he had a few friends and acquaintances such as Noel Fitzgerald (Boundary Road), Louis Fox (Belsize Park Gardens) and "Campbell and Rhona", a boxer and his girlfriend who lived at 100c Abbey Road. This was Selvin Campbell, born in Belize, who became Jamaican welterweight champion and moved to Britain in 1936; he fought as Lefty 'Satan' Flynn, "His Satanic Majesty". Crowley also notes an Adele Brand, who lived on Priory Road, and he had an "A1" sexual encounter with a woman called Julia at 37 Broadhurst Gardens.

Hampstead grows less expensive going west, shading across West Hampstead into the historically more down-at-heel Kilburn. In the spring of 1938 Crowley was ecstatic to meet a woman in her early thirties called Sally Pace, who was staying at number 55 Iverson Road, Kilburn, just by the railway bridge on the line to Kilburn station.

This was Sarah "Sally" Pace, aged 32, from Shrewsbury in Shropshire (where she was married to a considerably older publican who ran a pub called the Craven Arms; she may have run it with him).

---

1   e.g. with a bookbinders on Canonbury Road named Key and Whiting, and with W.L. Hershant at 236 Archway Road, who was involved in distributing *Magick*.

Crowley only had sex with her twice, in March and April, but he was very taken with her and she inspired some of his most enthused poetry since the days of 'Leah Sublime':

> Sally is a darlin' little bitch
> Slim and tall and wonderful, a witch.
> Her cunt is hot and slimy—
> She is ready to defy me
> To satisfy her everlasting itch.
> But I swear to God I'll put the matter right
> If I have to lick the bloody thing all night
> In an ecstasy of bliss
> Till she chokes me with her piss
> And a golden mess of hotly-scented shite.

After that he lowers the tone, and the second half is less suitable for quotation in a family book.

Sally probably didn't have a telephone, because Crowley also went up there (travelling by bus on a straight line up what is now the A5, along Edgware Road and Maida Vale) and didn't find her in. On the bus back he struck up an acquaintance with another woman, a Stella Hilling, who was in her late twenties and gave her address as 43 the Broadway, Cricklewood (a grocers, which she was either living above or working in). She later came to visit at Manor Place, but she was no Sally Pace. He asked his *I Ching* to divine the relative characters of Stella and Sally and, as he interpreted it, it came up with "idiot" and "hot stuff" respectively.

77

BLACKFRIARS ROAD, WATERLOO
Cath Falconer

One night in December 1938, during the Hasker Street period with Peggy and failing to get any further with Norah Knott ("futile"), Crowley went out and spent what seemed to be "two hours' futile hunt" looking for a pick-up in Hyde Park. At last he struck gold with a woman named Cath: not only would she be his main sexual partner through 1939, but it didn't end badly and she became a friend.

This was Katherine or Cathrine M. Falconer who lived on Blackfriars Rd, within the ambit of Waterloo rail terminus. This influenced the character of the area; George Burchett, the famous tattooist, was also nearby on Waterloo Road to cater for servicemen passing through. That same autumn Crowley had also visited a prostitute called Emmy Butler several times; she was even closer to the station on Lower Marsh, in Florence Davis's "Private Hotel" at number 141, next door to the Dover Castle pub (now the Walrus pub and hostel). Just across the road at number 9 Lower Marsh (demolished and now the site of a health centre; number 11 is still there) was the house where a few years earlier Maria Teresa de Miramar alleged to Gerald Yorke that she had been imprisoned for three months by "*tres mauvais*" Italians; the suggestion is that she was held captive by 'white slavers', until "*enfin je me suis escape*" [sic].

Cath Falconer lived at 83 Blackfriars Road in Harry Levy's "Women's Common Lodging House",[1] a few doors down from the Railway Tavern on the corner (now The Ring, opposite Southwark

---

1 'Common Lodging House' was a recognised, almost legalistic, term with the 'common' meaning communal eating and often sleeping. Jack the Ripper's victims relied on Common Lodging Houses. The nearest modern equivalent would be a hostel for the homeless.

underground station). Crowley found Cath to be "a lady & intelligent", and the operations (the first for "health") were "very first class" from the start. The only problem was Peggy, who was understandably jealous, and was expected to socialise with Cath. Crowley expected all his women friends around this time – Peggy, and Pearl, and Frieda, and Pat, and Ruby Melvill[2] – to get on under the same roof, and it didn't often work: "Cath back. Peggy insulted her all day", he writes in his diary, while on another occasion Pearl laid into Pat, "calling her trollop, harlot, whore, and slut in the course of a spate of venomous abuse." Cath was also jealous.

About a week into their relationship at Hasker Street, Cath was using a knife to cut up a tea cloth and accidentally stabbed Crowley deep in the face: he lost a good deal of blood and had to call Dr Cosgrove out again. After Peggy's earlier kitchen fire, it is almost surprising Crowley doesn't blame having Abramelin in the house for the accidents at Hasker.

Crowley invented a dish in Cath's honour[3] and took her to restaurants including the White Tower. Sex continued through 1939 and into 1940, overlapping with his later partner Alice, with Crowley praising Cath and her "cunt prehensile as ever".

Finally they stopped having sex but remained on cordial terms. A couple of years later Crowley was sorry to meet her again in a reduced state ("Ill-dressed, old, dirty, skin discoloured, smile and pawky speech quite gone")[4] and by then she had also been arrested for shoplifting, but they kept in touch. During the war she worked at the Royal Ordnance munitions factory at Swynnerton, Staffordshire, then joined the Women's Royal Naval Service (the WRNS or Wrens) and finally seems to have emigrated to Australia. She remains one of Crowley's happier relationships.

2   Ruby Melvill (1887-1939) was a former socialite and society beauty, painted by William Orpen, who travelled and wrote. She was also addicted to heroin. Crowley saw her on an almost daily basis for a couple of months in 1936 without it developing into a relationship.

3   The transcript ("Foudee Falconer") seems botched but it may be Fondue Falconer or Fondre Falconer ('Falconer melt'). It was fried mushrooms, cut small, with powdered chili, cooked in parmesan or preferably Cheshire cheese, then boiled up with the addition of cream, and eaten with fried French bread.

4   "Pawky" – a Scots word for playful, witty, drily humorous.

78

SOHO: JOSEPHINE BLACKLEY
The women of Soho

One night in October 1938 Crowley was out on an almost fruitless hunt when shortly before midnight he found a magnificent woman: "The most marvellous woman I have struck in years. But really too fat and ugly." This was Josephine Blackley, who lived at 256 Newport Buildings, a long-gone tenement – densely occupied, with a large proportion of Italians – almost at the junction of Charing Cross Road and Shaftesbury Avenue. He returned to her from time to time.

Inevitably Crowley met other women in the Soho area. Suggestive names and addresses in his 1930s diaries include "Lilian 40 Dean St top floor"; "Coloured girl 22 Windmill St."; "Dora Williams, 42 Rupert St"; "Betty Russell, 3 Brewer St."; "Jeanette, 72 Shaftesbury Avenue"; and "Gladys GER4602".[1]

It was probably the pursuit of women that led him to join the 'Social Dance Club' at 12 Little Newport Street (now, but not in Crowley's day, part of Chinatown, and where he had membership as A. Crowley Esq., valid until 22/6/1934) and to have dealings with the Colonial Club at 14 Bateman Street; he noted the club in his diary in 1938, and a few years earlier a girl named Millie Sharp had already given him the club's phone as her number: GER1441.

Josephine Blackley's story took a spectacular turn during the war. In the small hours of 17 April 1941, just before 3.30am, Newport Buildings was hit by a massive 1000kg parachute bomb (2,200lbs: a

1   i.e. the Gerrard Street telephone exchange: a West End number.

"landmine", as they were known) and completely destroyed,[2] leaving her under the rubble.

But she survived. Crowley was astonished to run into her again and learn what had happened: "Jo Blackley! disinterred after 2 hours under Newport Buildings!!! Now at 8 Marshall St."[3]

2   Roughly where Soho Fire Station is today, Newport Buildings was where the modern concrete development on the edge of Chinatown is now, including a multi-storey car park, by the church that still stands at the crossroads. There were over a hundred casualties.

3   Later to be well-known as the site of Cranks wholefood restaurant, but not in Josephine Blackley's day; born in 1899, and a widow when Crowley met her, she died in 1943. In official records her surname is Blatchly.

79

HYDE PARK
On shikar

Where was Crowley finding all these women? Postcards in newsagents' windows ("French Lessons", "Model", "Seats Caned" and the rest) have been a well-known London contact device (particularly after the Wolfenden Report advised taking prostitution off the streets, leading to the 1959 Street Offences Act) but in the first half of the century and before there was also a considerable trade on the street and in parks, particularly Hyde Park: "Bayswater Road, Hyde Park, Pimlico and the West End were seen as trouble spots, and the police had to respond to complaints from the public in these areas", leading to a crackdown in 1951. Hyde Park women were routinely arrested and fined, almost on a rota system, but to minimise this, and give minimum offence to the general public, they solicited as discreetly as possible with a nod, a "good evening", or a meaningful glance.

Hyde Park was one of Crowley's regular beats: "Shikar in park" he writes one night in 1940 (*Shikar* is an Anglo-Indian word, from Urdu, meaning to go on a hunt or a hunting expedition) and he refers to being on a bus with a "Hyde Park grasshopper" (grasshopper was German slang for a prostitute, particularly an outdoor one, from his Berlin days). He continued to seek Maisie in the park as her regular place even after he knew her, and if he couldn't find her or she declined him he might end up with someone else ("Emmy", or "Jessie Moran"). But shikars, in the park and elsewhere, were not always successful and he sometimes records "n.g." [no good] ("To park, late. N.G.") and shikars "in vain", "futile" or "fruitless." It was far from perfect, and when he went back to doing it after a break ("walked miles") it struck him "Stupidity of the park stands out immediately after an interval."

These safaris didn't have to be green and leafy. During the war he had a "Long shikar: Euston Road, Edgware Road, Marble Arch, the Dell" (the Dell, by the Serpentine, brings us back to the park). And on another occasion, failing to find a woman named Ruby Butler ("the Blonde Bombshell"), he set out on a definite quest:

> Determined on shikar
> Louisa 21 Lisle St.
> Millie 50 Langham St. Flat 5.
> Diona Compton Chambers 9.
> Found Ruby at Hop Poles. 40B Vereker Road.
> GER4994 Dora Williams 42 Rupert St – from the past.
> Mattie (basement) 62a Castletown Rd W14.

Pubs were another obvious hunting ground ("9.30 Fitzroy, on shikar"). He looked for women at the Swan in Hammersmith, a large Victorian pub with a dark wooden interior, and saw Ruby Butler, and on another occasion had a drink there with Rollo Ahmed and a Helen Fields ("huge lunar cow"). The Swan is still very much there, by Hammersmith tube station, as is the Hop Poles, another intact Victorian pub slightly further down King Street on the other side of the road. "Very disappointing shikar," he writes one night, "ending in an actual row at the Hop Poles."

80

THE FRENCH HOUSE, DEAN STREET, AND OTHER PUBS
Triple absinthe

The writer Maurice Richardson met Crowley one day in 1939 at the French Pub in Dean Street (then often known by its older name of the York Minster, or Berlemont's, after the landlord Victor Berlemont). Crowley was dressed, says Richardson, in a tail coat and striped grey 'sponge-bag' trousers, "like a duke in a musical comedy", and he smelled of ether, like an old-fashioned operating theatre. He told Richardson this was because he had started the day by drinking half a pint of ether (he had certainly used ether extensively when younger, but he was probably pulling Richardson's leg).[1] Asked what he wanted to drink, he plumped for a triple absinthe, followed by two more triple absinthes, and then they set off up the road for a gargantuan lunch at L'Escargot. On another occasion Crowley ate at the French with Louis Umfreville Wilkinson ("the beloved Umfreville"), and noted the toughness of the kidneys and the excellence of the Burgundy, a Volnay '34.

Crowley also drank at the nearby Dog and Duck on Bateman Street, with friends and associates including Driberg and Ahmed. In the earlier nineteenth century inns and taverns had been something

---

1   Gerald Hamilton also remembered an air of what he thought was ether, but may well have been a sweetish, piney, terpeney smell from Crowley's asthma inhalations.

There is nothing about ether in Crowley's later diaries, but his earlier use for introspection and mystical experience would make a book in itself, including a vision of existence as "nothingness with twinkles"; "a state of (visualized) mind"; "the old resolution of splendour into bliss"; and movie-like inner visions ("took Ethel to the cinema"). In the outer world, on a night-time hotel balcony in Tunisia, he writes "God! You ought to see Aldebaran from here... scarlet, azure, emerald violet – all by ether!"

any traveller might go into, but as the Victorian era went on, and into the early twentieth century, urban pubs had generally taken on a more proletarian character and were no longer something a man of Crowley's relatively gentlemanly status would go into (Golden Dawner Wynn Westcott lived almost next door to a pub on Camden Road but probably never went in, although his tradesmen might have done). This unacceptability of pubs thawed in Crowley's lifetime, particularly with Bohemian pubs such as the Fitzroy Tavern, and the Wheatsheaf.

Crowley was a familiar figure at the Fitzroy, as we have seen, although old Fitzrovia face Ruthven Todd remembers Crowley no longer going there in the late Thirties, so as not to meet Betty May, and going to the Wheatsheaf on Rathbone Place instead. This isn't borne out by his diaries, but he may have avoided it on nights when she was known to be in. He was safe in the Wheatsheaf, where she had been barred.

Crowley also knew the Old Cheshire Cheese well, on Fleet Street, a famous literary pub that would never have been too *déclassé* to go into. It was a pivotal venue in the 1890s, with the poets of the Rhymers Club including Yeats, Ernest Dowson and Lionel Johnson, and it was also well known to Arthur Machen and many others (even Picasso when he was in London). Crowley's invention of "Risotto Cheshire Cheese" is not about the cheese but the pub: it served a celebrated steak and kidney pudding, and his risotto recipe is steak and kidneys with chili, in rice.

El Vino's wine bar further along Fleet Street was similarly very acceptable, and both these venues – and Heneky's, now called the Cittie of Yorke – were well known to Crowley for much of his life, from the old Chancery Lane days to his friendship with Driberg, who had some work at the black glass Art Deco *Daily Express* building further along the street. El Vino's had another, smaller branch near Piccadilly, by the junction of Swallow Street and Vine Street (blitzed in the war) where Crowley would often meet friends before going on to the Café Royal and elsewhere.

There is a famous but largely apocryphal story about Crowley and Dylan Thomas (whose poetic career was launched by Crowley's friend Victor Neuburg, when he was poetry editor of the *Sunday Referee*). Thomas – who had no great respect for Crowley – was in a pub doodling on a piece of paper, with Crowley elsewhere in the room, and as Crowley left he dropped Thomas a copy of the doodle, 'as if by magic'. This is sometimes said to have been a poem rather than a doodle, and variously said to have happened at the Fitzroy, the French, or – most plausibly, as told by Thomas's friend Constantine Fitzgibbon, whose wife was there – at what was then the Swiss Pub, now the famous gay pub Comptons on Old Compton Street.

During his time in Paddington Crowley went to the Royal Oak (now just Oak) on York Street, Marylebone, and other occasional pubs there include the now gone Vintage Wine Lodge at 239 Baker Street, and the Horse and Sack at 36 Harrow Road, along with the Westbourne Hotel (where he lunched and went with Mattie, and which he knew familiarly as Peter Cable's, the name of the landlord) which is still a pub at 1 Craven Road, opposite the station on the junction with Praed Street, now called the Pride of Paddington.

Other pubs Crowley knew include the Adam and Eve, Green Man, and Yorkshire Grey, all in Fitzrovia; the Swan, the Hop Poles and the Dove in Hammersmith; the Mason's Arms in Maddox Street, when he lived in Hanover Square; the Windsor Castle ("fun on Sunday night", he thought, although it is not clear which of the several pubs with this name it is);[2] and the Antelope on Eaton Terrace, where he had a drink with Augustus John and occasionally took Peggy.

2   There is a famous one in Kensington near Holland Park but, since he was living in Manor Place at the time, it is more probably the now defunct one at 309 Harrow Road, once known for entertainment.

81

CHESTER TERRACE, BELGRAVIA:
The house on the borderland

After Hasker Street, Frieda Harris found Crowley a new lodging at number 24 Chester Terrace (now Chester Row). She found it in mid-February, and after a night at the Grosvenor Hotel and a few days at 20 Jermyn Street ('Gordon Chambers') he was fully moved in by the beginning of March 1939.

It was a furnished flat, high up in the building, with a little gas fire. Maurice Richardson remembers it as "on the borderland between Pimlico and Belgravia", a placing that is not just topographical but socially evocative, particularly in the period. On the one hand it was near Victoria Station and Victoria's bedsits, furnished rooms and cheap hotels, and on the other it was near Eaton Square in smart, aristocratic, virtually regal Belgravia.

Crowley was now in a relationship with Cath – Katherine Falconer – as his sexual partner, but Peggy was still on the scene, though not living with him. Now he found her annoying and "Peggisome", and her efforts to seduce him in lingerie repulsive ("Peggy abominable: in cheap *lingerie de cocotte* trying to seduce me!!!!! Rows & rows & rows"); "she would put off a satyr". He had what he called a 10 o'clock rule, which probably means he wanted her gone by ten. Sometimes she broke it, or caused trouble generally (asking to come in for just five minutes, and then threatening suicide) and when she was particularly troublesome he called out a Dr O'Hara who gave her Luminal, a barbiturate he used himself.[1]

He was still working on the tarot with Frieda, and he published

---

1   And Peggy fades from the scene. Sadly she was arrested in July 1941 (and described in court reportage as a 38-year-old housekeeper, of 45 Quarrendon Road, Fulham). In collusion with a postman of the same address, she had been stealing cash and postal orders from envelopes addressed to charities.

his Eiffel Tower lectures on yoga as *Eight Lectures on Yoga* by Mahatma Guru Sri Paramahamsa Shivaji; the appropriated name was a dig at the yogi of South Audley Street, nearly three decades earlier.

The Antelope on Eaton Terrace was now his favoured local pub. He was also eating out a great deal – Chez Victor, The White Tower and L'Escargot, among others – as if money was no object. It was feast or famine, and a couple of times he had to pawn his gold Ankh-f-n-Khonsu ring. When he wasn't eating out he was inventing and naming new dishes at home,[2] and the number of recipes lovingly recorded at Chester Terrace gives life there a rather leisurely and hospitable feel, although not always hospitable to everyone. Shortly after moving in he saw an occult student, Noel Fitzgerald. "Asked FitzGerald to drink: he asked himself to dinner: we asked him to fuck off."

That spring Crowley noticed a review in *The Observer* by Maurice Richardson, reviewing a biography of Soho character Ironfoot Jack,[3] in which Richardson compared him to Jack. Crowley took amiable offence at this, and invited Richardson to lunch at Chester Terrace. It was served by a woman called Kathy ("a Scots lady so indeterminate as to age, status and nubility that she seemed like one of those anthropological reconstructions with 'conjectural parts in black'"). Richardson thought she was just Crowley's housekeeper, but it sounds like his partner Cath. Falconer is a prevalent Scots surname, and she spoke to him familiarly, saying "Hurry up Aleister, the potatoes will be getting burned" when he led them through his "Do What Thou Wilt..." grace before lunch.

After a few large vodkas they had lobster bisque, roast duck, and a runny Brie, washed down with "several litres" of Chianti, followed by Cyprus brandy. Richardson was drunk, and Crowley produced a fountain pen with "Baphomet" on the side in gilt lettering. By now

2   Including *Cojones Mexicanos*; Risotto Cheshire Cheese (named after the pub); Turbot d'Urberville; Turbot Porterfield (named after his dentist); Sambar of Turbot and Mushroom; Goldfish Toast; Flying Fish; Capretto St George (goat); Fisherman's Daughter, a sole and lobster dish; *Escalopes de Veau Desespoir* (Veal Despair); *Pimentos Katarina a la St.Bartoleme*; *Biftek Crapaudine*; and others.

3   Mark Benney, *What Rough Beast?* (Peter Davies, 1939)

they were great chums, so Crowley wondered if Richardson could do him a personal favour and just scribble a little note of apology about the review. Fortunately Richardson was too drunk to write (Crowley was clearly thinking of a libel action against *The Observer*).

Crowley invited him to lunch again. This time Crowley's old Berlin friend Gerald Hamilton was present. Crowley brought the conversation around to Isherwood's Berlin, and assured Richardson that the real Mr Norris was far more wicked than the man in the book. Moreover, "If I was a real magician, I would be able to produce him for you at this table, would I not?" Again, after a drunken lunch, the fountain pen was produced. And again, Richardson said he was too drunk to write, with Hamilton catching his eye and making little 'Don't do it!' shakes of his head.

Privately, of course, Crowley was in total earnest about being a real magician. To counter nightmares at Chester Terrace he assumed the god-form of Harpocrates before sleep, to "make the real circle [real magic circle], i.e. the Aura of the Magus, impregnable" (and yet he still had them, with hallucinatory figures on waking). But for Richardson he clearly enjoyed camping it up. When it came to making coffee – Jamaica Blue Mountain, sometimes said to be the world's finest – Crowley mumbled occult incantations over the Cona machine, and seeing the tip of a claw protruding from the bisque, he said "Looks like a devil roasting in hell, does it not, Mr Richardson?"

82

WEST HALKIN STREET: DION FORTUNE
The Bat in the Belfry

Occultist and novelist Dion Fortune had been in the Stella Matutina, a Golden Dawn offshoot, and she went on to found her own Fraternity of the Inner Light; like Blavatsky with her hidden 'Masters' and the Golden Dawn with its 'Secret Chiefs', Fortune was in touch with her 'Ascended Masters'. Her magical thinking combined the Golden Dawn tradition with more psychoanalytic ideas, and she reformulated Crowley's definition of magick ("the science and art of causing change to occur in conformity with the Will") as "the art of causing changes in consciousness to occur in accordance with the will."

Fortune lived in a converted Presbyterian chapel named The Belfry at 11 West Halkin Street, Belgravia (it has subsequently been Anton Mosimann's private restaurant and dining club of the same name). On 30 March 1939 she gave a public talk there, and Crowley went along. "Public Bat No.1 at the Belfry", he thought. "Like a hippo with false teeth. Talk – bubbling of tinned tomato soup."

Crowley's relationships with other professional occultists were generally critical or adversarial. In his 1934 diary he encounters a "Dolores del Castro" 77 Holland Park (PAD9343) and notes she is "Crazier than ever – pure pathological lying." It sounds like the glamorous pseudonym of a prostitute, but it was a name used by the more 'popular' occultist Madeline Montalban, later to be known as The Witch of St.Giles.[1]

1   As if to confirm Crowley's complaint to Anthony Powell about the endless rivalry and one-upmanship of occultists, Montalban later pronounced her judgment on Crowley: "His principal trouble was his difficulty with astrology. He could never understand it, and astrology is, of course, the basis of successful magic."

As for Dion Fortune, he was on more cordial terms than his 'bat' comment might suggest, and as "Mr and Mrs Evans" (her original name was Violet Firth, and she married Tom Evans, a physician) Crowley had Fortune and her husband round to Chester Terrace for chili con carne on the evening of her talk.

83

MORTON HOUSE, CHISWICK: HOUSE OF LADY HARRIS
The Blackcurrant Pudding Brothers

Frieda Harris lived with Sir Percy at Morton House, The Mall, Chiswick, a terraced 17th century townhouse in this stretch running alongside the river. Crowley spent a great deal of time here, having lunches and dinners as well as working on the tarot card project with Frieda. Early on in his visiting, one day after lunch, he walked to see nearby Chiswick House and park.

Crowley appreciated her work, despite his occasional belittling comments ("simply a talented amateur groping about with the obscure Bloomsbury schools"; "silly woman... pointless daubs"; "Lady Harris did not *create* anything. She *executed* the paintings from my designs and descriptions under my constant supervision"). Frieda herself took it seriously enough to exclude Crowley from the exhibitions as a liability.

Frieda's peculiar sense of humour was on show when she had several people round for lunch in July 1939, including Crowley and Gerald Hamilton. She served blackcurrant suet pudding and Hamilton ate sparingly, wanting to leave room for his main course (he was thinking the meal began with something sweet; something he had known in China). But no; that was all there was going to be, and Frieda christened her luncheon a gathering of the "Black Currant Pudding Brothers", like an occult fraternity. The Masonic Fraters of the Most Holy and Thrice-Illuminated Black Currant Pudding, perhaps. Hamilton was a great bon viveur but largely dependent on his friends for food and other handouts, and he was not amused. Surprisingly, Crowley was: "A really great original meal & pleasant party".

84

THE PARAGON, PETERSHAM ROAD
The Holy Grail in Richmond

In August 1939 the Richmond period of Crowley's life began: "I have been guarding the Holy Grail in Richmond," he later wrote to Yorke. Lady Harris had a rented flat in this famously pleasant southwestern district at number 3 The Paragon, 57 Petersham Road, and Crowley had already been there: "delightful lunch in sunlit room overlooking the river." It was in the telephone book under the name of Chutney, from her pseudonym Jesus Chutney.

She lent it to him, and on 5 August 1939 he moved into a high room at the back of the building: "lovely flat, big windows, high above Thames". The next day he had two friends round for lunch, Hamilton and Louis Umfreville Wilkinson, for what he called "Nuncheon", an archaic word for a light midday snack. Crowley wrote up a little menu card for the occasion, typical of his sense of fun and the trouble he could go to for friends.

The idea that it was just Nuncheon may have been a modest little joke: it was a heavy lunch by any standards, with a starter followed by roast beef, Yorkshire pudding and two veg, all washed down with a serious Burgundy (a 1933 Gevrey Chambertin) then tiger melon and a cheese course before coffee and cognac. The starter was his own "Zakowski Louis LXIX", for which his recipe was "Herring Roes, Anchovies, Balachow, Curry powder, Red and Green Chillis cooked in butter. Serve hot on fried bread."

One night he had Tom Driberg round to the Paragon for curry, when Driberg played what he admits was "rather a mean trick". Unknown to Crowley, he had come into possession of a lost Crowley item (left behind with a landlady, according to Driberg, "either as payment in lieu of rent or in the course of a moonlight flit"). It was a little square book, "bound in red morocco and encased in baroque silver which must have held a missal or breviary" and it contained a Crowley diary.

Crowley would sometimes draw a little pentagram, then ask Driberg to look at the space in the centre and tell him what he could see. Driberg never saw anything. But this time he started speaking in an entranced voice, saying he could see a little book, with red leather, and shining baroque silver, and some writing inside which he couldn't *quite* read...

> I had never seen Crowley so staggered: he leaned forward in desperate eagerness. "Go on," he said, "go on." But the vision faded. Try again, he pleaded. "No" I said. I can't see anything more...

Driberg never let on, and years later he sold it to Jimmy Page.

Other events in the Paragon era include the appearance of Crowley's last significant sexual partner, Alice Speller (more about her later) and – no less important – the start of the Second World War.

85

THE GREEN, RICHMOND
Twenty-one again

Still in Richmond, in May 1940 Crowley moved to number 15, The Green, an eighteenth-century house with a fanlight over the door. The so-called Phoney War – the slow start – had run from September to May, but now things stepped up, with Germany moving on Belgium, Holland and France.

Crowley had already dreamed of Hitler in the late Thirties: "Elaborate dream about Hitler & cigars & Magick & my horse Sultan. I was running Germany for him." Another night, "I had several long talks with Hitler a very tall man... he was pleased & impressed: ordered all my books translated & made official in Germany. Later, a dusky night in a city. A man in gold-braid went round a corner, saw several horsemen, similarly gorgeous, one fired the first shot of the war."

In waking reality he had had some political hopes for Hitler and the cause of Thelema, and in May 1936 he met a man identified only as "Slippery Joe" in the Café Royal bar to have lunch and talk about "93 as base for Nazi New Order". Also in 1936 he asked his old First World War associate Viereck – now promoting National Socialism in America – to use any influence he might have with Hitler to bring *The Book of the Law* to his attention as a "philosophical basis for Nazi principles." Crowley was convinced he had influenced Hitler, probably through his German disciple Martha Küntzel. It is unlikely, but the correspondences are still remarkable. Küntzel saw Hitler and Thelema as one, and Crowley noted "astonishing" similarities between Hitler's thinking and *The Book of the Law* (also noticed by Gerald Yorke). Watching British propaganda, Crowley was impressed for what its makers would have seen as all the wrong reasons: "Saw show of cartoons lampooning *Mein Kampf*, with appropriate quotations. Taken in these selected doses, what a masterpiece! And how patent & profound a debt he owes to AL!"[1]

He felt the same way when he read *Hitler Speaks*, a 1939 book by Herman Rauschning, and annotated it enthusiastically ("true"; "yes"; "all very sound"; "excellent"; "For 'German people' read 'Thelemites'"). When Rauschning's Hitler says "After all these centuries of whining about the protection of the poor and lowly, it is about time we decided to protect the strong against the inferior" he wrote in the margin "Yes!"

Despite all that, at the onset of war he wrote to Martha Küntzel saying Britain would "knock Hitler for a six" and that Germany owed any high culture it had to Jews. Although he was capable of intense casual anti-Semitism, as we have seen with Michael Houghton at Atlantis, he had no interest in any systematic absurdities about an Aryan master race ("Nordic Aryan nonsense").

Nor did he like Hitler's "demoniac foaming-at-the-mouth expression", and he said the trouble with Hitler was that he didn't understand "the rights of the individual". Above all Nazism, or National Socialism, was too collective for Crowley, and instead he wished Germany had been able to restore the Hohenzollern monarchy.

From now on Crowley was a loud and publicity-seeking patriot, trying to interest the British government in Thelema, writing songs and verses for Britain and France, and claiming to have invented the 'V for Victory' sign (more usually credited to Victor de Laveleye, an anti-Nazi Belgian who broadcast for the BBC; Crowley also claimed to have invented the Nazi use of the swastika, having allegedly suggested it to Ludendorff[2] around 1925). Nevertheless, one of his most interesting and far-reaching comments comes when he explained to Germer why, in his anti-Nazi propaganda writing, he was still unable to attack Hitler by name: going back to the old Golden Dawn idea of trans-human 'Secret Chiefs' (of whom he thought Aiwass was one) he writes that he couldn't attack "a man who may be, for all I know, working directly under one of my own chiefs!"

1   i.e. *Liber Al, The Book of the Law.*

2   Erich Friedrich Wilhelm Ludendorff (1865-1937), German general and politician.

With his asthma in particular, for which he had started using heroin again, along with heavy drinking and gargantuan eating, Crowley's health was bad and he was not ageing well. At one point he congratulates himself on walking from Richmond Green to Richmond Bridge, which is no great distance. But Charles Cammell remembers his excitement during a bombing raid, when they saw a German bomber shot down in flames by anti-aircraft guns.

Here was a man who had been gasping his life away all through the night; and now at the crack of dawn he ran downstairs two steps at a time, and was shouting Hooray! And waving his arms skyward in a passion of boyish excitement and jubilation. No trace of asthma; it was gone to whence it came. Crowley was twenty-one again...

86

FITZWILLIAM HOUSE, RICHMOND: CHARLES CAMMELL
Drinks with the Reverend

Charles Cammell (father of Donald Cammell, who made the cult film *Performance*) was an associate editor of *The Connoisseur*, the art and antiques journal, and he was an admirer of Crowley's poetry. After meeting at Gwen Otter's they became friends, drinking and eating occasionally at El Vino's and the Café Royal. It was through Cammell that Crowley found his lodging on Richmond Green. Cammell lived across the Green on the Little Green at number 4 Fitzwilliam House, a more modern 1930s building in red brick.

Crowley sometimes went over to Fitzwilliam House – probably trying to cadge a free dinner, says underground filmmaker and Thelemite Kenneth Anger – and on at least one occasion Cammell had him round with the Reverend Montague Summers, the witchcraft and demonology writer remembered for books such as *The History of Witchcraft and Demonology* (1926) and *The Vampire in Europe* (1929); he also lived in Richmond at 4 Dynevor Road. Summers was a bizarre figure in his own right, affecting eighteenth-century clothing, and he was so High Church that religion was a kind of fetish.

Summers was also ultra-reactionary in his politics and is remembered for his fire-and-brimstone hatred of witches and Satanists, associating them with communism and anarchy. It was less well-known in his lifetime that he was a former practising Satanist himself, of a distinctly 1890s-ish persuasion.[1] It was Summers who conducted the first Black Mass in Britain for which there is any real evidence, and later than one would imagine, in Eton Road, Hampstead, on Boxing Day 1918.

[1] And in line with this he was no mean poet, in the decadent-Satanic vein: see *Antinous and Other Poems* (1907).

In public Summers disapproved of Crowley, but in private things had been more cordial. Dining with Summers in 1929, Crowley recorded "The most amusing evening I have spent in decades!" (they seem to have talked about Crowley's plans for a universal sex-appeal perfume called 'It').[2] He was less effusive about seeing him at Fitzwilliam House with "Mrs Forbes" – a reference to Summers's secretary-companion Hector Stuart Forbes – and noted only that the sherry was indifferent.

There was also a Continental restaurant called Valchera's, just along from Richmond Station and handy for the Green, where Crowley dined on a couple of different occasions with Cammell and Summers (separately). I can dimly remember it in the 1990s with thickish – possibly velvet – café curtains, and I regret not going in when I had the chance. Symptomatic of the way London has changed, the building is now the Richmond branch of McDonald's.

Like so many of Crowley's friendships, especially if money was involved, his relationship with Cammell ended badly. He bought a quantity of expensive hand-made tweed from Cammell's wife Iona but failed to pay for it, instead writing "Ha Ha" in his diary and selling it on to other people in smaller batches. When she asked for the money he became abusive, and that was the end of friendship with the Cammells.

Under no illusions about Crowley ("No sense of honour, friendship or virtue of any kind"), Cammell nevertheless wrote a fair and even affectionate 1951 memoir of him, *Aleister Crowley: The Man The Mage The Poet.*

2   As in Hollywood "It girl" Clara Bow and her 1927 movie *It*, in tandem with Elinor Glyn's sensational novel of the same year and title. Glyn defines "it" as "that strange magnetism which attracts both sexes".

87

DUKE STREET, MAYFAIR: DR THOMSON
Death of a doctor

Crowley's final years were shadowed by heroin addiction. The first doctor to prescribe it seems to have been Harold Batty Shaw, based at 122 Harley Street, whom Crowley had been seeing since 1898 and who prescribed it for bronchitis at Christmas 1919. But Crowley had a longer relationship with opiates: he had experimented with laudanum in 1907, and his diary suggests he was also using heroin by the time of his first Jermyn Street lodging in the same year (he includes it in a list of things 'allowed' by his health regime, mainly directed towards dieting).

In a 1924 Paris diary he discusses his astrological and elemental "idiosyncrasy" for heroin, and he also records tremendous pleasure, writing what could be described as happy nonsense: "It has been like thirteen masturbations, a menstruation orgie, a five-man buggery competition, sixteen rapes of assorted quadrupeds [etc.]... and a pot of marmalade thrown in." Heroin users often experience pleasurable itching, leading to very pleasurable light scratching, and Crowley writes "I itch marvellously lewdly, and to scratch – Ah! But for to scratch, it is to scratch!"

Unfortunately by this time he was addicted: "I seriously dread the failure of supply." He managed to beat it and stay clean for some years, but by 1936 if not earlier he was driven back to morphine for asthma relief, and by 1939 he was injecting regularly, with the return of a full habit. His most distressing withdrawal symptom was the return of asthma. Crowley obtained heroin from Heppell's chemist, with branches at 169 Piccadilly, 35 Haymarket and elsewhere, and in his final years they posted it to him.

His health – surprisingly delicate all his life – was very bad in later years, with teeth regularly breaking or falling out and an injection abscess on his leg, on top of asthma and lifelong bowel troubles and vomiting, never adequately diagnosed. He would be woken by diarrhoea, and vomited on the floor in theatres and cinemas, attributing it to excitement. A whole troupe of doctors have walk-on parts in the later diaries – Crawshaw (heroin), Lodge (morphine sulphate), Vernon, Peacock, Macdonald and others – but one late doctor in particular is remembered, due to a gutter press story that Crowley had put a curse on him. As James Laver remembers it, "the story was current (I do not vouch for it) that, shortly before his end, his doctor had said to him: 'I am going to cut off your heroin.' Crowley replied: 'If you do I shall die – and I shall take you with me.' He did die, and the doctor died a fortnight later."[1]

In fact, the doctor coincidentally died not just within two weeks, but within a day. He was found dead in his bath. This was Dr William Brown Thomson, a man Crowley liked ("Charming humorous lowland Scot, very clever and thorough"). He was at two Mayfair practices, 15 Half Moon Street, running between Piccadilly and Curzon Street, and 83 Duke Street (not the one off Jermyn Street), near Grosvenor Square, from where he told Crowley he was going to reduce his dose.

---

1   The widest circulation for this story probably came from the *Daily Express*, 4 December 1947, 'Magician Put Curse On Him'. The version given doesn't really add up: allegedly Dr Thomson had started personally chaperoning Crowley to the "West-End chemist" in the last year of his life (which sounds unlikely anyway, as if doctors have nothing else to do) but Crowley was by then living in Hastings, and even in London Heppell's had started sending his heroin by post.

88

HANOVER SQUARE, MAYFAIR
Tamasha dreaming

After Richmond, Crowley spent the winter of 1940-41 down in Torquay, attended by the usual troubles with money. At first he moved in to the Grand Hotel ("Food excellent – beyond praise!") but he was unable to pay: "No money, Paul, manager Hotel, most kind, let me go." While in Torquay he tried to establish a more modest Abbey of Thelema, with all members pooling their resources in "aristocratic communism", but noted all too realistically that the "worst snag in England about the Abbey is the social gap between classes, as regards members... it is hard to extend the [Thelemite] principle to menials." He also went on "shikar" quite purposefully, and was directed by a sympathetic taxi-driver to the evocatively named "Belgravia Club".

In July 1941 he returned to London, taking a serviced flat for 3½ guineas a week (about £200 today) at 10 Hanover Square W1, in the area of Mayfair between Regent Street and Bond Street. Now completely redeveloped, the large house at number 10 on the corner with Princes Street was then akin to a cheap hotel, with a telephone switchboard and meals.

Crowley lost no time being back in town, going to the nearby Café Royal, Oddenino's, and the French Pub (on one occasion too crowded, so he went on to the Fitzroy Tavern). Soho was just across Regent Street, and one afternoon, with an associate named Morrison, he had tea at Maison Bertaux, a long talk in Soho Square, and a drink at the Shakespeare's Head pub on Great Marlborough Street: all "Very pleasant."

He also visited the famous, or notorious, publisher R.A. Caton of the Fortune Press at 12 Buckingham Palace Road, a publisher associated with Montague Summers. Along with a couple of famous names such as Dylan Thomas, his list had a strong leaning towards more niche-market gay titles, and sadistic books such as *Nell in Bridewell* and the like. He combined this with a career as a slum landlord, boasting that he owned 91 houses and not one with a bathroom. Crowley visited him several times and hoped he might re-publish his *Diary of a Drug Fiend* and his earlier pornographic novel *Not the Life and Adventures of Sir Roger Bloxam*, as well as his tarot project, but found him to be a "seedy fraud" who finally admitted he had no interest in tarot and just wanted books about "torture and flagellation."

His local pub was now the Mason's Arms on Maddox Street (where the landlord took two copies of his patriotic poem *England Stand Fast* to display in the pub) and it was on Maddox Street at Christmas 1941 that he records the Epiphany-like fragment of someone (perhaps a street vendor of some kind; perhaps Italian) saying "Take 'ome a Chreesmas pooding?", working it up into a short comic poem.

Crowley's main sexual partner through this period – seemingly the last of his life – was Alice Speller, a secretary in her early fifties whom he had met up in Highgate in October 1939. She lived in Effingham Road, Crouch End. John Symonds changes her name to Alice Upham: she was still very much alive when his 1951 biography came out, not dying until 1969. One wonders if she ever knew her Aleister was on the cover of the Beatles' *Sergeant Pepper's Lonely Hearts Club Band*.

On their first date in town, two days later, they had gone at lunchtime to the Yorkshire Grey in Langham Street, and then had difficulty finding a room to go to bed; they finally managed "*chez* Jeanette", a woman he'd met a while earlier, who was at 72 Shaftesbury Avenue. She was possibly involved with a club there called the 72 Club (no doubt by analogy with the notorious or glamorous "43 Club" just behind it at 43 Gerrard Street) or Ida's Club.

Crowley was alternately amused and appalled by Alice's ignorance and her malapropisms, or "Spellerisms" ("Really I should collect them"). He noted some of them in his diary, and she clearly had a very eccentric and childlike understanding of what jealous, covet and reactionary might mean, for example. In conversation, "she says something and you realise she's not understood a word of the last five minutes". He was far from romantically engrossed with her ("Saw coloured girl I wanted twice while with Alice. Hell!") but nevertheless they became old friends (he nicknames her "Tub"); they often ate out together, and she visited him in Torquay.

Crowley liked to birch Alice by way of foreplay, and bought a birch specially, but his erections were failing with age, and increasingly his diary reports "frigged her for politeness sake" (and similar; "on compassionate grounds" or "for human kindness sake"). In December 1941 "Alice generously offered a banquet on her birthday. She didn't care what it cost her – the world well lost for love.¹ Cost: sherry 8/4d: lunch £1/3/- : smokes 9/9d: taxi 1/-. Total: £2/2/1. Her contribution 12/6d. Lady Bountiful! Cunnilingus: damned decent of me!" And then on 23 December 1941 he reports "Alice here: frigged her." This, in Hanover Square, seems to be his last sexual act.

✛

Crowley suffered from poor health and intermittent depression at Hanover Square, but he did have the most extraordinary and vivid dreams. In July 1941 he had

> a wonderful novelette-length dream in which I was pursued by an American girl-detective in bombed city. It was all framed by me and her father to get her married to me!

and a couple of nights earlier "one very wonderful dream about an hermaphrodite." Later he had

> Marvellous dream: young strong tall woman and [magical sign] fucking – I gave her (and myself later) to an animal which we called a hog, but wasn't exactly a hog. Intense lust. All this out-of-doors somewhere in the East – N. Africa, I think.

1   An allusion to *All for Love: or The World Well Lost* (1678), Dryden's play inspired by Shakespeare's play about great lovers, *Antony and Cleopatra*.

The complexity of a dream from early the following year recalls Clifford Bax on the impressive 'voltage' of Crowley's mind. It was an "A1 dream" of what he recognised as a type:

> This type of dream begins with presentation of extremely vivid miniature "freaks-of-nature" or sculptures in curious rare gems, usually semi-precious. These objects are then read as symbols of phrases: e.g. "while runs the sacred river" etc.
>
> This is then *recomposed* into single picture. Gamekeeper, thanking squarson for christening his firstborn (throaty – autumn tints – nutbrown ale – rich dark greens, reds, & browns) "with care & the Church of England, your arse, sir, as you may say, sir, the country's safe."
>
> This is heard, felt & seen all at once: and understood as the perfect presentation of the poem, as each phrase of that is to be the original sculptures in miniature.

"While runs the sacred river" sounds like an echo of Coleridge's *Kubla Khan*. One reason Crowley's dreams were so vivid and complex at this stage of his life was that he was using opiates; back in 1915 he had noted "Began morphia... with 1/6 grain. Many dreams at first of the annoying type. Afterwards extraordinarily vivid and delightful."

His dreaming at Hanover Square (where he also had nightmares) may have been further exacerbated by the fact that he seems to have been constantly on the cusp of withdrawal: he seems to have been scraping by most of the time on never-quite-enough, prescribed not to maintain an addict but to bring temporary relief for his asthma.

Crowley's word for all-out extravaganza-spectacle dreams was *tamasha*, an Anglo-Indian word for a show:

> Woke 2.10 from very wonderful dream: cunt, buggery, cocaine, beautiful places & things – real tamasha.

> Dreamt last night that I was with Frieda who told me in a very off-hand way that all the [tarot] cards were finished. After lunch – lots of 1834 Brandy! – slept for 1½ hours. Great Tamasha: very

> long & full of religious activities: intrigues of vile Christians in a vast country house largely composed of antique ruins.

> ...terrific Tamasha with Anti-Christian fights. A long series. At one Christian meeting I altered a hymn & a woman got hysterics & vomited – oh! enough to write a long novel.

> Woke from long fantastic Tamasha with terrific diarrhoea (I foresaw this) & long fit of savage coughing. 1/6 [grain heroin] restored calm – incomplete – after half hour pretty bad.

His appreciation of vivid and often beautiful dreams continued right through the final years of his life:

> Marvellous dream of Himalayan heights & abysses – a train on some high slopes – I am sending a letter, or resending, by affixing stamps of solid gold foil – to Allan Bennett!

> Sex-and-naval-war dreams

> Quite the most magnificent tamasha of my life. Location: Paris.

> Strangest dreams some very gorgeous, some sexual. One about a cable that nearly went astray, owing to an erasure and the name "Bishop".

> Superb dream. With Leah Hirsig? Took room in London slum, low tide. Flood brought royal dolphins majestically swimming past – amid thousands of other marvels.

✛

Crowley's time at Hanover Square was also brightened by Gerald Hamilton moving in as a fellow lodger; he had previously been lodging in Half Moon Street. Hamilton was a very camp and eccentric character in his own right, and like Crowley he lived from hand to mouth while maintaining a serious interest in wine and food. Crowley sometimes grew tired of Hamilton ("Ham like a crazed bluebottle") but he was more often cheered by him: bored by Alice, and his dull disciple Bayley, he adds "Hamilton dropped in and brightened things up from time to time".

Hamilton had been a communist when Crowley knew him in Berlin, but he had now gravitated to the far-right and put his faith in the "sacred cause" of absolute monarchy. Hamilton's politics were well off any serious scale: he was not only an obsessive and boring anti-Semite, but he regretted the end of slavery, and in the 1950s he championed apartheid, affecting a black armband when South African premier Johannes Strydom died. Nevertheless he had a certain charm, and John Symonds – who knew them both – records them having a "similar radiance".

In July 1941 Crowley reports Hamilton foolishly getting himself nabbed under "18B", the wartime regulation for dealing with individuals who were potential security risks, and Hamilton spent time interned in Brixton prison along with Sir Oswald Mosley, the British Fascist leader. Hamilton made an official complaint when his bottle of Gevrey Chambertin 1916, sent by a well-wisher, was decanted into a tin by prison authorities, and Tom Driberg, who wrote the incident up in his *Daily Express* gossip column, commented "It's a grim martyrdom."

It was after his release he moved to Hanover Square and started seeing Crowley almost daily ("Alice and Ham as usual", Crowley writes). On Easter Sunday 1942 Hamilton was walking past Crowley's room on his way to Mass and Holy Communion at St. James's, Spanish Place, Marylebone, when Crowley – who left his door ajar because of his asthma – heard him and shouted out "Is that you, Gerald? Where are you going?" Hamilton said he was going to communion. "I hope your god tastes nice," said Crowley, "You're such a gourmet."

He also gave Crowley his wartime sugar ration, and once when stocks were running low Crowley sent him a note:

I am looking forward to our solitary encounter at 6 on Tuesday. Can you sweeten it literally as well as metaphorically... for of late so many people, encouraged by your report of the deliciousness of Mrs Speller's chatamasha, have thronged my ancestral halls at the strygogemous hour of four,[2] that my combinations of Carbon, Hydrogen and Oxygen in the proportions of 12, 22, and 11 respectively are quantitively inadequate. Angelice, can you bring some shong-shong?

Chatamasha seems to mean Alice Speller's wonderful tea, from the Anglo-Indian "*cha*". Cha plus tamasha may be Crowley's own coinage, a tiny part of his larger "high-imperial, occult-exotic" cultural booty from the Empire, along with curry, yoga and yogic meditation, going on shikar, practising quasi-tantric sex magic,[3] and dreaming *tamashas*

2   Four p.m., or teatime. Strygogemous is a wonderfully rare (possibly unknown) word, which may be derived from the Homeric Greek, meaning exhausted or squeezed out drop by drop. I am indebted to Timothy d'Arch Smith for this information.

3   See note to Reuss and 93 Regent Street: site 33.

89

DOVER STREET, PICCADILLY
A very short stay

The set-up at Hanover Square fell to pieces after the manageress, one Lily Hubard, was arrested for fraud. Hamilton was arrested again for bad debts and fraud shortly afterwards.

Crowley then shifted to Arlington Chambers, Dover Street (at number 5, now redeveloped). He was helped to move by a friend or associate of Hamilton's named Eric Jackson, whom Crowley found he rather fancied: "Eric interests the ageing Alys"[1] he wrote; "Is it too silly? Is it merely cerebral?"

Arlington Chambers didn't last – the chambermaid complained about his hygiene, and he was out again within a week – but it was a stopgap address on what had become Crowley's 'manor' on the long main drag of Piccadilly with Mayfair behind it.

Crowley sometimes went to Hatchett's restaurant on the corner of Dover Street and Piccadilly, and to a restaurant called Maison Basque, at number 11, where his dining partners included Collin Brooks, an editor he wanted to cultivate. Brooks was a bon viveur and old Café Royal habitué, a friend of Louis Umfreville Wilkinson's, and he had also written a cheap thriller – a "shocker" – called *Mad-Doctor Merciful* (Hutchinson, 1932) which compared the symptoms of lunacy and mysticism. Not a man to be intimidated by Crowley, he had a rather hearty and hard manner, and one of the intriguing lines lurking in his memoirs is "You don't need a revolver often, but when you do, you need it damned badly."

Brooks and Crowley also went to what Brooks describes as a "that new Latin Quarter which has grown up around Portland

---

1   His feminine alter ego.

Place" (a mini-Bohemia taking its character from the BBC staff at Broadcasting House) and in particular to a bar and restaurant attached to the Langham Hotel called the Bolivar, which was on the corner of Portland Place and Chandos Place. Crowley already knew this area at the far end of Regent Street well, and this restaurant, and it was here Brooks introduced him to the spy-traitor Guy Burgess and his partner Peter Pollock: "one or two of the younger generation who wished to meet him", as Brooks calls them.

Crowley pulled out his new party trick of putting methylene blue dye in his drink, perhaps to give the impression it was some strange potion, from a little phial labelled 'Lady Astor'. The humour of this is a mystery, but probably related to the fact that Lady Astor was famously teetotal.

Brooks writes in his memoirs that by now Crowley could be something of a bore. Nevertheless, after dining, "we would go to his chambers in Piccadilly, where he would produce some exotic wine... he always gave the impression of having somebody hidden in his bedroom, perhaps a virgin goat."

90

HAMILTON HOUSE, PICCADILLY
The abiding rapture

After Dover Street, in May 1942 Crowley moved further west along
Piccadilly to Hamilton House, number 140, right down at the Hyde
Park Corner end near the present-day Hard Rock Café. Number 140
is on the corner with Hamilton Place. He wasn't impressed to begin
with; there was no phone, and "not even brekker in bedroom".

After a week he moved from suite 105 to a better one at 111, and
he praised the location to Germer, with its views: "If I want country,
I look over to Green Park; if sculpture, I gaze on the Quadriga; if
religion, across to the campanile".[1] More than that, if he wanted a
bath he had Lord Byron's old bath to climb into.

He was still on his old territory: up at the Circus end he was
going regularly to the Café Royal and Oddenino's, where the stranger
told him he looked like Churchill, and occasionally with Hamilton to
a large subterranean pub under Piccadilly Circus called Ward's Irish
House, while down at this western end he also went occasionally to
the Hyde Park Grill inside the Hyde Park Hotel at 66 Knightsbridge,
and occasionally went for a now innocent stroll in the park.

Crowley was getting old, and in one of his more sensitive
moments he asked himself "Why do I fail to appreciate lovely glass
and china? Because I can't get rid of the agony of their perishability."
His health was getting worse, along with his addiction. Regularly
logging his doses, he sometimes adds comments such as "This just
WILL NOT DO", while in a less regretful moment he notes that
there is no food left, but ample tobacco, and "oodles" of heroin. His

---

1   The Quadriga is the four-horse chariot sculpture on top of Wellington Arch,
at Hyde Park Corner, and the campanile is the striped brick tower of Westminster
cathedral, visible further across on the other side of Victoria station.

regular circle of friends – most of whom regularly disappointed, bored, appalled, and disgusted him – was now diminished in quality as well as quantity. His reliable but stodgy disciple Bayley, Cath when she was in London, and a woman called Deborah Hogg[2] all figure regularly in his diaries, along with Hamilton, Alice 'Tub' Speller, and a couple of chess-playing cronies. Film makers Paul Rotha and Karl Meyer were supposed to call on him at Hamilton House to talk about a tarot film, but cancelled, but he did have a fruitful visit from theatre director Peter Brook and a more surprising one from actors Tyrone Power and Charles Boyer, who seem to have been sent by American friends as possible investors or backers.

Things were very rocky with Frieda ("sly treacherous vixen"), who didn't want Crowley's presence undoing her work on the tarot paintings. In July 1942 she mounted a show of them at the Berkeley Galleries, 20 Davies Street, just near Berkeley Square, and Crowley found out ("amazing treachery"; "Frieda's sneaking treachery"). She did it again in August at the Royal Watercolours Painters Society, 26 Conduit Street; this time Collin Brooks tipped him off, and on 4 August Crowley walked in and "caught her", as he thought of it. One of Crowley's less appealing traits was a willingness to take legal action against friends, and he wasted no time going round to consult "Ikey" Kerman.

Louis Wilkinson and his partner Joan Lamburn (eventually to be his fourth and final wife) visited Crowley at Hamilton House one night in June 1942, and Joan included an atmospheric if distinctly odd account of their visit in a letter to a friend. First of all, she was convinced the place was "really a brothel": as soon as she took in the "cheaply furnished hall with its dusty palm tree in the middle and its Lloyd Loom chairs and insolent looking porter in gold braid I knew where I was." This doesn't seem to have struck other visitors such as Peter Brook. As for Crowley, they went upstairs and met him in "a sort of ante-chamber with a filthy uncurtained window looking on to Piccadilly" which had a

2   Crowley never has anything good to say about the "Hoggess" or "She-Hog", and doesn't seem to have enjoyed her company. She was an upper-class morphine addict, daughter of a major-general and married to a brigadier-general, Rudolph Edward Trower Hogg C.M.G.

few stuffed chairs and a sofa on a bare wooden floor. Crowley came out of his room to meet them, and sat down: "in the fading light there was a touching dignity in the dumpy little figure by the window." She knew of his fancied resemblance to Churchill, "but I thought he seemed more like Queen Victoria – an ageing, pettish, harassed queen robbed of her happiness...". Altogether, and perhaps fearing his influence on Louis, she found him "repulsive."

That June he felt "Mental state v. bad: no clearness, no power to concentrate... I feel the need of a loyal friend as never before. Not one in England who really cared a nickel" (oblivious of the fact that the loyal Tub was round that same afternoon to see him). And yet at the same time he still took the trouble to make ordinary life sacramental: going to see Wilde's play *The Importance of Being Earnest* at the Phoenix Theatre, Charing Cross Road (in the celebrated production with John Gielgud and Edith Evans) he decided to make the whole outing "a magical ceremony", not stinting: "Chambolle-Musigny for lunch, taxis all the time, melon— all regardless."

His dreams were still nourishing: "Saw and saluted new moon, very large and very misty. First dream of the kind that I remember." And whatever life threw at him in the way of disappointments, the almost bipolar glory was still there, and often, in a landscape like the London of Blake or Machen. Looking through his diary, he noticed it was "mostly complaints", or "odd bits of pleasure or good luck":

Nothing at all of the reality, of the abiding rapture which makes a 'bus in the street sound like an angel choir!

91

WILTON PLACE
Doctor Faustus

In July 1942 Crowley was contacted by a bold and enterprising Oxford undergraduate: it was Peter Brook, later to become one of Britain's greatest theatre directors. Brook was putting on a production of *Doctor Faustus*, Marlowe's play about a man who sells his soul to the devil, and he wanted Crowley to be the play's "magical advisor".

Brook called to see him at Hamilton House ("where gentlemen-about-town lived in expensive service flats") and found him "elderly, green-tweeded and courteous" with an air not of being wicked but of being down on his luck. They met several times and lunched at the Piccadilly Brasserie, inside the Piccadilly Hotel (now Le Meridien). As they walked along Piccadilly, Brook was embarrassed by Crowley raising his walking stick at noon and chanting praise to the sun, and similarly in the restaurant by Crowley declaiming what Brook remembers as "a conjuration" across the soup (more probably his own version of grace).

The Torch Theatre was a theatre club in a private house at 37 Wilton Place, just across Hyde Park Corner from Hamilton House. The Berkeley Hotel wasn't there in Crowley's day, being built over a demolished strip which by the 1960s included Esmeralda's Barn, the Kray Twins' nightclub, but Wilton Place is otherwise much as it was, with the mews-like Kinnerton Street (where the ubiquitous Gerald Hamilton had been living at the start of the war) just around the corner.

Crowley attended rehearsals, and "helped with conjuring and stage effects". At one point, when Faustus began his incantation to conjure up Mephistopheles[1] Crowley shouted out that you need a bowl of blood to bring real spirits. Then he added "Even at a matinee...", and winked.

"He had demystified himself," says Brook, "and we laughed together." It was inspired of Brook to bring Crowley on board, getting the greatest magician of the twentieth century to advise on Marlowe's sublime Renaissance tragedy. Crowley had given his life to the Great Work, and almost every year he noted two dates in his diary. One was the death of his father, and how old he would have been, and the other was his own "birth" on 18 November. This wasn't his actual birth in 1875, but his 1898 birth into the Golden Dawn, back in Great Queen Street. That was where he counted the beginning of his great lifelong magical adventure.

The *Faustus* premiere was on 1 October, and Crowley took Tub and Bayley, his magical student since the old Argenteum Astrum days. As they walked to the theatre Crowley stopped on the pavement to say his 'Evening Adoration' but – as he complains in his diary – when it came to Bayley and Alice, "they sauntered on, and pretended not to belong to me. What a herd!"

1   Scene 3, lines 16-25.

92

LEVY'S SOUND STUDIO, NEW BOND STREET
The magical voice

In the same October as *Faustus*, Crowley wanted to make some recordings. On Friday 16th he went to Star Sound Studios at 17 Cavendish Square (LANgham 2201), where he recorded his 'Hymn to Pan' and the First Call in Enochian, the angelic language of Renaissance magicians Dr Dee and Sir Edward Kelley. Perhaps ironically, Star Studios had been the meeting hall of the Theosophical Society, an organisation of which Crowley had a very low opinion. It lived up to this inauspicious start on the following Monday, when Star refused to cut Crowley's 78rpm disc or let him have his recording. There may have been trouble about money, or perhaps they understood enough of 'Hymn to Pan' to decide it was obscene.

Crowley did better on his familiar territory of Bond Street, where he went on the 27th and recorded the First and Second Enochian Calls at Levy's Sound Studio, 73 New Bond Street (MAYfair 8521). These survive.[1]

Louis Umfreville Wilkinson remembers a reading of these same texts after lunch with Lady Aberconway: "more than once I have seen him under the sudden stress of his inspiration. He was controlled, I was sure of it then, by something that was in truth religious, that had the quality, the motive force of Oriental religious ecstasy... he read aloud to us from an enormous Magical Book which he supported on his knees. What he read to us was in a strange language, a language unknown. It was of a singular vibrant beauty and power... 'What is that language?' [Lady Aberconway] asked. 'It is the language of the angels,' replied Crowley."

---

1   And can be heard on Youtube. They have been released in several editions over the years, sometimes described as wax cylinder recordings and misdated to 1910-1914, perhaps to give the impression of a man in his prime.

Crowley performed his reading and recordings in a deliberately sonorous, incantatory voice that he called his "Magical Voice". There are varying accounts of his normal voice. Viola Bankes describes it as light and high, and Yorke remembers his telephone voice was quite high and pleasantly melodious, while his former secretary Israel Regardie remembered that outside of the Magical Voice, "Crowley in reality possessed a thin, effeminate, rather squeaky voice. This was one of the most obvious areas where his homosexual component emerged. I would never have thought that his was a strong masculine voice, capable of booming out a sonorous invocation."

Arthur Calder-Marshall and Anthony Powell remember his voice as more nasal and Cockney, although Cockney is misleading today. It seemed Cockney to them, compared to the rather extreme, cut-glass standards of pre-war upper class speech. Certainly Crowley wasn't out of the very top drawer (a man as snobbish as Powell would have noticed this at once). But he wasn't today's idea of Cockney either. And to many of the working- or lower-middle-class women he picked up, part of his appeal must have been that he seemed like a 'real gent'.

93

93 JERMYN STREET
The Valley of the Shadow of Death

On 16 November 1942 Crowley moved into his last London address at 93 Jermyn Street, behind Paxton & Whitfield's eighteenth-century cheese shop. Alice "Tub" Speller and a friend helped. His new landlady Miss Manning lived in the basement ("Cave-Woman", in his diary, seems to be a reference to her) and she turned out to be a spiritualist.

Living in a world of numbers, planets and correspondences, Crowley was delighted that his new phone number was 9331 (WHItehall 9331), adding 31 – the numerical key to the Book of the Law that had attracted him to 31 Wellington Square – to 93. He sometimes went to the all-in wrestling – "three hours of sweetness and light", as he nicely calls it – at the Piccadilly Pavilion by Piccadilly Circus, and he'd been similarly gratified to be the holder of lucky ticket 93, winning him two free seats the following week.

He was at 93 Jermyn Street for almost a year and a half; in the second winter he notes London fog so thick that his powerful torch beam couldn't reach the pavement. It was a street and an area he knew very well by now, and his diaries expand into almost villagey and novelistic detail. Next door was the Savoy Turkish Bath and a chemist called Rawlinson's, where he was puzzled to find a man gazing cluelessly into the window one morning and asking "Do you think they're open?" Across the road was the church of St. James, with the font where William Blake was baptised, where Crowley slipped and banged his head quite badly walking across the churchyard. On a luckier note he records finding a silver threepenny piece there.

Crowley had used Davies, a highly respected tailor 'By Appointment' to the King, and even dreamed about them while he was in Torquay, but his main tailor at this late period was called Bright, of Bright & Paul, just across Piccadilly at 8a Sackville Street:

Crowley had a phone conversation with Bright when he was clearly drunk ("It's my birthday today, Sir!"; "You sound to me blind drunk!"; "Yes Sir!"). He went bankrupt shortly afterwards; perhaps fortunately, the Tailors' Benevolent Fund was at 9a.[1]

Astley's pipe shop was at 109 Jermyn Street ("Pleasant talk with Astley about pipes") and the whole area is given over to gentlemanly commodities, but more unexpected items include a Nepalese kukri (a Gurkha knife) from Cogswell and Harrison's gun shop at 68 Piccadilly (on the corner with Dover Street, now Korean Air) which Crowley bought after some deliberation with the *I Ching*. He was also very interested in an image of Pope Alexander VI ("Rodrigo Borgia", one of the more controversial and notorious popes) which came up at auction not far away. Crowley believed he was Alexander's reincarnation, and made him one of his 'Gnostic Saints', crediting him with having stood as a "Satanfather" to the Renaissance. This was sold by Glendinning's auctions at 7 Argyll Street, near Liberty's – they specialised in coins and medals, so it may have been a medallion of some kind – and he was interested enough to trace the buyer.

Being told he looked like Churchill had stimulated Crowley's interest in his own image, and he had a series of photographic sittings with a photographer named – auspiciously enough – William Churchill. He was on the Holborn edge of Covent Garden above a grocery at 42 New Compton Street, and Crowley was impressed with his work, dubbing him "Cambyses Daguerre Churchill".

Behind St. Giles' church, up at the quieter end of Shaftesbury Avenue, New Compton Street had already figured on Crowley's mental map: a couple of years earlier, after a day of "futile raids on old yonis" (and "possible later Jeannine REG0775") he noted in contrast

---

1   Inevitably tailoring had been important to Crowley-as-gent, and as well as Davies in Hanover Street he had used Tom Brown in Conduit Street, Henry Poole on Savile Row, Sulka's on Bond Street, Rogers of New Burlington Street, and Henry Heath ("Hat makers to the King") at 62a Piccadilly. He was also very pleased with a pair of handmade shoes from Lobb on St. James's Street, then at 55 (now at 9, still shoeing the rich): "Lobb made good shoes!"

"Interesting hope for real liaison Henriette Mrs. H. Barnitt 56 New Compton St. WC2".[2] But nothing seems to have come of it.

Crowley was still writing and working hard: he was anxious to press on with the tarot project, for which he consulted bookbinders Sangorski and Sutcliffe at 1-5 Poland Street ("most friendly and helpful") and he published his old poems about Russia, *City of God* and *The Fun of the Fair* as independent booklets, with frontispieces of Crowley smoking his meerschaum credited to Cambyses Daguerre Churchill. For a couple of years he had been using a printer called Apex at 53 Monmouth Street, Covent Garden, until they refused to set his additional 'Political Note' for *Fun of the Fair*. Terminating the relationship with a fulminating letter, and signing off with "Yours, really concerned about your future in the workhouse infirmary", he now had to use a cheap firm called Fermaprint, just across Piccadilly in Quadrant Arcade,[3] running beside the Café Royal between Regent Street and Glasshouse Street. One copy went to the Soviet ambassador Maisky, and Crowley was delighted when the bookseller in Jermyn Street's Princes Arcade, Francis at number 6, bought one for himself.

Crowley was also thinking about a further series of pamphlets on various subjects including the politics of Thelema as "golden mean" between the Bolshevik Trotsky and the Fascist Mosley, and on his own poetry, championing himself as the last great poet working in the "classical tradition." He had no time for the Modernists such as T.S. Eliot; *The Waste Land* left him "nauseated and ineffably contemptuous", and by his own understanding of poetry he was the greatest living poet. This made it all the more unjust that he was "England's literary martyr", after the long unfair blackening of his reputation.

His greatest project of the period began as a series of letters to an Australian seeker named Ann Macky, a musician with an interest in Rudolf Steiner who was living in Britain at Hemel Hempstead. Crowley found her irritating ("imbecile hag") and thought of her as "poor old

2   "Yoni" is vagina in Sanskrit and Hindi; REG0775 is a Regent Street telephone exchange number, covering West Soho.

3   Currently being revamped as "80 Regent Street" arcade.

Wallaby" and the "Wailing Wombat of Wagga-Wagga", but there was money in her family and she entered into a contract with him to provide a course of spiritual instruction by regular letter for £26 (well over a thousand pounds today). Written in an avuncular style and originally entitled 'Aleister Explains Everything', it became *Magick Without Tears*.

Louis Umfreville Wilkinson remembers there was a pathos about Crowley in old age: "I had always felt that there was something of pathos about him but in his last years this element seemed to me much stronger and he was in consequence lovable as I had not known him to be before." At any rate, says Wilkinson, although he felt a sense of failure, at least he never played for pity and "he never resorted to 'repentance.'"

It was at Jermyn Street that Crowley read to Wilkinson and Lady Aberconway in Enochian. Her later account of it is more patronising than Wilkinson's description would suggest ("Her lovely eyes were large with an emotion that I shared"), but even Wilkinson was struck, amid the grandeur of the moment, with a sense of something picturesque, incongruous and 'period':

> Impressed though I was by the exaltation, the irradiation... I could not help reflecting on what an admirable subject the scene would have made for a cartoon by Max Beerbohm. 'Aleister Crowley reciting to Lady Aberconway in the Language of the Angels.'"

He was thinking of Beerbohm drawings like his 1904 'Yeats Presenting George Moore to the Queen of the Fairies'.

Crowley's health was still declining, and his heroin habit growing ever more central. His teeth were still bad and – since his friendly dentist Porterfield had joined the army[4] – on Hamilton's recommendation he went to a new dentist named Wallis at 93 Cornwall Gardens,

---

4   Morris Fraser Porterfield, a young dentist (born 1910 and still in his twenties) who practised at 65 Elgin Mansions, Elgin Avenue, Maida Vale. Crowley had seen a lot of him since 1937 and got to know him socially. He seems to have been gay – Crowley refers to running into him with the "thicket of thorns" boys, a reference to his own homo-erotic poem 'The Priestess of Panormita' – and he was friendly with Crowley's acquaintance Tom Wyllie (1910-1948), a member of Guy Burgess's circle.

Kensington. He was considering one in Welbeck Street, but plumped for the man at 93 as "probably my cuppa tea".

Socially he still saw people, including Bayley and Frieda Harris, and played word games and spelling bees as well as chess, but he also recorded days of desolation: hardly anyone "bar the Tub", the loyal Alice; "complete (bar Tub) desolation". At one point, in the spring of 1943, he felt there was "no news, no tobacco, no friends, no printer, no hope, no bloody nothing."

Crowley now found that when he was "free of the sexual impulse" a whole group of ideas were now "'obscene' 'disgusting', and 'revolting'" – the quotation marks are his, as if he was considering the whole business critically. This included contemplation of the vagina (but the phallus less so, he noted) along with disease, accidents, meat, warfare, and physical pain. From this he concluded "humanitarianism, pacifism – all such feelings – are functions of sexual weakness." He'd had a related idea back in Berlin, when Bertha Busch stabbed him and Hamilton was appalled to hear about the blood: "This is all his complex – homosexuality and pacifism etc."

Crowley was an avid cinema-goer in this late period, writing notes and mini-reviews of what he'd seen. He felt *This Gun for Hire* at the long-gone Blue Hall cinema, 194 Edgware Road (PAD7188) suffered by having its London assassin story (from Graham Greene's novel *A Gun for Sale*) transplanted to Los Angeles, and that the French classic *Carnet du Bal*, about an older woman looking back on the lovers in her life with a mixture of nostalgia and disenchantment, was just too sad (he'd gone to it "hoping to cure melancholy", but now at this age, he said, "I seem to want pleasant things"). Others included *Brighton Rock, Derriere la Façade, The Man Who Came to Dinner, Striptease Lady, Margin for Error, Arsenic and Old Lace* and the war film *Five Graves to Cairo*, but his particular favourites seem to have been *A Night to Remember* (1942), seen at least six times in various places, from King's Cross to the Elephant and Castle, and the 1943 Bob Hope film *They Got Me Covered*, seen eight or nine times at various places including the Rialto on Coventry Street (now Grosvenor Casino).

Food was an abiding interest: along with the usual haunts there were notable lunches at Hatchett's, with a Hoyo de Monterrey cigar afterwards, The Ivy, and the nearby Ritz ("A1 lunch"), as well as the

American-themed Potomac, which was at 40 Jermyn Street ("good appelstrudel!") and the Chicken Inn ("vile"). Best of all, perhaps, was the classic French fish restaurant Prunier's on St. James's Street, which redeemed a whole day. It was "Another dreadfully blank day till 8," when his friend Cordelia took him to Prunier's: "Food A1 Green oysters! Joy!!" – then they went back to number 93, and played chess through an air raid until midnight: "A glorious evening."

There is something endearing about these late flashes of a tweedy lust for life. He was now receiving what must have been cheering parcels from disciples in America, with regular supplies of crystallised fruit, figs, caviar, and Perique tobacco, and they were also sending him money, totalling over £800 a year (towards £40,000 today). In Britain he might have gone from being (in the words of Arthur Calder-Marshall) the Great Beast to the Great Joke and finally the Great Bore, but Thelema was finding more fertile ground in California.

Crowley was in two minds about Americans: on the one hand he could joke about a plan to civilise them – "a 5,000 year plan" ("Sanguine, I know, but I'm always an optimist") – while on the other he could also say, more sincerely, "Discovered why I like Americans. They are *friendly*." Crowley's correspondence with America was subject to attention from the wartime censor, and he fell foul of a rule that forbade people expressing "willingness to receive" food parcels. What should he write instead, he wondered – perhaps "My dear Aunt, I don't want your beastly food: stuff it up your arse."

Horse meat and whale were both being served in wartime, and Crowley noticed odd meat being served at the Piccadilly Brasserie, where he had "coupe je ne sais quoi" (i.e. a Frenchified fillet of I-don't-know-what). But all things considered, living the life of a West End gentleman, Crowley managed remarkable well with wartime privations: "This desolating war!" he writes cheerfully after a lunch of game pie, grapes, 1858 cognac and a Cabanas cigar.

Crowley leaves a vivid picture of the West End in wartime, with fewer cars in the blackout but travelling faster, and an increase in hit-and-run accidents. The real ordeal was bombing or, as he puts it with classic British understatement, he found the "entertainment value of these raids rather low". Trying to analyse his "blue funk", he felt the worst thing was fear of a hit with "HE", high explosive, particularly the 1000 kg bombs (the so-called landmines) rather than incendiaries and the fire afterwards, because it was random and there was nothing to be done about it. The West End was not a specific target like the docks, but the Jermyn Street hammam at 72 (another Turkish bath) had already been hit and destroyed, with popular singer Al Bowlly killed in a nearby flat, and while Crowley was living there a bomb took out Christopher and Co. wine merchants just to the south at 43 Pall Mall; one night the dreaded "HE" caused great destruction at the foot of nearby Duke Street, blowing out one of Crowley's windows and bringing a rain of small debris down like hail.

Crowley found his fellow tenants at 93 a depressing bunch, especially when they held hands in fear during raids. On one occasion he asked Miss Manning for her Bible and read aloud to them, with the sound of planes overhead and bombs exploding, from the 23rd Psalm: "Yea, though I walk through the valley of the shadow of death, I will fear no evil: for thou art with me..."

Others were not so lucky. There were 81 killed and 248 injured when a bomb struck Putney High Street, hitting the Cinderella Dance Club and the Black and White Milk Bar (both in the same building). It was a site of what would soon be called 'youth culture', and Crowley noted rather misanthropically "100 morons killed in Putney".

Finally he'd had enough, leaving London first for Aston Clinton, near Aylesbury, and then to Hastings for a final decline; he died in 1947. He was cremated in Brighton, with about a dozen mourners, largely from London. Louis Umfreville Wilkinson read his 'Hymn to Pan' and remembered the more emotional mourners shouting "Io Pan!" as he read, and then "a beautiful girl" throwing red flowers "upon the coffin as it slid downwards."

Shortly before he died he said, with Frieda Harris holding his hands, "I am perplexed."[5] While in Jermyn Street he had written a poem, beginning

---

5   But these were not, as sometimes reported, quite his 'last words'; neither was the often quoted "Sometimes I hate myself", which he also seems to have said. In the event he seems to have subsided peacefully a day or two later with Deirdre "Pat" Doherty present, and without any dramatic final utterance.

I often wish I could divine
What's in this funny head of mine,
This complicated tangled brain
That is? is not? or is it? sane.
No one has ever understood
Why I was never any good,
Or why my diamond brilliance
Was dulled by causal circumstance.

At the end he imagines leaving his brain to the College of Surgeons, but even that won't help:

Being dead, I may not know
What engine made the damn thing go.

As his old opponent W.B. Yeats had written, back in his 1901 essay 'Magic', "Man can embody truth but he cannot know it."

✝

There is one more site that belongs in Crowley's story, the long-gone New Delhi Durbar Indian restaurant which was at 179 Hampstead Road (not in Hampstead, but on a bleak strip running north of King's Cross between Euston Road and Mornington Crescent, now being redeveloped). In memory of Crowley and his love of curry, Frieda Harris rallied some friends to go there a year after his death. One of them was Gerald Hamilton, but he didn't enjoy himself – he may have found it a rather melancholy event – and he went home early.

NOTES

Crowley's *Confessions* (Cape, 1969) – which he liked to refer to as his autohagiography, the autobiography of a saint – are abbreviated simply Hag. with page number.

Crowley's 'Royal Court' diaries of the 1930s and 1940s (with transcripts in the Yorke collection as their standard referent, although now superseded in places by the OTO edition-in-progress that I have used) are cited simply by dates thus: 27.vi.32.

Ordo Templi Orientis archive material is indicated with {OTO}.

Magick Without Tears has appeared in several editions but is in 83 very short chapters, so in preference to any particular pagination I have cited by chapter.

John Symonds' several biographies are cited by dates, from *The Great Beast* (1951) to *The Beast 666* (1997), and Richard Kaczynski's *Perdurabo* as Kac.

"I dreamed I was paying a visit...": *The Magical Record of the Beast 666* (Duckworth, 1972) p.157.

INTRODUCTION: MAGUS ABOUT TOWN

"The very streets testify....": Hag.118.

Singing and dancing: Hag.216.

"...I am a reactionary Tory...": to George Cowie, 29 May 1913, Yorke NS4.

"...114, 278, 394 years penal servitude...": letter to JFC Fuller re 1907 diary, in Hogg, *Bibliotheca Crowleyana* [individual items not numbered] p.22.

Jardins de Ste.-Clair: 25.xi.38.

baron's crown: 23. viii.39.

fictional entry for partner to find: 25.iv.30, to put his wife Maria off the trail of his feelings for Hanni Jaeger.

lost court case: 13.iv.34.

asthma in witness box: 25.vii.34.

"...very dangerous to print...": to Grady McMurtry, 25 September 1945 {OTO}.

"the 'cat-feeling'...": 29.i.35.

"untrodden regions of the mind": Preface to 'John St. John', *Equinox*, Vol.1, No.1.
Or as a later generation would put it, that of Alexander Trocchi and William
Burroughs in the early 1960s, he was "a cosmonaut of inner space" (see Ted
Morgan, *Literary Outlaw*, p.335).
"...Eleven things went wrong...": 18.xii.36.
"a really charming gesture of the Gods...": 11.iii.38.
"'Small restraint' at South Kensington Station...": 9.x.39.
"...in London I have to swank": to Karl Germer, c. 20 Sept 1930 {OTO}.
'Diabolic Dandy': published in *The Bon-Mots of Samuel Foote and Theodore Hooke*
(Dent, 1894) p.104; sold by Sotheby's London *Aubrey Beardsley* 10 November
1999 Lot 18 untitled; catalogued with this title by Chris Beetles Gallery, London,
2000; also known as 'Devil in a Morning Coat' (1893), *Aubrey Beardsley: A
Catalogue Raisonné* ed. Zatlin Vol.1, item 810, p.476.
Beerbohm's caricature of Matthew Arnold: letter to Ann Macky, published as
Magick Without Tears Ch. XLIV.
"Far-off indeed..."; "...to whom the world was gracious": ibid.
Symons, 'Décor de Theatre: I: Behind the Scenes: Empire'; Wratislaw, 'Etchings:
3: At the Empire': *Poetry of the Nineties*, ed. R.K.R. Thornton (Penguin, 1970)
pp.42; 74.
"...but in Jermyn Street...": Bernard Bromage, 'Aleister Crowley', *Light* Vol.
LXXXIX no.3440 (Autumn 1959) p.159.
"Suppose I were to start from Scott's..." John St.John, 'Sixth Day'.
"...two dozen oysters and a pheasant...": Hag.570.
Haymarket stores, Mapleton House etc: receipts, bills, correspondence: Yorke
OS E10.
"...odd bits of London": to McMurtry 29 Nov 1943 {OTO}.
"Brixton need not envy Bayswater...": draft of *Confessions*, typescript p.321, not in
published version. Yorke OS L14.
"Transitional space": see Winnicott, 'Transitional Objects and Transitional
Phenomena' [1953] reprinted in *Playing and Reality* (Tavistock Publications, 1971).
Psychoanalyst Winnicott derives the idea of transitional phenomena from what
he calls 'transitional objects', neither entirely me nor entirely not-me, such as an
infant's comforting piece of cloth. The idea of this intermediate space has since
been applied to areas as varied as play, art, culture, fantasy, lying, drug taking,
gambling, and more. It is certainly relevant to religious and occult experience;
Winnicott is only in the second paragraph of his introduction when he raises
the theological issue of transubstantiation.
Novel with Soho door: M. John Harrison, *The Course of the Heart* (Gollancz, 1992).
Gentleman: the idea of being a gentleman is central to Crowley, running like
a motif through the *Confessions* and elsewhere: his much-admired father was
a "gentleman" [Hag.40]; Douglas, his splendid tutor who advocated "smoking,
drinking...racing, billiards, betting, cards and women" was a gentleman [Hag.75];
MacGregor Mathers, for all his faults, was a "scholar and gentleman" [Hag.194];
his friend "J-" in Paris is a "great surgeon and a true gentleman" [Hag.346];
when Crowley himself shoots at "a band of common robbers" in India with his

Webley revolver, he does so in the persona of "English gentleman" [Hag.455]; thinking of his future career as an advocate of Magick, walking across Spain in 1908, he decides firstly "the most important point was never to forget that I was a gentleman" [Hag.582]; travelling in remote China, "I knew, as I know that two and two make four, that it is only necessary to behave like a gentleman in order to calm the apprehensions of the aborigines" [Hag.466-67]. This is not to be confused with being overbred or gently behaved, which overlaps with what Crowley means when he sent Gerald Kelly a manifesto-paean to the idea of a new and ultra-virile magic in 1905, just after the disastrous Kanchenjunga expedition: "I want blasphemy, murder, rape, revolution, anything, good or bad, but strong. I want men behind me, or before me if they can surpass me, but men, men not gentlemen." (to Gerald Kelly, 31 October 1905, Yorke OS D6). Most telling of all, perhaps, in a dignified and affectionate first letter to his ten-year-old son Ataturk, he insists on the importance of learning Latin, even though some people might say it is not useful, "and that is quite true if you are going to be some commonplace person like a tradesman or a bank clerk. But you are a gentleman, and if you want to be an educated gentleman, you must know Latin." [reproduced Kac.545] Meanwhile, in a characteristic irony of the British class system (difficult to explain, and not to be confused with socio-economic status), people slightly higher – Anthony Powell, Gerald Kelly, Augustus John, even Arthur Calder-Marshall – seem to have been uniformly struck by the sense that Crowley *wasn't* quite a gentleman.

" ...as many miracles in London...": 'Preface' to 'John St.John' *Equinox* Vol.1 no.1.

I   TOMB OF BURTON
"...every sin in the Decalogue": Brodie, *The Devil Drives*, p.3.
"Quite jolly, what about you?": widely cited in this form with no reference. The most primary source seems to be (to a Doctor Bird) "Oh, quite jolly! How do you?" in *The Romance of Isabel, Lady Burton*, by Isabel Burton Vol.1 [Ch.X, At Last] (Hutchinson, 1897), p.166.
"the scrotum...": *The Book of the Thousand Nights and a Night* (Benares, Kamashastra Society, 1885), Vol.X, Terminal Essay, Section D, p.205 n.2.
"...whole life and all my life blood...": T. Wright, *The Life of Sir Richard Burton* Vol.2 p.317, cited in Jason Thompson, 'Burton, Sir Richard Francis', *Oxford Dictionary of National Biography*.
"not one dull paragraph": Hag.375.
model for Dracula: see e.g. Paul Murray, *From The Shadow of Dracula* (Cape, 2004) p.178.
"the perfect pioneer...": Hag.27.

2   DRAYTON GARDENS
railway shares: 'Preface' to *The World's Tragedy*.
"No more cruel fanatic...": Hag.55.
"...lachrymal glands of a crocodile..."; "what he called sin..."; "nondescript...": Hag.54-56.

"dinginess": Hag.58. cf *Equinox* Vol.1 no.8 (1912), pp.248-9.
"...name has since been changed...": Hag.55.
"London's most suburban 'subbub'": 'My Crapulous Contemporaries no.VI: An Obituary', *The Equinox* Vol.1 no.8 (1912), p.248.

3   ROYAL ARCADE

Tarrasch trap: Hag.48.
took up climbing: *Magick Without Tears* Ch. LXIII 'Fear'.
"what all the others are afraid to touch": Stephen Calloway, *Aubrey Beardsley* (V&A, 2020) p.18.
Wilde on limited editions: Wilde to Smithers, May 1898, *Complete Letters of Oscar Wilde* p.1063.
Gladstone bags: James G. Nelson, *Publisher to the Decadents*, p.55.
Peter Fryer, "the filthiest verse in the English language": cited Symonds (1971) p.16.
"...hys fyrst booke": cited d'Arch Smith, *Books of the Beast*, p.24.
"jobbing printer in the Brompton Road" and Murray details: d'Arch Smith, *The Times Deceas'd*, p.112.
Sangorski for vellum: to Grady McMurtry, 25 Sept 1940 {OTO}.
"...truly spiritual intercourse": Hag.148.
"...destinies drew apart": Hag.149.
"...lifelong regret...": ibid.

4   WATKINS BOOKSHOP

"It was a windy night...": *Aceldama* [p.5, unpaginated].
"...communication with the devil...": Hag.126.
"...foolish mysteries...": Waite, *The Book of Black Magic and Pacts*, p.232.
"...ignorant and affected dipsomaniac...": Hag.126.
"if it had not been for Waite...": to Louis Wilkinson 7 April 1945, cited in Gilbert, *A.E. Waite: Magician of Many Parts*, p.11.
"emblazoned over, within and without...": *Waite, Shadows of Life and Thought*, p.71.
Jagger and "stack of occult books": Devereux, *The Long Trip*, Introduction p.14, cited in Lachman, *Turn Off Your Mind*, p.294.
Black Arts bedside reading in 1969: Richard Cavendish obituary, *Daily Telegraph*, 3 November 2016.
Symonds' Watkins story: Symonds (1971) p.361.

5   DOUGLAS ROAD

"...Eckenstein his modern representative": Hag.166.
"...immense amount in his life mysterious and extraordinary...": Hag.155.
Eckenstein story, and discussion: Hag.156-58.
"Suddenly, at the end of one of these alleys...": Proust, 'The Fugitive' [Albertine Disparue, 1927], *Remembrance of Things Past* Vol.3 (Chatto and Windus, 1982) p.665.
"extraordinarily gripping" etc.; "City of God": Hag.158.
Eckenstein public house story: Hag.161.

6   HOTEL CECIL and THE STRAND
Meets Baker and Jones: Hag.164-5; 172-3.
entomb body in a secret place: 1905 instructions quoted in Symonds (1971) p.75.
"Feminine Hermes on cubic stone...": diary November 1898, no date, next entry
14.xi.1898.
"...sky above Cecil": ibid.
"Beware of Sods" signs around Charing Cross in later nineteenth century: see
Colin Simpson et al, *The Cleveland Street Affair*, pp.5-6.
"...as if it were the Strand": Hag.495.
Milliken and Lawley skeleton: recalled by Crowley during the 1934 'Black Magic
libel case', cited Booth, *A Magick Life*, p.449.
"The city is monstrous and misshapen...": *Moonchild* (Sphere, 1972) p.19.

7   FARRINGDON ROAD
a "club": as Jones described it to Symonds, quoted Symonds (1971) p.17.
Cipher Manuscript and Kenneth Mackenzie: see e.g. R.A Gilbert, *Golden Dawn
Scrapbook* p.5.
"...found on a bookstall...": Hag.175.
"...nothing dishonest about the Farringdon Road...": early typescript draft of *The
Book of Thoth*, 'Prefatory Note' p.4: Yorke OS L11.
"church and university": see Brenda Maddox, *George's Ghosts*, p.8, and Roy
Foster, *Yeats: A Life: The Apprentice Mage*, p.106.
"obvious and melodramatic...": Yeats, 'The Hermetic Brotherhood' note for 'The
Trembling of the Veil', *Autobiographies* (Macmillan, 1955) p.576.
"...a stumer...did nobody any harm.": Arthur Machen, *Things Near and Far*, p.153.
He discreetly calls it The Order of the Twilight Star.

8   GREAT QUEEN STREET
asked Baker if anyone had died: Hag.176.
"...deadly and hostile current of will...": Hag.177.
"any schoolboy in the lower fourth could memorize the whole lecture": Hag.177.
"...abject assemblage of nonentities...": Hag.177
"...British middle-class dullness": Maud Gonne, *A Servant of the Queen:
Reminiscences* (1938) p.258.

9   BARROW ROAD
"at some ceremony or other": Hag.178.
"Little Brother": ibid.
"a tiny tenement in Southwark or Lambeth...": Hag.179.
"If his talents had been less varied...": ibid.

10   CHANCERY LANE
"...altar supported...": Hag.182.
Milliken and Lawley: Booth, *A Magick Life*, p.449.
"demon servant"; "not a real cat, either"; "Round and round the big library

tramped the devils...": 'The Revival of Magick' Part 1, *The International*, Vol.XI, no.8. August 1917.

"As we went out, we noticed semi-solid shadows on the stairs...": Hag.182.

"...talismans which got on the job, and stayed on the job": 'My Wanderings in Search of the Absolute', *Sunday Referee*, 10 March 1935.

11   LOWE'S CHEMIST

"...cycle of life...": Hag.180.

"...World behind the Veil of Matter": Bennett (via Crowley), widely cited e.g. Symonds (1971) p.24; Regardie, *Eye in the Triangle* p.117.

"exploring the pharmacopoeia for the means of grace": Hag.386.

"...Chancery Lane rule...": Crowley, 'The Herb Dangerous: The Psychology of Hashish', reprinted in *Roll Away the Stone*, ed. Regardie, p.102.

"...favourite rendezvous...": Hag.546.

"People of all ranks"; "...understood human frailty...": ibid.

'A Pharmaceutical Study of Cannabis Sativa' by E. Whineray (Part I of 'The Herb Dangerous', with Haddo [Crowley], Baudelaire, and Ludlow), *The Equinox*, Vol.1, No.1 (1909). Whineray's firm, Lowe's, also advertised in *The Equinox*: Vol.1, nos. 3, 4, 5 and 6.

Warlock rhyme: letter to Cecil Gray, 22 January 1923, *The Collected Letters of Peter Warlock* Vol.IV 1922-30, p.65.

Abramelin dabbling and suicide (re "the late Philip Heseltine, a composer of genius") see *Magick Without Tears*, Ch.XX, 'Talismans [...]'

"...'wish-fulfilment' (no doubt) dream...": 17 July 1920, *Magickal Record of the Beast 666*, p.222.

1924 heroin letter: to Norman Mudd from Paris, 18 March 1924, Yorke NS 5.

Whineray and trouble with the police: Booth, *Cannabis* (2003), p.107.

Whineray review of *Chronicles of Pharmacy* by A.C. Wotton, *Equinox* Vol.I no.VI. p.170.

"such as *kyfi* ...onycha...": Hag.546.

"Dear Sir Aleister...": Driberg letter 7 April 1926, Christ Church Library, Oxford.

12   BLYTHE ROAD

investigating corpses and not raising them: "paid to sit on corpses not raise them" [in the sense of a court sitting] Crowley, *The Rosicrucian Scandal* [1911] reproduced in Robertson, *The Aleister Crowley Scrapbook* pp.64-81; quote on p.68.

"...human and living upon this earth...": Howe, *Magicians of the Golden Dawn*, p.129.

"...no Golden Dawn and no nuffin'": Howe op.cit. p.37.

"a reformatory": Yeats to Lady Gregory, 25 April 1900 ("We did not admit him because we did not think a mystical society was intended to be a reformatory.") *Collected Letters of W.B. Yeats*, Vol.2 1896-1900, p.515.

"black, bilious rage": Hag.166.

"lank, dishevelled demonologist": Hag.177.

"...the Order in its existing form came to grief...": draft 'Preface' to *The Book of Thoth* (typescript p.8). Yorke OS LII.

13 RANDOLPH ROAD
HGA definitions: to Frank Bennett, see Kac. 374-76, Symonds (1997) 290-97; to Ann Macky, see *Magick Without Tears*, Chapter XLIII, 'The Holy Guardian Angel is not the "Higher Self" but an Objective Individual'.
Paddington Hotel: 13.iv.1900.
Baptising dried peas, see e.g. Francis King, *Ritual Magic in England: 1887 to the Present Day* pp.71-2, and Gerald Yorke, 'Magic and the Golden Dawn' in *Aleister Crowley, The Golden Dawn and Buddhism*, p.75. Crowley seems to launch this story in 'The Magician', a section of 'The Temple of Solomon the King' in *The Equinox*, Vol.I no.3 (March, 1910).
Georg Witkowski, *Von Menschen und Buchern* (Leipzig, 2000) p.161, translation courtesy William Breeze.
entering daughter's room in astral body: Hag.225; Kac.92.
Horses, cab lamps, fires, mackintosh etc: 13/14/16.iv.1900. {OTO}

14 GOWER STREET
Horos case: see Gilbert, *Golden Dawn Scrapbook* pp.7-20.
"...most powerful medium living": Mathers to Yeats 12 January 1901, cited Howe, *Magicians of the Golden Dawn* p.203.
Lola Montez: *Golden Dawn Scrapbook* p.14.
"I, Vera Croysdale...": *Golden Dawn Scrapbook* p.8.
"Keep quiet, you reptiles!": *Golden Dawn Scrapbook* p.10.

15 THE CAFÉ ROYAL
"...exuberant vista of gilding and crimson velvet...": Beerbohm 'Enoch Soames', in *Seven Men and Two Others* (Heinemann, 1950) [1919], pp.3-51. Quotation pp.5-6; 15; 8-9.
"EPICURES are invited to taste the special dishes invented...": e.g. *Equinox* Vol.1. No.8, cf draft in Yorke PD72 c.2.
Betty May: *Tiger Woman* p.43.
Crowley's account: Hag.644-46; 648;
Epstein's brief neutral account: *Jacob Epstein, An Autobiography* p.54.
Entertained a party of guests: Guy Deghy and Keith Waterhouse, *Café Royal: Ninety Years of Bohemia*, p.186. There is an entire if not entirely reliable chapter on Crowley, 'The Magus of the Café Royal', pp.177-186. Deghy and Waterhouse also recount the story of Crowley's "6oth" (in fact sixty-first) dinner for about twenty people when Countess Lewenhaupt picked up the bill as intended, but the management were reluctant to accept it (p.185), also remembered by Cammell, 177-79 and in diaries 12.x.36.
Conical hat with stars: Deghy and Waterhouse op.cit. p.177; quoted as joke by Cammell p.164.
"That's just Mr. Crowley being invisible." I used this particular wording in a book on Austin Osman Spare, and now see it drifting around the internet from that book. It is from a man at the Secret Chiefs speaker meetings, Princess Louise pub, Holborn; the same man who said "Have a fuck and make a wish." See p.100, footnote 1.

16   ST. MARY'S TERRACE
Fancy dress contest: Hag.230.
"...eyes of Jesus": *The Book of the Law* (Liber AL) III 51.
"...face of Mohammed...": AL III 52.
"...crapulous creeds": AL III 54.
"...I was Ankh-f-n-khonsu...": Hag. 665.
"To worship me take wine and strange drugs...":, AL II.22, p.41.
"The kings of the earth shall be Kings forever...": AL II.58, p.47.
"We have nothing with the outcast and the unfit...": AL II.21 p.41.
"...between Wilde and Hitler": Cyril Connolly, 'Engendering monsters' [review of
Symonds' *The Great Beast* and other books] *Sunday Times* 14 Nov 1971.
"acute nomenclature": cited e.g. Symonds (1997) p.102.
Opal in Bond Street: 12.iii.07. Possibly in the window of Hunt and Roskell,
jewellers to Queen Victoria, a shop Crowley certainly knew: their name is jotted
on an unrelated scrap among his papers in the Yorke collection. But there were
other jewellers, including Asprey's.
Vow of silence: 7.iii.07.
Razor cuts; Rose angry: 9.iii.07.
Crowley moves out: 23-24.iii.07.
"...obvious from the style, in Paddington": 'Preface' to *The World's Tragedy*,
p.xxxvii.

17   WARWICK ROAD
Earl of Coke and Crankum: Hag.547.
150 bottles of whisky (figures for this vary from 120 to 159 – Symonds (1997) p.132
– but in the *Confessions* Crowley goes for a round 150): Hag.535.
Burlington Arcade girl: Miss Zwee, widely reported in accounts of the divorce
proceedings, e.g. *Dundee Courier*, Nov 25 1909, 'Amusing Divorce Evidence'.
Having met in Soho, they had tea at the Criterion Brasserie, still there, and
dinner at the long-gone Restaurant Venice, off Oxford Street, in what was then
the notorious institution in restaurants of a 'private room' where sex took place,
as well as at Warwick Road and 3-5 Orange Street, Haymarket, where Crowley
had rooms. She lived at 48 King's Cross Mansions, Hastings Street, where
Crowley also visited her, and they had a son on 28 October 1909. I am very
grateful to William Breeze for sharing the divorce court papers with me.
Layout of house at no.21: Hag.569.
"prestidigitation" : ibid.
"life with Rose is intolerable...": to Dr Murray Leslie, June 3 1908, copy in Fuller
papers, King's College, item 4/12/18.
The servant or charlady was Bella Danby (or Dauby; variously transcribed in
records) and the bejewelled woman she remembered was Jenny Zwee.

18   VICTORIA STREET
Two Englishmen invited: Symonds (1997) p.104. The other was Lord Brocket.
"abyss after abyss"; "ledge labelled Battersea': 'The Bismarck of Battersea',
Equinox Vol 1. No.7, p.403.

"moral pygmies": Gilbert, *Golden Dawn Scrapbook* p.184.
"one too many": Hag.589.
"A room, she reflected...": Ethel Archer, *The Hieroglyph*, pp.7-9.

19 HENRIETTA STREET
Northam's advert: in several issues, e.g. Vol.I, no.7, unpaginated advert section in final pages.
Dressing up box: d'Arch Smith, *The Times Deceas'd*, p.79.
Four Red Monks Carrying a Black Goat: illustrated e.g. Symonds (1997) facing p.244, and sampled on the cover of Symonds's *The Magic of Aleister Crowley* (Muller, 1958).
"...in horror stories by Dennis Wheatley...": Jean La Fontaine, *Speak of the Devil: Tales of Satanic Abuse in Contemporary England*, p.53.
There is more on the popular Dennis Wheatley aspect in Peter Bradshaw's comic novel *Lucky Baby Jesus*: "... these recovered memory yarns were about as real as the ones with which the apple-cheeked bairns of Orkney or whey-faced pre-school shoplifters of Middlesborough had once regaled their social workers: the ones about them dancing in a circle around their tumescent scout-master in his front room with the curtains drawn, dressed up in little Dennis Wheatley outfits his wife had run up." *Lucky Baby Jesus* (Little, Brown, 1999) p.64.

20 SOUTH AUDLEY STREET
"If you are the one I seek...": 13.xi.06.
"You pig-faced man!...": Fuller with Crowley, 'Half Hours with Famous Mahatmas', *The Equinox*, Vol.1 no.4. (September 1910).
"Fuller at 60": 17.xi.07.
Guru's later downfall: Dick Weindling and Marianne Colloms, 'Remembering the West Hampstead "holy man" and his cult of women', *Hampstead and Highgate Express* online https://www.hamhigh.co.uk/lifestyle/heritage/remembering-the-west-hampstead-holy-man-and-his-cult-of-3488096. He was convicted of indecently assaulting Suzanne Allaveue and Maud Anderson at 110 Goldhurst Road.

21 BRUTON STREET
"...management of line...": *The World*, 29 October 1907.
"Mr. Spare's art is abnormal...": *Observer*, 3 November 1907.
"Vicegerent of God...": cited in Grant, *Zos Speaks!* p.43.
"...cannot afford the robe...": cited in Semple, *Two Tracts on Cartomancy* p.19; Keith Richmond, 'Discord in the Garden of Janus', note 13.
"An artist. Can't understand organisation...": Richmond op.cit. unpaginated.
Spaghetti; invisibility; "if I had to go to all that effort...": Grant, *Zos Speaks!* p.43.

22 TOOK'S COURT
"Orridge": Anthony Curtis, *Lit. Ed.: On Reviewing and Reviewers* (Carcanet, 1998) p.163.

23   BRITISH LIBRARY
"flies caught in a huge web": Gissing, *New Grub Street* (Smith, Elder & Co., 1891), vol. i, pp.193-6.
"velveteen coat": for Yeats on Mathers see 'The Trembling of the Veil', *Autobiographies* (Macmillan 1955) pp.182ff.
"...flavour that manuscripts only have in dreams": 'Diary of a Magus' (Liber 63) 12.ix.16 {OTO}.
"One thing you can say about Satanists...": Robert Irwin, *Satan Wants Me*, p.95.

24   THE BRITISH MUSEUM
Pearson's Magazine, August 1909.
discovered sarcophagus: 25.viii.30.
"imminence of world catastrophe"; "the New Zealander": Hag.542.
Thomas Macaulay review of von Ranke's *History of the Popes*, *The Edinburgh Review* no.72 October 1840.
"...to sketch the ruins of St. Paul's": Macaulay op.cit., cited David Skilton, 'Contemplating the Ruins of London: Macaulay's New Zealander and Others', *Literary London: Interdisciplinary Studies in the Representation of London* Vol.2 no.1 (March, 2004).
Walpole, "curious traveller from Lima" and visitor "from the banks of the Oronooko", both in 1770s letters, Skilton op.cit.
"...Professor of Archaeology in the University of Lhasa...": Hag.542.

25   ROYAL COURTS OF JUSTICE
"...wish to keep dark.": Hag.268.
"...affection of a judge": Symonds, e.g. *Great Beast* (1971) p.121.
'Rosicrucian Rites: The Dread Secrets of the Order Revealed': *Morning Leader*, 23 March 1910.

26   CAXTON HALL
keeping probationers and higher grades apart: Hag.629.
"shameless masturbation or indecent advances": Crowley, 'Energized Enthusiasm', *The Equinox* Vol.1 No.9, p.33.
"...throbbing with jungle drums...": Robert Fabian, *London After Dark*, p.77.
"...may be on to something": Kac.216.
Account of performance: Raymond Radclyffe, 'Aleister Crowley's 'Rite of Artemis'', *The Sketch* August 24 1910.
"By the power in me vested...": Radclyffe op.cit.
"...elixir introduced by me to Europe": 'Energized Enthusiasm', *The Equinox* Vol.1 No.9. In fact Crowley hadn't introduced peyote or mescaline to Europe: W.B. Yeats, Arthur Symons and Havelock Ellis had experimented with it in the 1890s. Nevertheless, as Mike Jay writes in *Mescaline: A Global History*, it is "probably true to say he was the first westerner to take peyote methodically over a period of years, and the first to adopt it as a ritual sacrament" (p.107). Crowley's first recorded use seems to be on the 12 March 1907, on the day he saw the opal in

New Bond Street (see site 16); on the same day he had also visited Whineray, the drug supplier, at Lowe's chemist just off Bond Street. He mentions using a commercially prepared tincture ("presumably that of Parke, Davis": Jay, p.108). Potter & Clarke at 60-64 Artillery Lane, near Liverpool Street station, were also noted suppliers of peyote at this time. Best known for Potter's Asthma Mixture and Potter's Asthma Cigarettes, which contained belladonna, they sold peyote buttons over the counter by the bagful.

27 THE LOOKING GLASS
Grave Diggers Journal: cover cartoon, *The Looking Glass*, Vol.II no.65, 23 December 1911.
"sham Buddhist monk...": *The Looking Glass*, 'An Amazing Sect no.3' 26 Nov 1910 p.268.
"...notoriously evil character": court transcript cited Kac.233, cf "one Crowley, who was alleged to be a person of disgraceful and criminal character", *Times* April 27 1911 p.4.
'The Rosicrucian Scandal', reproduced Robertston, *Aleister Crowley Scrapbook*, pp.64-79.
"...trial in Alice in Wonderland": Kac.232 cf Hag.641.
relative of Alice Liddell: I am indebted to Cecil Court bookseller Jake Fior for this information.
"...associate of the notorious Jones": 'Rosicrucian Scandal', Robertson *Scrapbook*, p.79.
Postcards: Jean Overton Fuller, *The Magical Dilemma of Victor Neuburg*, p.165.
"If you wish to hoorosh down...": Fuller to Crowley 2 May 1911 cited Symonds (1997) p.136.

28 RALSTON STREET
"...wonderful days in Chelsea...": Neuburg in Calder-Marshall, *The Magic of My Youth*, p.60.
Pocahontas: Kac.221.
"piles of tasselled cushions...": Evelyn Waugh, *A Little Learning*, p.212.
"Pity that stuff had no effect.": Laver, *Museum Piece*, pp.118-19.
Bankes on Crowley: *Why Not?* pp.160; 201-11. Bankes description of Crowley's eyes as green seems to be fanciful; Cammell and others remember them as brown.
"...always Sunday afternoon"; "...high priest of black magic...": Ethel Mannin, *Confessions and Impressions*, p.195. "Gwen Otter represents that *fin-de-siècle* tradition of the 1890s, a tradition fast fading into the background.": p.194.
not in love and never lent money: Laver p.117.

29 SAVOY HOTEL
"artistic furniture throughout": advert in *The Times*, 6 August 1889 p.1 (and purely electricity: "no gas or other artificial light used").
"exchanging electricity": Hag.676.
Desti's nightclub: diary entry 1 Jan 1920 in *The Magical Record of the Beast 666*, p.88.
"morning Sun Room": 6.v.41.

30 SIMPSON'S-IN-THE-STRAND
"great dinner at Simpson's...": *Magical Record of the Beast 666* p.88.
dream of being hanged: 4.iv.41.
Powell's account in *Messengers of Day* (1978): "...false top to his head" p.82;
"horrible baby" p.83; "sinister if gifted buffoon" p.152; "ponderous gags" p.82;
"unkindness and backbiting" p.83.
"boiled toads, Mother, or fried Jesus": Fuller, *Magical Dilemma of Victor Neuburg*
p.183. The published quote in Fuller is 'Jesu', coming second-hand via Preston,
but Crowley refers to his childhood diet of "cold boiled Jesus" four times within
a dozen lines of the 'Preface' to *The World's Tragedy* (xix-xx) so I have taken the
liberty of normalising it.

31 OLD TIVOLI THEATRE
three dipsomaniacs and four nymphomaniacs: Hag.711.
taking London by storm: Hag 690. He is joking.

32 ROSSETTI STUDIOS, FLOOD STREET
Calder-Marshall's account: *Magic of My Youth*, 168-171.
Jean Overton Fuller's account: *Magical Dilemma of Victor Neuburg*, 171-3.
"...adept known to THE MASTER THERION...": *Magick*, p.298.

33 REGENT STREET
Account of Reuss: Howe and Moller, 'Theodor Reuss: Irregular Freemasonry in
Germany' (1978).
"one of the greatest shocks of my life": letter to Henri Birven, October 1929,
cited Kac.252.
BABALON *manibus*: Rex de Arte Regia diary, 7 February 1915 (*Manibus*, i.e. by hand,
solitary masturbation; concentrating on the idea of Babalon, the Scarlet Woman;
in the hope of manifesting $20,000). *Magical Record of the Beast 666*, p.18.
Shivalingam temple: Hag.257.
"...far-off Jerusalem or Bethlehem...": Paschal Beverley Randolph, *Eulis*, cited in
Hugh Urban, *Magia Sexualis* (2006) p.66. Curiously the relevant page of *Eulis* is
excised and replaced with a blank in the British Library copy.
Reuss as "Supreme and Holy King of Germany": Hag.701.
"Supreme and Holy King of Ireland, Ionia, and all the Britains...": King, *Magical
World of Aleister Crowley*, p.81.
"There could hardly be a nicer set..."; "swank!": Cowie to Crowley undated [late
1916] Yorke NS4.
"motherly old fool" and tea-leaf reader: Hag.756.
Crowley accuses Cowie of being anti-German: e.g. undated letters c. May 1913,
Yorke NS4.
"severe shock"; "that use to be made of your stuff": Cowie to Crowley 8 March
1917, Yorke NS4.

City of the Beast: The London of Aleister Crowley

34 PICCADILLY

Christine Rosalie Byrne: *Magical Record of the Beast 666*, p.4.
"...an element of atomic weight...": Hag.702.
"principal engine": Hag.694.
inspiration and energy to write *De Arte Magica*: "...might the ill-health be part of the success...?": *Magical Record of the Beast 666*, p.4.
Violet Duval and Leila Waddell: ibid.
Mona Lisa and Piccadilly prostitution: 'The Herb Dangerous: The Psychology of Hashish', from *Equinox* Vol.1 no.1 (1909), reprinted in *Roll Away the Stone*, ed. Regardie (1968) p.118.
Shift from Strand to Piccadilly: Collin Brooks, *Tavern Talk*, p.174.
"Save us from every evil demon", Greek Orthodox liturgy: Symonds (1951) p.387.

35 AVENUE STUDIOS

Real number noted: Crowley annotations to *Drug Fiend*, p.31.Yorke Collection.
"Most Holy, Most Illustrious, Most Illuminated..."; "Gnostic Catholic Church...": *Oriflamme* 'Jubilee Edition', reproduced in Howe and Moller (1978).
"Our Order possesses the KEY...": Reuss in Howe and Moller op.cit.
"...caught the old cats": Trevor Blakemore in Symonds (1997) p.203.
"evil bleating": 'Weird Rites of Devil Worshippers Revealed by an Eye Witness': Harry Kemp, *New York World* 2 August 1914, in Symonds (1997) p.203.
"...the most elementary type...": Elliott O'Donnell, *Rooms of Mystery* (1931), p.257.
"...regular rendezvous for spies...": Hag.888.

36 OUTRAM ROAD

Crowley, 'The Green Goddess', *The International*, February 1918.
'La legende de l'Absinthe', Crowley (as 'Jeanne la Goulue') *The International*, February 1918.
"...in their last Zeppelin raid...": Crowley, 'Behind The Front: Impressions of a Tourist in Western Europe' *The Fatherland* (New York) Vol.III no.21, 29 December 1915.
"Not only has the war changed nothing...": Booth, p.355.

37 WELLINGTON SQUARE

"wholly free from all limitations soever...": *Magick*, pp.329-30.
"the fiend, Satan-Alostrael": *Magical Record of the Beast 666*, pp.251-2.
"...dull ugly school-teacher, ignorant, tired, old and common...": Magical Diary, March 1922, holograph Yorke OS A4, typed OS H3.
Goat details disputed: the account in Symonds's books (e.g. 1997, pp.298-99) draws on a fictionalised account by Mary Butts in her novel *South Lodge*. See Kac. pp.373; 386.
"...concubine Dionysus Ganymede": Cefalu diary, Yorke OS H4.
Rembrandt, *The Abduction of Ganymede* (1635), Old Masters Gallery, Dresden.
"...Half a woman made with half a god": 21 April 1920, *Magical Record of the Beast 666*, p.110.
"a horrible hotel in Russell Square...": Hag.889.

Grant Richards: Hag.895-6.
"nice quiet house"; "Hero's Bride": to Jane Wolfe, n.d. [c. May 1922; between
letters of 7 and 12 May] {OTO}.

38   CLEVELAND GARDENS
"Sex maniac. Moved to British Columbia.": AC annotation to Probationer's Oath
form, December 1912 {OTO}.
"begged me to stay..."; "I went round...": Hag.901-2.
malevolent influence of Sheila: Hag.907.

39   HARLEQUIN CLUB
"...best tits in Europe": Daniel Farson, *Soho in the Fifties*, (1987) p.54.
Betty May's account of visit: *Tiger Woman*, pp.131-32.
Crowley's account: "fatal folly..."; "...swine of Soho": Hag.904-5.
Death of Yannis Papani: May, *Tiger Woman*, p.129.

40   EIFFEL TOWER RESTAURANT
"I begged her to introduce me..." and subsequent account: Calder-Marshall,
Magic of My Youth, pp.177ff.
"most criminal street in London": ten-page deposition against Gerald Yorke, p.9.
Yorke Collection OS.F1. The hotel was literally on Percy Street, but in context he
means it was at the end of Charlotte Street.
"stew in the stinking slum of Charlotte Street...": 23.vi.32.
"At the Eiffel Tower!": Yorke annotation ibid.
"I feel his day is rather over": Lawrence to P.R. Stephensen, 5 September 1929.
The Letters of D.H. Lawrence, vol.7 p.469. He also mentions that out of 3000
copies of Crowley's *Confessions*, only 200 have sold (*Letters* pp.557-58).
"Goodbye to Stulik...": 7.viii.37.

41   DUKE'S HOTEL
Oddenino's, Yeoman House, etc.: receipts, bills, cheque stubs, etc in Yorke
OS E10.

42   MANSFIELD STREET
Eton curse: see e.g. Gordon Bowker, *George Orwell* (Abacus, 2003), p.56.
Lance Sieveking, *Eye of the Beholder*, p.254.
"rat": 22.viii.32; "skunk": 15.ix 32; "utter shit": 7.iv.38; "heartless cad": 21.vi.32;
"unspeakably treacherous swine": 28.vii.32. Just a sample.
"Forced to smoke that beastly stuff...": d'Arch Smith, *Books of the Beast* p.108.

43   MUSEUM STREET
John Bull cannibal story, April 1932: account from Cammell p.157.
"'ninetyish romantic bravado" [i.e. 1890s-ish]: Stephensen, *Legend* p.22, cf
"Ninetyish and Edwardian" p.23.

"every phenomenon should be an orgasm of its kind": 'Questions Put to E.A.C. by J.W.N. Sullivan'. Yorke NS18.

44 ATLANTIS BOOKSHOP
"...negroes and dwarfs...": Burra to Anthony Powell, Marseilles 1930, in Jane Stevenson, *Edward Burra*, p.154.
"Brazen Head..."; "At the sign of the Beast 666" etc: circa 1937 notes, Yorke OS EE2.
"...Grumpy in *Snow White*": d'Arch Smith, *Books of the Beast*, p.109.
"A dwarf kike, who called himself Houghton!...": 23.x.34.
"These low Jew thieves...": to Germer n.d. May 1937 [replying to letter of 12 May and before Germer's subsequent letter of 17 May] {OTO}.
"...Send us a Hitler!": 24.vi.1944.
Michaud in diaries: e.g. 28.xii.41.
"Let's leave": Jean Overton Fuller, *Magical Dilemma*, p.232.
Run-in with Buddhist bookshop etc: 22.x.07; 22.xi.07; 2.xii.12 {OTO}. It is not clear how far the dispute is with Rost himself, or whether Crowley hopes Rost will intervene.
"Mike still thieving in Museum Street...": to Edward Fitzgerald, 27 February 1943. Yorke NS117.
"...Oriental bookshops by the British Museum...": Calder-Marshall, *Magic of My Youth* p.94.
Plough pub: e.g. 2.v.34. I am told a member of staff showed an enquirer where Crowley used to sit; this sounds optimistic.

45 LANGHAM HOTEL
Dinner with Carter: Tom Cullen, *Man Who Was Norris*, p.143.
Hoped to take Aquila Press over for premises: to Germer, 19 May 1930, Yorke NS13.
Carter amused; infiltration plan; subscription paid for: Tom Cullen, *Norris* ibid.; letter from Carter to Yorke re subscription Yorke OS D4.
"Israel Regudy"; "Darling Alice": reproduced in part in e.g. Regardie, *Eye in the Triangle*, pp.8-9.
Jean Ross in Hatchett's: 24.vii.32.
fig leaf: Cullen op.cit. p.26.

46 PARK MANSIONS
"...on the verge of some sort of hysteria...": Yorke 'Introduction', *Aleister Crowley, The Golden Dawn and Buddhism*, p.xvii.
"...sensed a Being, Presence, or Force...": Yorke, 'A Lecture on Aleister Crowley', *Aleister Crowley, The Golden Dawn and Buddhism*, p.8.
Carter living at apartment 8: Crowley address book, Yorke OS43.
Mrs Stuart's Domestic Agency: receipts Yorke OSE11.
"insane swine": 12.ix.31; "unclean masturbating pimp": 1.ix.31; "utterly unimaginable shit": 11.xii.30. A sample.
"...most nauseating thing I have ever read..."; slaves and kings: to Germer, 22 June 1930 {OTO}.

"educated person expects a bath to be clean": to Germer 27 June 1930 {OTO}.
attended a number of times: e.g. 19.ix.37; 13.x.37; 31.x.37; 17.xi.37.
Ngaio Marsh e.g. Anson, *Wandering Bishops*, p.370 n.17.
arsenic and strychnine order to chemist: e.g. 5 December 1929, Yorke NS13.
"AC is died for me...": Maria letter to a Mr Foreman, n.d., Yorke OS D4.
"Bug House": 18.vii.1931.
"...in Colney Hatch": 18.vii.31.
earthquake in Managua: in deposition against Yorke, Yorke OS F1.
"lots of loonies": 23.vii.31.
married to the Beast 666: Yorke interview with David Tibet in *Aleister Crowley, The Golden Dawn and Buddhism*, p.218.

47 FRIBOURG AND TREYER

"...typical *bon bourgeois*": Cullen, *The Man Who Was Norris*, p.142.
London shopping list: Cullen op.cit. 143.
stranger in Oddenino's: 21.i.42.
"Churchill's own Cigar Merchant!!!...": 30.i.42.
name like Zanoni: 1.ii.42.
"...facts and suggestions about Mysticism.": *Magick*, Appendix 1, p.310.
"Soul of mine, the luminous, the Augoeides": *Zanoni*, (Blackwood, 1861), Book II Ch,IV, p.113.

48 L'ESCARGOT

"admirable" 28.ii.38; "magnificent": 31.iii.38; "A1" 14.iv.38; "excellent": 16.iii.38.
"...old brandy, caviar and truffles in Hell": to Gerald Kelly from Boleskine, n.d. [1903] Yorke NS4.
" ...oysters, caviar, foie gras": 28.ii.32.
"...stuff a chicken with oysters?": 1.ix.38.
"Caviar, lobster, foie gras...": 27.vii.37.
"...kings in exile are always beggars": to Germer 14 Sept 1930 {OTO}.
"anti-Christmas cards": e.g. recipient list at end of 1941 diary.
"...robber Santi Romani": 25.xii.37. There was also a restaurant called Santi Romano on Greek Street (literally 'Roman Saints') but that seems not to be the object of Crowley's joke.
Astoria Hotel: 7.iv.33.
"hoolie-goolie"; bats squeaking: Cunard 'Thoughts About Aleister Crowley' (10 November 1954) to Gerald Yorke. Yorke NS1.
"Soho with a Mayfair accent"; "well-cut coats": Jackson, *Indiscreet Guide to Soho*, pp.81; 83.
looking like hell: 31.i.42.
"White's Oysters...": 23.xi.37.
"...after a struggle....": 3.ii.38.
Canape Talisman: 26.viii.39.
Biftek Crapaudine: 4.vi.39.

49 SHANGHAI RESTAURANT
Shanghai as 'favourite' in terms of how often he went there, e.g. at least eight times in 1937 (8.iv; 7.ix; 16.ix; 8.x; 8.xi; 11.xi; 28.xi; 17.xii).
Ley-On's: 10.ix.37; 22.ix.37.
Young's: e.g. 19.xii.39.
"coarse and bad as ever": 16.xii.41.
accused them of serving rabbit: 19.i.42.
"...murder, rape, revolution, anything, bad or good, but strong": to Gerald Kelly, 31 October 1905, Yorke OS D6.
"...Ordeal by Curry": 22.xi.36.
"Last week, a man called Mulk Raj Anand...": Dylan Thomas to Pamela Hansford Johnson, 6 Aug 1937, *Letters*, p.296.
"Romanticism led to the unconscious...": Anand, *Conversations in Bloomsbury*, pp.41; 145.
Sunningfields Road: 6.x.32.
"...sting like serpents...": Hag.232.
"at the first mouthful...": Burnett-Rae, *A Memoir of 666* (London, Victim Press, 1971), reproduced in Robertson, *Crowley Scrapbook*, pp.23-27; quotation p.27.
Wilkinson best friend: Crowley, "greatest" friend, in Louis Marlow [pseud. Wilkinson], *Seven Friends*, p.52.
"astounding"; "moving"; "excessiveness": *Seven Friends*, p.46.
Black Magic Restaurant plans: Yorke OS EE2.
Clay Street as location for Exotic Restaurant: 20.i.36.
Further restaurant plans: manuscript offered for sale by Adrian Harrington Rare Books, Tunbridge Wells, 2007, together with *Konx Om Pax*.
"Zambar of Lobster": 10.vi.36.
Madras curry powder etc: shopping lists, Yorke NS 117.
"...memorably exotic...": 2.vi.36.
Pot au feu Ang-Kor: 12.i.39.
My new savoury: 23.ii.36.
My savoury: 9.v.36.
Gold fish toast: 21.vii.39.
Almond Chicken: 16.ix.38.

50 WESTMINSTER ABBEY
Bertha Busch stabbing: 6.xii.31.
Will of 22 December: cited Sutin pp.362-63.
Eliphas Levi story: 'Necromancy' in Levi, *Doctrine of Transcendental Magic*, pp.151-56.
Lord Haw-Haw and Black Mass: e.g. Cammell p.143; Marlow p.42; Symonds (1997) p.531 n.1.

51 ALBEMARLE STREET
"...Vile Bodies to the Cavendish hotel": 28.vi.32
"...man wot owes me money!": Jeremy Lewis, *Cyril Connolly* p.233 n.1.

"...classic of subjective idealism" (re Berkeley's *Three Dialogues*): *Magick*, Appendix I, p.309; other mentions in *Magick*, pp.24; 258; 331.
"...Success to 15 Sept. speech": 2.ix.32.

52 GROSVENOR HOUSE HOTEL
"ransack Charing X Road": to Grady McMurtry, 29 November 1943 {OTO}.
200 copies of *Magick*: 22.viii.32.
"...swine feeding": 21.v.36.

53 PRAED STREET
moved to Queen's House Hotel: 26.ix.32 (and again in May 1933).
Park Lane Hotel: 5.i.33.
Grosvenor Hospital For Women: 3.i.33.
window in Praed Street: 7.i.33.
"...not the smallest ground...": *Daily Telegraph* 11 May 1933; slight variant Symonds (1997) p.495.

54 CUMBERLAND TERRACE
Meets Brooksmith: 3.vii.33.
"Here lies a Pearl of a woman...": 18.viii.33.
"Success": 16.viii.33; "Lust": 27.viii.33; "Love": 2.ix.33.
Opus 7: 4.ix.33.
"marvellous lust": 6.ix.33.
"...flame of fornication...": 3.ix.33.

55 CARLOS PLACE
"Your interest in Magick...": flyer, private collection, London.
Desolation over death of daughter: Hamnett, *Laughing Torso*, p.175; "flag in space": p.69.
"abominable libels": 7.ix.32.
"...baby was said to have disappeared mysteriously": Hamnett op.cit. p.163.
top hat in court: Symonds (1997) p.505.
"...consternation of Constable & Co.": 13.iv.34.
"...His Satanic Majesty...": Mannin, *Confessions and Impressions*, p.195.
"South Sea stick" at auction: 6.iii.39.
Kerman details from obituary by Stephen Aris, *The Independent*, 20 August 1998.

56 UPPER MONTAGU STREET
"...so bloody lonely!": 21.xii.33.
"run on the assumption...": 20.ix.33.
"...money question is the very devil...": Brooksmith to W.T. Smith, 12 August 1934.
Yorke NS 15.
syndicated reportage: e.g. 'Explorer Granted Bail', *Sunderland Echo*, 22 June 1934.

57   THE OLD BAILEY
"Attack of asthma...": 25.vii.34.
"Thank you...": e.g. Symonds (1997) p.505; Kac.487.

58   HUNGARIA RESTAURANT
"Member of Parliament Z": Wheatley in e.g. *The Devil and All His Works*, pp.273; 276.
"Ipsissimus": *The Devil Rides Out* (Hutchinson, 1934), pp.72, 84.
"Published for Subscribers Only 1929" etc.: Sold at Blackwells Oxford. Catalogue
A1136 *A Catalogue of Books from the Library of Dennis Wheatley* (1979) item 433.
Private collection, Hampshire.
Title page reproduced in *The Devil and All His Works*, p.275.

59   CURZON STREET
"...really a little Ely Culbertson...": note on Claridge's hotel notepaper, May 1934,
sold at Sotheby's with Wheatley's copy of Crowley's *Mortadello*, 7 December
2007, lot 146; formerly Blackwells item 534.
Donegall and Punch's Club: 22.x.32.
"Rumpus at Tombstone"; "Farewell speech": 29.x.34.
"Hotel chucks me out!!": 9.xi.34.
"Dear Dennis Wheatley...": note on Hotel Washington notepaper, 1 November
1934; private collection.

60   MAYFAIR HOTEL
"...eminent mental specialist...": Wheatley, *The Devil Rides Out* (1934), p.33.
"...two other ladies doing it...": 5.vii.32.
Levitation, Burnett-Rae: (in Robertson, *Scrapbook*) p.23.
"Rollo Ahmed...V. good"; Cannon "bowled out...": 13.v.34.

61   REDBURN STREET
four deformed men: Symonds (1997) p.182.
"understood for the first time...": Mudd to Charles Stansfeld Jones, cited Kac.175.
"...hate to live in Chelsea....": Greene to Vivien Greene 20 March 1945, in *Graham
Greene: A Life In Letters* ed. Richard Greene (Little, Brown 2007), p.133.
"...religious maniac": to Germer, 16 September 1929 {OTO}.
"...amorphous mollusc quality...": and limerick: Diary 666, March 1924, Yorke OS A11.
"...commonly called Norman Mudd": Kac.416.
"...define the term Lyg...": Symonds (1997) p.409.
"...long, elaborate, mathematical proof...": Kac.422.

62   CAREY STREET BANKRUPTCY COURT
"...well-known to prosperous Hebrews..." *The Book of Lies*, Ch.74, 'Carey Street'.
"author and psychiatrist": syndicated e.g. 'Aleister Crowley's Affairs', *Evening
Telegraph*, Dundee, 14 February 1935.
noblest prose in the English language: deposition re bankruptcy, Yorke YC NS 117.
"...selling me cigars?" (re Philip Morris): 6.i.42.

"...spirit of the Jew...": 7.iv.41.
Francis of Assisi: 13.xii.40.

63 GREAT ORMOND STREET
"...creditors are unable to ascertain": syndicated e.g. 'Edward Alexander Crowley', *Daily Herald*, 6 February 1935.
"...corner of Primrose Hill...": to Andre Pigné, 6 March 1936, Yorke NS117.
"...old and rather dilapidated house"; "wandering about Piccadilly wearing the same suit...": Bernard Bromage, 'Aleister Crowley', *Light* Vol. LXXXIX no.3440 (Autumn 1959) pp.149-61, all Bromage quotation from this source.
"...Pearl struck me": 7.ix.34.
"...resistance to analysis in André...": 27.iv.36.
"...prolonged wild visions...": 5.xii.33.
"...symptoms of insanity": 12.v.36.
"...Bat Club": 29.ii.36.
"...the filth of London...": 24.vii.36.

64 WELBECK STREET
Burnett-Rae, *A Memoir of 666*, reproduced in Robertson, *Crowley Scrapbook*, pp.23-27: "highly evolved": p.23; "...nuisance...strange foods and drinks": p.23; "as if unconscious": p.24; "middle-aged widow": p.24.
Cockren: AC has a number of meetings and treatments between 18.i.33 and 2.v.33, when he accuses Cockren – Cochran in the transcript – of bruising his colon (by abdominal massage).
'Amrita Elixir' scheme: Yorke NS3, and self-testimonials e.g. 27.ii.33, and 'Memoranda for 1936' in 1936 Royal Court Diary.
Grant and Arnsohn: e.g. 9.ix.36.
Amie McClymont: 6.vi.38.
"...'Good morrow, fair sir": 4.ix.36.
"...perfectly amicable...": Burnett-Rae op.cit. p.24.
May said she would kill him: op.cit. 27.

65 WARREN DRIVE
"...Doomed Bastion...": 28.x.36.
"amazing treachery": 20.xii.36.
Further Richardson details from Weiser Antiquarian cataloguing of Richardson's copy of Stephensen, *The Legend of Aleister Crowley*, item 57449 (2020).

66 REDCLIFFE GARDENS
"entrenched": 16.xii.36.
"biting girl...": in notebook of 1916-17, Yorke OS31.
Warrilow: 14.i.36.
Elsie Morris:14.vi.36. There was also an attempt to persuade her to abort with two boxes of "female pills", and an associate of Crowley's named Rutherford frightened her with details of St. Philip's hospital for women – mainly for

prostitutes with venereal disease – at Sheffield Street, a backstreet in WC2 near
Kingsway (6.vii.36).
scene at Eiffel Tower ("Pearl went nearly insane"): 24.ii.37.
Meg Usher: 19.xii.36.

67 FAIRHAZEL GARDENS
Typescript flyer, private collection.
"...white Yogi in the West": *Daily Mirror*, March 9 1936, p.11.
"good visions"; "great success": 17.iii.37.

68 DUKE STREET
"Turker": e.g. a spell from 15.iv.37 to 18.iv.37.
"...living in a Turkish bath...": to Germer, 26 February 1937 {OTO}.
"...down to 6d": 10.v.37.
"no money for bath": 3.xii.36.

69 MANOR PLACE
"Except once...": Louis Marlow [Wilkinson], *Seven Friends*, p.51.
Number 10 with Evans: 29.iv.37.
'London medium snaps his own levitation', *Life*, 4 July 1938.
40 Cambridge Terrace: e.g. letter to Germer 11 September 1933 {OTO}.
"...next few days...": to Germer 22 May 1937 {OTO}.
Fortune-telling and fish paste: Anthony Powell, *The Acceptance World*
(Heinemann, 1955), pp.5; 6-7. James Laver also notes an association between
seedy Bayswater and fortune telling: "a whole variety of rather depressed
fortune tellers who eked out a living in the less fashionable parts of Bayswater."
Museum Piece, p.220.
"Through those broad streets...": Betjeman cited in *The London Encyclopaedia*,
'Paddington', p.590.
"...stench is ghastly": to Germer 22 May 1937 {OTO}.
"fluid margin in which sank or swam...": William Plomer, *At Home: Memoirs*
(Cape, 1958), p.220.
"ambiguous or transitional districts": Burroughs, *Junky* (Penguin, 1977), p.111.
"Met Camille Comer...": 18.ix.37.
"...sacred character of the Office": 'Of the Second Party to This Art [...]', *De Arte
Magica*, p.10.
Lola Breton: 31.v.33.
Hilda Goodwin: 5.xii.38.
Pat Harvey: 25.xi.38; 1.xii.38; 4.xii.38.
"...perhaps flagellation": 18.ix.37.
Marianne: meets her 29.i.33; "fuckstress" 13.ii.33; and after a number of works she
returns to the continent in March, going to Paris before Budapest. It is not clear
who she was: Crowley refers to a Marie of Bulgaria (possibly a jokey name, based
on the once-famous "Marie of Romania") and this may be the same person. There
is also a hint that he has met her before ("after all these years"), perhaps in Europe,

and that she might be aristocratic (or some very minor royal, perhaps seen in Berlin; the kind of person Gerald Hamilton cultivated). Nevertheless it is hard to imagine a bona fide royal in Room 2 of Augusta Faillie's Boarding House.
Miss Cooper: 29.vi.33. The unidentified word seems to be '*kala*' in Greek, which is hard to make direct sense of (generally an adjective or adverb meaning 'good' or 'well') and the context suggests a physical feature. It may be a bilingual word-play alluding to the word kala in another language. *Kala* means time in Sanskrit (and has had some currency with modern Western occultists, via the British occult writer Kenneth Grant, to mean sexual fluids) but this is hard to make sense of as 'pretty'. It also means black in Urdu, a language Crowley had encountered, but if Miss Cooper herself was black, judging by other references, Crowley would have simply said so. He elsewhere uses black or dark as an anal allusion: e.g., in an early diary, March 24 1900 {OTO}, he uses the Welsh *twll du* (black hole) seemingly not to refer to the geographical feature in Snowdonia but to sodomy. And in the Thirties he refers to a male visitor as "one of the [*kala*] legion" (27.v.36), perhaps judging his sexuality. In context, Miss Cooper of Howland Street seems to have had the most attractive anus Crowley had ever seen. Lying awake in February of the same year, Crowley had a dream-like fancy of going around "the Grill" – probably Café Royal or Berkeley – and judging "the best anus, the wittiest word, etc. I give present to one I choose." [II. ii.33]. It remains a mystery. No mystery about Miss Cooper's lodging though – above what was then a confectioner's, between Howland Mews East and the Carpenter's Arms pub on the corner of Whitfield Street, it is long gone in the redevelopment of Howland Street, as is that of Lillian Williams at number 41.
Lilian Williams: 11.vii.37.
Lily Parker: 3.vi.40.
Marta Allen: 5.viii.41.
Paula Fyffe [Figffe in transcription]: 5.viii.41.
Hilda...Rita...Isabel...: 7.ii.33.
Susie King: 2.vii.33. AC goes to Colombo's a couple of times with a Susie, and writes an obscene rhyme for a Susan.
Gipsy Rae: 1.viii.41.
Violet at Jamaica International Hotel: 18.xi.37.
Violet Davidson "stupid": 28.iii.38.
rang from police custody: 12.v.38.
Meets Evelyn Harley: 14.ix.37.
Joan Dobson: 19.xii.37.
Argyle Street: 19.iii.38.

70 RAC CLUB
"voltage": Clifford Bax, *Inland Far* (Heinemann, 1925) p.42.
"seriously on the Path": 18.ii.38.
Dhyana: 7.i.44.
"...*This is the Great Work*.": undated letter to Harris circa 1941, formerly in the collection of Clive Harper, catalogued by Weiser Antiquarian 2020 item #65121.

"...Jew she married": 7.iv.42.
Thelemite candidate for Bethnal Green: 20.v.43.
'Housemaid': Driberg, *Ruling Passions*, p.86.
"...dangerous lunatic, the most treacherous and deceitful person...": to Germer, 19 July 1945 {OTO}.
"constant thieving": to Germer, 25 September 1945 {OTO}.
"...disloyal but imbecile intrigue": 4.v.42.
"...Frieda's savage ravings": 12.i.42.

71 SANDWICH STREET
Meets Barfoot : 25.vi.37.
Ruthvah: see Symonds's, e.g. 1997 pp.445-6. Symonds' ratios may be a misunderstanding from Crowley's 1[full stop] ambergris, 2[full stop] musk, 3 [full stop] civet. These are very possibly not proportions, but an emphatic sequence simply naming three ingredients. The detail of eyebrows is in Iain Coster 'The Worst Man in London', *The Inky Way Annual* II c.1948.
"...uncultivated": 25.vi.37.
"power over men": 27.vi.37; "money": 23.i.38; "health and strength": 31.vii.38; "health especially for Pearl": 5.viii.38.
"told her how...": 18.xii.37.

72 CHEPSTOW VILLAS
"...poor zebu...": 17.x.37. Crowley had a particular distaste for Eurasians, people of mixed European and Indian descent, which Phyllis clearly fell foul of. "I am not a snob or a puritan," he writes in the *Confessions*, "but Eurasians do get on my nerves. I do not believe that their universally admitted baseness is due to a mixture of blood or the presumable peculiarity of their parents; but that they are forced into vileness by the attitude of both their white and coloured neighbours." [Hag 468-9] Crowley and race is a large and nuanced subject outside the present book, but the abrasiveness of his expressed opinions goes well beyond the ambient attitudes of his time. John Symonds, unpopular with Thelemites for his critical attitude to Crowley, was one of the very few people to 'call' him on this. When he challenged Crowley on his comments about Jews (at least one of Symonds's wives was Jewish, and his mother) Crowley made jokes about it, but when it came to Crowley calling Symonds's friend Tambimuttu (Ceylonese-born poet and founder of *Poetry London* magazine) a "drunken nigger", he dug in harder and said "THEY ARE – education only makes it worse." In context he seems to have meant the Ceylonese were as hopeless intellectually as sub-Saharan Africans were sometimes thought to be. Crowley to Symonds, 9 October 1946, Yorke NS 117.
"Phyllis has disappeared!": 31.x.37.
Symonds asserts: Symonds (1997) p.527.
"The girl who stood before me, smiling with big red lips...": Cammell p.181.
Beryl Drayton, Hyde Park: 9.ix.39.
"the name of a jewel that has magical attributes": Cammell p.181.

"coloured girl": 11.vii.37.
Marie Johnson: 26.v.33.
Blowzabella: 21.xi.37.
"...many whores...": 9.iv.33.
"...nigger whore": 26.x.42.
"Fuck negress...": Magical Record of Ankh-f-n-Khonsu (1927-29 diary) 22 August
1927 {OTO}, re *I Ching* LXI.
"Began by kissing...": 1.i.39.
Mary Wilson: 20.ii.39.

73   THE OBELISK
"An Englishman, a Jew, an Indian...": Tom Driberg, 'A Mixed Bag of Early Birds',
Daily Express, 23 December 1937.
"I, Ankh-f-n-Khonsu...": Kac.499.
Joan Dobson: 19.xii.37; 20. xii.37.

74   ALDERNEY STREET
slept on chair in clothes: 24.ix.37.
Joan Gibbons: 4.iii.1938; 5.iii.38.
"...Gibbons alias Brooks": 30.iv.38.
"not worthwhile competing": 19.iv.38.
meets Mattie: 12.iv.38.
"pure Thelemite"; "...stranger start to convert me": to Germer, 22 April 1938 {OTO}.
"...first truly sympathetic woman...": 2.v.38.
"health – power &c": 2.v.38; "health and energy": 2.v.38; "health and au.": 25.v.38;
"money for new lodgings" (i.e. seemingly together): 16.v.38; "...superb artist": 12.v.38.
"both completely entranced": 29.v.38.
"think she was doing au." (while he was doing "power – health"): 14.v.38.
"Letter from Miss Stanton...": 14.v.38.
"Rude letter from Mattie...": 15.viii.38.
"...came astrally to caress me...": 31.vi.38.
"...whiskey and *The Author of Trixie*...": 31.vii.38.
"Nurse M. Pickett. Basement...": 2.ix.39.
Abramelin dabbler: alleged by Crowley, *Magick Without Tears* Ch.XX
'Talismans'.
"...Moreland agreed...": Anthony Powell, *Casanova's Chinese Restaurant*, p.106.
Ethel Donley: 29/30.vi.38.
Peggy Young: 14.iv.39.
Rose Wilson: 20.viii.38.
Works for "A1 War": e.g. 13/15/20.ix.39.
Maisie weeps: 23.ix.38.
Maise "Superb opus": e.g. 1.ix.38.
Mary Wilcox as "possible Maisie": 23.iii.40.
Peche Maisie: 20.ix.38.
"...getting really keen...": 16.vii.37.

"...the hand that used to pet children and animals": picture reproduced in alostfilm.com [blog] as from *Flaming Sex*, but possibly from a French true crime magazine such as *Detective* 26 February 1931.
Allegedly living with a boxer: letter to Yorke 17 June 1935, Yorke NS115, cf Symonds (1997) p.494.
Works for Memodial invention: 29.x.39; 2.xi.39; and with Alice 30.x.39.

75   HASKER STREET
"Two or three really bad nightmares...": 25.ix.38.
"Kempinski A.1 wild duck": 12.ii.39.
"Peggy hopelessly drunk...": 13.ii.39.
"Peggy raving...": 18.ii.39.
"...admirable dinner...": 19.ii.39.
"heroic and unselfish": 14.xi.38.
Charing Cross Hospital: 16.xi.38.
"...curiously peaceful...": 19.xi.38.
"...paradise for Peggy": 30.xi.38.
Norah Knott, "complex": 28.xi.38.
Blackley "*Wunderschon!*": 16.xi.38.
Marie-Louise Draghici: first contact 16.xi.38.
to "get" Maria-Louise : 2.ix.38.
Peggy falls down steps: 23.x.38.
Maisie: 19.viii.38; Jessie Moran: 15.viii.38; Rose Wilson: 20.viii.38; Angela Considine: 21-22.viii.38.
"John Jameson shows...": 13.ii.39.

76   LOVE IN HAMPSTEAD
"...love in Hampstead": 19.vi.37.
(I am indebted to William Breeze for details of Selvin Campbell)
Adele Brand: 2.vii.37.
"A1" Broadhurst Gardens: 22.vi.37.
Sally Pace: 25.iii.1938; 7.iv.38.
"Sally is a darlin' little bitch": in the back of 1938 Royal Court diary. Yorke Collection. Close variant in 1938 Appointments book sold by Weiser Antiquarian 2007 item #62528.
Stella Hilling: 3.iv.38.
Stella at Manor Place: 6 .iv.38.
I Ching: Stella "idiot" [Hexagram 2] and Sally "hot stuff" [Hexagram 51]: 3.iv.38.

77   BLACKFRIAR'S ROAD
"...futile hunt": 8.xii.38.
Norah "futile": 8.xii.38.
Meets Cath: 9.xii.38.
Emmy Butler: 7.ix.38; 12.ix.38; 1.x.38.
Marie imprisoned; "*tres mauvais*": to Yorke 25 May 1931, Yorke NS117.

"a lady & intelligent"; health"; "very first class": 9.xii.38.
"...insulted her all day": 7.ii.39 (Peggy insults Cathrine; cf "Peggy and Cathrine fought for me all day" 4.ii.39): "...spate of venomous abuse": 31.vii.36 (Pearl insults Pat).
stabbed Crowley in face: recounted in letter to Germer 19 December 1938 {OTO}.
Falconer recipe: 31.xii.38.
"prehensile": 1.vi.40.
"...smile and pawky speech...": 31.iii.42.
shoplifting: recounted to Crowley at their meeting 10.iv.42. The magistrate noted that she was an intelligent, hard-working woman come down in the world, and gave her a year's probation.
Royal Ordnance at Swynnerton: recounted to Crowley 9.v.42.
Women's Royal Naval Service: letter from Cathrine ("Wren C Falconer") in WRNS noted 30.vi.43.

78 JOSEPHINE BLACKLEY
"...marvellous woman...": 6.x.38.
"Lilian 40 Dean St...": 8.iii.40.
"Coloured girl...": 11.vii.37.
Dora Williams: 5.x.39.
Betty Russell: 11.vi.33.
Jeanette: 12.x.39.
"Gladys GER4602": 22.iii.38.
Colonial Club: 31.xii.38.
Millie Sharp: 10.iii.33.
"Jo Blackley!...": 30.viii.41.
Blatchly was her correct name, from her dead husband.

79 HYDE PARK
"Bayswater Road, Hyde Park, Pimlico...": Helen Self, *Prostitution, Women and Misuse of the Law*, p.101.
"...meaningful glance": J. Laite, *Common Prostitutes and Ordinary Citizens 1885-1960*, p.84.
"Shikar in park": e.g. 23.iii.40.
"Hyde Park grasshopper": 10.vii.37.
"Emmy": 7, 8, 12.ix.1938; 1.x.38.
"Jessie Moran": 15.viii.38.
"To park, late. N.G.": 10.i.38.
"fruitless": e.g. 1.x.39.
"Stupidity of the park...": 22.xi.38.
"Long shikar...": 2.viii.42.
"Blonde Bombshell": 4.vi.40.
"Determined on shikar...": 24.ii.40.
"9.30 Fitzroy, on shikar": 5.x.38.
Swan in Hammersmith: 9.ix.39.
"...lunar cow": 6.ii.40.
"...row at the Hop Poles": 4.x.39.

80   THE FRENCH HOUSE
"...duke in a musical comedy": Richardson, 'Luncheon with Beast 666' in *Fits and Starts*, p.113.
Hamilton and ether: e.g. Cullen, *Norris*, p.199.
"nothingness with twinkles"; "(visualized) mind"; "...splendour into bliss": 'Diary of a Magus' [Liber 63], August 23 1916 {OTO}.
"...Ethel to the cinema": 24.ii.24, Yorke OS H4.
"Aldebaran": to Mudd from Tunisia October 1924, cited Symonds (1997) p.354.
"...beloved Umfreville": 21.vi.42.
Kidneys and Volnay: 27.vi.42.
Dog and Duck: e.g. 1.i.38.
Ruthven Todd, *Fitzrovia and the Road to the York Minster*, Section I 'Fitzrovia', unpaginated.
Risotto Cheshire Cheese: 16.v.39.
Crowley and Dylan Thomas: Constantine Fitzgibbon, *The Life of Dylan Thomas*, p.174.
Royal Oak (now just Oak): e.g. with Fitzgerald 14.vii.37.
Vintage Wine Lodge: 27.ii.38.
Horse and Sack: 10.iii.38.
Westbourne Hotel: 16.iv.38.
"fun on Sunday night": 27.iii.38.

81   CHESTER TERRACE
"on the borderland...": Richardson, 'Luncheon with Beast 666', p.113.
"Peggisome": 8.iii.39.
"abominable": 16.v.39.
"put off a satyr": 10.iii.39.
Ten o' clock rule; threatening suicide: 12.iv.39.
Dr O'Hara, Luminal: 27.iii.39.
Peggy arrested: *Westminster and Pimlico News* 4 July 1941.
Antelope on Eaton Terrace: e.g. 23.iii.39.
pawned ring: e.g. 11.v.39.
Cojones Mexicanos 26.vii.39; Risotto Cheshire Cheese: 16.v.39; Turbot d'Urberville: 15. v.39; Turbot Porterfield: 21.iv.39; Sambar of Turbot and Mushroom: 4.vii.39; Goldfish Toast, Flying Fish: 28.v.39; Capretto St George: 23.iv.39; Fisherman's Daughter: 20.v.39; Escalopes de Veau Desespoir: 26.v.39; Pimentos Katarina a la St.Bartoleme: 24.vii.39; Biftek Crapaudine: 4.vi.39.
Fitzgerald: 2.iii.39.
"a Scots lady so indeterminate...": Richardson, 'Luncheon with Beast 666', p.114.
"...real circle, i.e. the Aura of the Magus": *Magick*, p.222.
hallucinatory figures on waking: e.g. 15.iv.39.
"...like a devil roasting in hell...": Richardson op.cit. p.114.

82   WEST HALKIN STREET
Dolores del Castro: 11.viii.34.

"...principal trouble was...": 'Frontiers of Belief: Madeline Montalban' in *Man Myth and Magic* no.23, 1970.

83 MORTON HOUSE
walked to see Chiswick House: 27.xii.39.
"...talented amateur..."; "pointless daubs": to Germer 24 July 142 {OTO}.
"...did not *create* anything": to Germer 30 September 1942 {OTO}.
"Black Currant Pudding Brothers"; "really great original meal": 18.vii.39.

84 THE PARAGON
"...guarding the Holy Grail in Richmond": to Yorke 25 Jan 1940 from Petersham Road, Yorke OS D5.
"...lunch in sunlit room...": 18.ii.38.
"...big windows, high above Thames": to Germer 9 August 1939 {OTO}.
Nuncheon menu: formerly in the collection of David Tibet, sold by Weiser Antiquarian, item #64333.
"rather a mean trick": Driberg story, *Ruling Passions* pp.85-86.

85 THE GREEN, RICHMOND
Moved to no.15: 23.v.40.
"Elaborate dream...": 4.ii.38.
"...long talks with Hitler a very tall man...": 2.vi.39.
Viereck and "philosophical basis": cited Sutin p.250.
Slippery Joe and "93 as base for Nazi New Order": 5.v.36.
Alleged influence through Küntzel: e.g. Symonds (1997) 518.
"astonishing" similarities: to Jane Wolfe, 12 February 1941 re Rauschning {OTO}.
"...cartoons lampooning *Mein Kampf*...": 29.viii.43.
Hitler Speaks by Rauschning is now thought to be of dubious authenticity, although this is irrelevant to Crowley's responses: "true", re Austria rotten with Jews p.92; "yes", re protecting strong against weak p.141; "all very sound" and "excellent", re political economy and inspiration 180, 181; "For 'German people' read 'Thelemites'" p.48; "After all these centuries of whining...Yes!", p.141.
"knock Hitler for a six": to Martha Küntzel, cited Kac.505.
"Nordic Aryan nonsense": to Germer 5 December 1939 {OTO}.
"demoniac foaming-at-the-mouth...": to Germer 11 July 1933 {OTO}.
"rights of the individual": to Germer 5 December 1939 {OTO}.
Hohenzollern monarchy: to Germer, undated, received 24 September 1939 {OTO}.
Suggested swastika to Ludendorff: annotation in *Hitler Speaks*, p.212. There is also a strikingly early use of the swastika in a pro-German rather than Eastern context on the cover of *The International*, the propaganda paper Crowley was involved with, Vol.XI no.8, August 1917.
"...directly under one of my own chiefs!": to Germer 4 March 1942 {OTO}.
Richmond Green to Richmond Bridge: 8.ix.40.
"...twenty-one again [...]": Cammell p.187.

86   FITZWILLIAM HOUSE, RICHMOND GREEN
Kenneth Anger: cited Mick Brown, *Performance*, p.56.
Summers and Black Mass: see d'Arch Smith, *Books of the Beast*, pp.56-57.
Described as earliest: Gareth Medway, *Lure of the Sinister*, p.382.
"...most amusing evening...": 5.vii.29.
"Mrs Forbes": 19.viii.40.
Valchera's: with Cammell 10.vi.40. As for Summers, this is something I've long
'known', but with no reference: it may be something I was told by the late
and much-missed Roger Dobson of *The Lost Club Journal*, who led Montague
Summers walks around Richmond.
"Ha Ha": 28.vii.41.
Sold to other people: e.g. chess crony Sutherland 27.vii.41 and ("last piece")
Bayley 22.ix.41.
"...honour, friendship or virtue...": Cammell to Yorke, undated, cited Symonds
(1997) p.587.

87   DUKE STREET
Harold Batty Shaw: Appendix to Notebook 9, April 3 to May 16 1924, Yorke OS H4.
Laudanum 1907: 'Experiment with Laudanum', 28-29 September 1907, Yorke OS22.
Heroin noted in Jermyn Street diary, 21 March 1907 {OTO}.
astrological "idiosyncrasy" for heroin, Paris diary/notebook March 25 to April 3
1924, Yorke OS A12.
"...thirteen masturbations...": Diary 666 rue Vavin March 20-25, 1924, Yorke OS
A11. "Menstruation orgie": this might look like a possible mistranscription of
'Restoration orgie', i.e. the orgiastic later 17thC in Britain, the era of Charles II's
Restoration and Lord Rochester, which would make more conventional sense,
but the holograph is definitely menstruation.
"...itch marvellously lewdly...": Diary 666 as above; same night.
"...dread the failure of supply": to Mudd from rue Vavin 18 March 1924, Yorke NS5.
Teeth breaking e.g. 28.xii.41; 23.vii.43; 17.v.44; 17.vi.44; 23.vi.44; woken by "terrific"
and "extreme" diarrhoea in sleep e.g. 21.viii.40; 5.vi.41; 15.x. 41; vomiting e.g.
sick in cinema at *No Orchids For Miss Blandish* 13.x.42, and notes it happening
recently during *Macbeth* and a gangster film.
Walk-on parts, e.g. Crawshaw with at least 37 diary entries.
"...story was current...": Laver, *Museum Piece* p.231.
"...humorous lowland Scot...": 2.ix.43.

88   HANOVER SQUARE
"Food excellent...": 26.ix.40.
"...most kind, let me go": 1.x.40.
"aristocratic communism": 3.iv.41.
"worst snag in England...": 20.iv.41.
"Belgravia Club": 24.x.40.
French Pub crowded, on to Fitzroy: 14.vii.41.
"Very pleasant": 11.ix.41.

Caton: first contact 21.viii.41. "...flagellation": 26.viii.41; "seedy fraud": 13.vi.42.
Mason's Arms, *England Stand Fast*: 1.viii.41.
"...Chreesmas pooding?": 'Christmas in Maddox Street' at end of 1941 diary.
Meets Alice Speller: 18.x.39.
date at Yorkshire Grey: 18.x.39.
Spellerisms: "...must collect a few of these Spellerisms" memo at end of 1942 diary, with a collection.
"...a word of the last five minutes": memo note to September 1942.
"Saw coloured girl I wanted...": 15.viii.40.
Birch: e.g. Sutin p.391 cf Symonds's inuendoes (e.g. 1997, pp.541; 546): Sutin follows Symonds in calling her Upham. Crowley buys "birch for Alice" in Torquay – 28.iv.41 – in anticipation of her visit next day.
"...compassionate grounds": 5.viii.41; "...human kindness sake" 1.viii.40.
"...offered a banquet...": 2.xii.41.
"...frigged her": 23.xii.41.
"...novelette-length dream": 29.vii.41.
"...about an hermaphrodite": 27.vii.41.
"...young strong tall woman...": 13.ix.41.
"This type of dream begins...": 23.ii.42.
"Began morphia...": 'Notes from the Diary of the Candidate Nemo 8=3 during his Initiation to the Grade of Magus' 1 February 1915 Yorke OS C3.
"Woke 2.10": 21.vii.41.
"Dreamt last night...": 9.viii.41.
"...terrific Tamasha": 10.viii.41.
"...long fantastic Tamasha...": 10.viii.41.
"...dream of Himalayan heights...": 1.vii.40.
"Sex-and-naval-war dreams": 11.ii.42.
"...the most magnificent tamasha...": 4.i.46.
"Strangest dreams some very gorgeous": 1.ii.43.
Superb dream: 12.viii.45.
"...like a crazed bluebottle": 31.iii.42.
"...dropped in and brightened things up": 28.ii.42.
armband: Symonds, *Conversations with Gerald*, p.78.
"similar radiance": Symonds op.cit. p.112.
"18B": 22.vii.41.
Gevrey Chambertin and Driberg: Symonds op.cit. p.144.
"Alice and Ham as usual": 2.v.42.
"...looking forward to our solitary encounter...": Cullen, *The Man Who Was Norris*, p.200
I have borrowed the terms "High-Imperial, Occult-Exotic" from John Bramble's *Modernism and the Occult* [p.10] where he discusses Modernism's indebtedness to the imperial occult and what Patrick Brantlinger has defined as Imperial Gothic.

89   DOVER STREET
(Dover Street also went a long way back with Crowley as the site of the
photographer he used for pictures of himself in yoga postures, reproduced in
The Equinox, along with Leila Waddell, and a widely reproduced 'happy family'
portrait of himself, Rose, and baby. It was the Dover Street Studio at number 38,
now Erco; the early 20thC 'artistic' style of the 38 numeral on the frontage may be
contemporary. Like Lowe's chemist, the Studios placed advertising in *The Equinox*.)
"...interests the ageing Alys": 1.v.42.
chambermaid complained: 6.v.42.
Collin Brooks dinners e.g. 26.v.42, Maison Basque; 8.vii.42 Bolivar.
"...don't need a revolver often...": Brooks, *More Tavern Talk*, p.9.
"Latin Quarter around Portland Place": Brooks op.cit. p.98.
"...the younger generation..."; 'Lady Astor': Brooks, *Tavern Talk* p.65. There were
wheels within wheels, because Burgess had covertly pro-Soviet reasons of his
own for wanting to cultivate Brooks as a media figure and may have been using
Crowley as a pretext for this.
Bore; "virgin goat": Brooks op.cit. p.64.

90   HAMILTON HOUSE, PICCADILLY
"...brekker in bedroom": 7.v.42.
"If I want country..."; Byron's bath: to Germer, 11 May 1942.
Ward's Irish House: e.g. 9.v.42; 16.vi.42.
"...lovely glass and china": 29.x.42.
"...just WILL NOT DO": 16.vi.42.
"oodles": 3.viii.42.
"Hoggess": 29.v.42; "She-Hogg": 30.vi.42.
Rotha and Meyer: 13.i.42.
Power and Boyer: 17.x.42.
"sly treacherous vixen": 21.vii.42.
"amazing treachery"; "Frieda's sneaking treachery": 31.vii.42.
"really a brothel": Lamburn, Joan, 'Letters to Alyse Gregory 1941-1943', *The Powys
Journal*, XXVI (2016) pp. 156-57; "repulsive"p.170.
"Mental state v. bad...": 25.vi.42.
Importance of Being Earnest and theatre outing as "magical ceremony": 21.x.42.
"...saluted new moon...": 30.ix.42.
"...an angel choir!": 11.vi.42.

91   WILTON PLACE
Brook calls by appointment: 6.45pm, 28.vii.42.
From "magical advisor" to "demystified himself": Peter Brook, *Threads of Time*, p.9.
"What a herd!": 10.x.42.

92   LEVY'S SOUND STUDIO
"more than once I have seen him...": Louis Marlow [Wilkinson], *Seven Friends*, p.54.
"Magical Voice": Regardie, *The Eye in the Triangle*, p.388.

"...rather high for a man": Bankes, *Why Not?*, p.202.
"... effeminate, rather squeaky": Regardie op. cit. p.388.
Calder-Marshall, *The Magic of My Youth*, p.118.
"celebrated near-Cockney accent": Powell, *Messengers of Day*, p.82.

93 93 JERMYN STREET
"cave woman": e.g. 13.ii.44.
Delighted with 9331: e.g. to Germer, undated, received 26 October 1942; to Jane Wolfe, n.d. October 1942 {OTO}.
"...sweetness and light": 24.i.39.
lucky ticket 93: 22.ii.39.
fog: 27.viii.43.
chemist's window: 27.viii.43.
slipped and hit head: 21.x.43.
threepenny piece: 6.i.44. The word he uses is "tickey", of mainly South African usage, but the sense of it being a small coin seems confirmed by a reference (15. iv.41) to counting all his money and also having a "numismatic hoard of tickeys", in the sense that one might put small change in a jar.
dreams of Davies tailor: 14.i.41.
"birthday today": 2.xii. 43.
Lobb shoes: 30.vii.38.
talk with Astley: 3.iv.42.
Gurkha knife: 30.iii.44.
Alexander VI at auction: 2.xii.43.
"Satanfather" to the Renaissance: Crowley in draft of 'William Blake, by a Mental Traveller', pp.22-23, Yorke OS C1.
Sold by Glendinning's, and Crowley traced the buyer as Baldwin, 3 Robert Street, Adelphi TEM[ple] 1611: 2.xii.43.
Cambyses etc: 15.xii.42.
Henriette Barnitt: 21.v.40.
Sangorski: 14.iii.44.
"...in the workhouse infirmary": 6.iii.42, sold by Weiser Antiquarian item #60765.
Fermaprint: this might look like a mistranscription for Permaprint but the business really was Ferma-.
Maisky: 6.i.43; Francis: 30.xii.42.
Thelema as "golden mean": in 'Memo' section of 1943 diary.
"classical tradition": ibid.
"nauseated" by Eliot: 13.iv.42.
"England's literary martyr": to Grady McMurtry, postmark 3 August 1945 {OTO}; (Crowley was drafting 'The Strategic Implications of a "Clear Crowley's Name" Campaign' – McMurtry was at the time a lieutenant in the US Army).
"imbecile hag": 23.iv.44.
"poor old Wallaby": 8.vi.43.
"Wombat of Wagga-Wagga": 8.viii.43.
"...something of pathos...": Marlow, *Seven Friends*, p.53.

"poor old Aleister Crowley": Aberconway, *A Wiser Woman?*, p.45.
"Her lovely eyes were large...": *Seven Friends*, p.55.
"impressed though I was by the exaltation...": ibid.
"...Willey, Porterfield and boys: 'Thicket of thorns crowd'": 25.vii.37.
"...my cuppa tea": 30.vii.45.
"bar the Tub": 4.iii.44.
"complete (bar Tub) desolation": 11.iii.44.
"no news, no tobacco, no friends...": 9.v.43.
"free of the sexual impulse": 25.i.43.
"...homosexuality and pacifism etc.": 15.xii.31.
This Gun for Hire: (Graham Greene) 4.x.43; *Carnet du Bal*: 22.xii.43; *Brighton Rock*: 13.iv.43; *Derriere la Façade*: 2.ii.43 ("A1"); *The Man Who Came to Dinner*: 30.vii.43 film (and stage play three times); *Striptease Lady*: 1.viii.43; *Margin for Error*: 6.viii.43; *Arsenic and Old Lace*: 6.v.43; *Five Graves to Cairo*: 9.vii.43; *A Night to Remember*: (1942) 4.v.43, seen at least six time at venues including the New Vic, King's Cross Cinema with Alice, and the Elephant and Castle with Cath, though to sixth viewing 11.vi.43; *They've Got Me Covered*, with Bob Hope, from 8.vii.43 to 7.iv.44 ("8th or 9th time"; "it gets better").
"...appelstrudel!": 10.i.44.
Chicken Inn: 3.v.43.
Prunier's and glorious evening: 29.ii.44.
"Great Joke" etc.: Calder-Marshall reviewing *Magick*, *Times Literary Supplement* 27 July 1973 p.871.
"5,000 year plan": 27.viii.44.
"Discovered why I like Americans...": 10.ix.44.
"My dear Aunt...": 12.xii.42.
"coupe je ne sais quoi": 25.iv.42.
"This desolating war!": 24.x.42.
West End in wartime: to Germer, undated, received October 1942.
"entertainment value of these raids...": 17.iii.44.
"blue funk": 22.iii.44.
Bomb at foot of Duke Street ("Where you and Cora stayed – I was there too"): to Germer 19 March 1944 {OTO}.
"...valley of the shadow of death...": Miss Manning ("Cave Woman") to Symonds, in Symonds (1997) p.573.
"100 morons killed...": 7.xi.43.
"I am perplexed" to Lady Harris: Symonds (1997) p.585.
"sometimes I hate myself" to a Mr Rowe, ibid.
"I often wish I could divine...": 24.x.43: the transcript has 'causal', but it is just possible the circumstance was 'casual'.
"Man can embody truth...": Yeats, 'Magic', in *Essays and Introductions*
New Delhi Durbar Indian: an invite survives (Yorke OS EE2).
Hamilton leaves early: Cullen, *The Man Who Was Norris*, p.201.

A WORD IN WILDE HASTE:
Crowley, London and the 1890s

Crowley's affinity with the culture of the 1890s was more obvious in his lifetime: the novelist Anthony Powell, who met him between the wars, has described him as "what might be called a 'post-decadent', representing a curious residue of the nineties that lived on into Edwardian days, side by side with early elements just beginning to take shape, of the 'Modern Movement'....". Crowley's Nineties quality has been noticed in passing,[1] but it is more central and important to his identity than is usually acknowledged.

Remembered as the time of Aubrey Beardsley, absinthe, *The Yellow Book* and the Café Royal, the Nineties were as significant in their way as the 1960s, a decade they prefigure with their sense of 'liberation', more open sexuality, critical social thinking, drug use, and an occult revival. London was central to both decades: it was the capital of the Nineties as it was of the Swinging Sixties. And just as "the Sixties" really lasted until around 1974, so the currents of the Nineties lasted into the Edwardian period and, in Crowley's case, well beyond.

Along with real social change, such as the rise of the bold and independent 'New Woman' in the later nineteenth century, the Nineties in their more decadent aspect were a time of sexual irregularity (already encoded in the queer tendencies of the

---

1   For example Timothy d'Arch Smith, "Crowley is to be recognized as a 'nineties' figure even if he arrived on the scene rather late"; and Christopher Partridge, "Aleister Crowley was the epitome of the *fin de siecle* occultist...In several respects, he was a good example of the 'the tragic generation' eulogized by W.B. Yeats." Partridge compares him to J.K. Huysmans' decadent hero Des Esseintes in his novel *Against Nature* (*A Rebours*, 1884). Alex Owen similarly notes he was "wedded throughout his life to the outlook and modus operandi of the 'Decadent' movement."

'aesthetic movement' in the 1880s); High Church religiosity and a Catholic, Latinate aesthetic co-existing with an anti-Christian spirit; esotericism; French influence, notably with the Symbolist movement; a fascination with the *femme fatale*; an aura of corruption and glamorous evil; an entwining of sex and death; and a 'beyond good and evil' ethos.

The spirit of the *fin-de-siècle* went well beyond simple decadence, and its wider tendencies – all visible in Crowley – include romantic Celtic revivalism; "paganism" and the cult of Pan; mediaevalism; Orientalism and Egyptomania (the latter already with its own history in occult thinking); Social Darwinism ('the survival of the fittest'); eugenics (subject of a Crowley poem of that title, where he expresses scepticism at social reform of the lower classes); and the rise of the unconscious.

W.B. Yeats recalled later that "My friends believed that the dark portion of the mind – the subconscious – had an incalculable power, and even over events. To influence events or one's own mind, one had to draw the attention of that dark portion, to turn it, as it were, in a new direction." He is writing about the revival of magic that reached its high point in the 1890s with the Golden Dawn, and friends such as MacGregor Mathers in particular. And Crowley himself, with a greater knowledge of Freud and Jung, later wrote "I have shown a way of bringing the unconscious into the conscious. That is why I am a hierophant." This newer approach could combine the powers of the unconscious with mediaevalism, bringing a transformed understanding to old magical grimoires, so Crowley could re-interpret the Holy Guardian Angel – a key idea in the Golden Dawn and associated with *The Magic of Abramelin*, a text traditionally dated to 1458 – as the unconscious mind.

The period's magical revival was accompanied by a wider idea of Satanism, although as usual with Satanism it was more rumoured than real. But the idea was in the air: man-of-letters Richard Le Gallienne was offered absinthe one night in 1890 by poet Lionel Johnson, and recalled "I had just heard of it, as a drink mysteriously sophisticated and even Satanic...in the '90s it was spoken of with a self-conscious sense of one's being desperately wicked, suggesting diabolism and nameless iniquity." The great commentator on the period, Max Beerbohm, remembered Yeats, at an 1896 party for *The Savoy* magazine in Coventry Street, near Piccadilly, talking in his grand voice to Aubrey Beardsley about "Dyahbolism". Beerbohm reports that Beardsley wasn't very interested, although he went on to be labelled after his death as the "Fra Angelico of Satanism".

Like a watermark, the era put its indelible print into a Nineties style, with a distinctive diction. The touchstone of the period is Max Beerbohm's fictional creation Enoch Soames, the quintessential doomed Nineties poet, devil-worshipper, and "Catholic diabolist". Beerbohm meets Soames in the Café Royal, where he is drinking absinthe, and Soames explains that good and evil are merely illusions. His poems ("strange growths" as he calls them) in slim books of verse such as *Fungoids* have a strangely distinctive style, convoluted and antique ("Thou hast not been nor art!").

Crowley hits the same unmistakable note in collections such as his 1906 *Gargoyles*, with its subtitle *Being Strangely Wrought Images of Life and Death* (and poems including 'Patchouli', 'Rosa Inferni', 'The Eyes of the Pharaoh', 'Ave Mors' and 'Le Jour des Morts'). It is particularly manifest in his 1918 essay 'Absinthe: The Green Goddess', where he advises readers to drink absinthe "till you become as gods, knowing good and evil, and this also – that they are not two but one." This is the point of view of the artist, he says, and "solves every problem of life and of death – which two also are one."

There are sustained flashes of this style in *The Book of the Law*, Crowley's holy book (notionally the speech of a long-dead Egyptian or other spirit, with Crowley taking dictation): "To worship me take wine and strange drugs...and be drunk thereof."

"Burn to me perfumes!", says *The Book of the Law*, blending orientalism with the high church aesthetic of the period. Also central to 'high' Satanism, or at least the idea of it, this aesthetic can similarly be seen in Crowley's more casual references, over the next couple of decades, to opium as "Our Lady of Dreams". Among his most intense treatments of this Catholic aesthetic, ultimately coming from France, is the depiction of opium as "Our Lady of Darkness" in his prose-poem 'At the Feet of Our Lady of Darkness', a paean to opium smoking supposedly translated from the French of Izeh Kranil. It is not clear how much the final work owes to Kranil, but she was a real woman: part of London's Bohemian scene before the First War, she died in Islington in 1958.[2] Crowley published 'At the Feet of Our Lady of Darkness' in *The International*, February 1918. Opening with Verlaine, moving through "strange floating perfumes" and an opium pipe prepared by an "epicene boy", it must have been a period piece by the time it appeared.

✝

Nineties writing was also notable for a new attention to urban squalor, and a combination of a 'high' style with 'low' subjects, as in the poetry of Ernest Dowson, with his Latinate treatment of infidelity with prostitutes,[3] or Arthur Symons; a man as quintessential in his way as Enoch Soames. As well as editing *The Savoy* with Beardsley, Symons wrote *The Symbolist Movement in Literature* (1899), introducing Baudelaire, Rimbaud, Verlaine and others to a wider Anglophone audience, and published his own poems in collections such as *London Nights* (1895), recording a demi-monde of streetwalkers, music halls, and the Café Royal, along with poems such as 'The Absinthe Drinker', and 'The Opium Smoker'. Accused by a critic of having written poems with "a faint smell of patchouli", a scent particularly associated with the Nineties, he defended himself in a new preface to his collection *Silhouettes*, 'Being A Word On Behalf of Patchouli'.

The high style/low subject tendency of the era is extraordinarily concentrated in Crowley's poem '*In Manu Dominae*: A Black Mass' ("In the Hand of the Mistress"), which records a handjob from a girl who is

2   Largely forgotten, she was born around 1888, probably Hungarian, and may originally have been called Vaghya, but Crowley knew her in her French-Algerian persona (she is the basis for Fatma Hallaj in his novel *Diary of a Drug Fiend*). She adopted her name and substantially her identity from a character – Izé Kranil, a music-hall dancer and prostitute – in the novel *Monsieur de Phocas* (serialised in Paris in 1899) by the ether-drinking Symbolist-Decadent writer Jean Lorrain. I am indebted to William Breeze for knowledge of Kranil.

3   As in his best known poem, entitled '*Non sum qualis eram bonae sub regno Cynarae*' (1896), or Cynara, with its refrain "I have been faithful to thee, Cynara! In my fashion."

clearly tubercular (she is wasted, with feverish "glittering eyes", a bad cough and a deathly pallor but for the symptomatic red patches on her cheeks: "The frightful flush...the rouge of the White Scourge"). She is exquisitely described: the poem manages to include incense, a Circean smile, and repeated attention to jewels ("She hath divers jewels crusted on"). She is also dying ("the dying priestess" in fact) but at the same time dominant and evil ("The snake-cold hate and stealth of her") and "Her slim transparent hand is wan, / As a moonstone, as blue ice": this is the all-important "mystic hand", and the job in hand is "sceptre to sepulchre". "In the half-light her jewels flame / Like stars that presage pestilence...Her death's-head grins the gargoyle shame / Of her virile virulence." She is a *femme fatale* in every sense, in a poem which totally out-Symonses Symons and might even have shocked him.

Not published until 1910, it exceeds the major Nineties writers in its Nineties traits, like a late parody, or decadence itself gone decadently to seed, and if it was by almost anyone but Crowley – buried in a vast corpus of largely disregarded and disreputable witing – it might be better known.

✛

The public fortunes of Nineties decadence rose and fell with those of Oscar Wilde, crashing with Wilde's arrest for homosexual offences in 1895. Crowley had mixed feelings about Wilde. He disliked the later repentant Wilde, but his championing of the earlier Wilde was central, although it is probably fair to say he was at least as interested in the cause as the writing (when it came to literature, he preferred Arthur Machen).[4] The Wilde case was a rallying point for queer identity, and Crowley was the man who proclaimed in 1909 "I shall fight openly for that which no living Englishman dare defend, even in secret – sodomy!"

4   Machen was one of the most notable authors in publisher John Lane's influential Keynotes series, including *The Great God Pan* and *The Three Impostors* (both published by Lane in 1895), and Crowley later included him on the A∴A∴ reading list. He drafted a letter to King George V in July 1930, urging him to grant Machen a Civil List pension as "the greatest living stylist in English prose."

Wilde's supporters saw Lord Alfred Douglas ("Bosie", one of his younger lovers) as the Judas responsible for his downfall, and Crowley wrote two pieces attacking Douglas. His poem 'A Slim Gilt Soul' (1910) takes its title from a phrase in a Wilde letter to Bosie, dragged up by the prosecution during Wilde's trial at the Old Bailey trial fifteen years earlier. His 1913 prose attack 'A Galahad in Gomorrah' (as in Sodom and Gomorrah) confronts the later moralising Douglas (how lucky England is, says Crowley, to have such a "noble soul to protest against decadence") with his earlier homo-erotic poetry.

Crowley was at the 1908 London Ritz dinner for Wildeans, a select event celebrating the posthumous publication of Wilde's *Collected Works*: other guests included Max Beerbohm; Osbert Burdett, author of *The Beardsley Period*; Somerset Maugham; Wilde's early biographer Frank Harris (a friend of Crowley, who considered his Wilde biography "sublime"); H.G. Wells; and Robert Ross, Wilde's more loyal friend. And a few years later in 1914 it was Crowley who staged a dramatic coup at Wilde's tomb in Paris, removing the bronze butterfly – added by the authorities, and acting as a fig leaf – from the tomb's Jacob Epstein sculpture, presenting it to Epstein one night in the Café Royal.

Crowley was, to say the least, intensely aware of Wilde. And like a little insistent voice, quietly lurking in Crowley's later correspondence to his disciple Karl Germer, there is an intriguing slip in a 1925 letter from Tunisia: Crowley is leaving Tunis for Kairouan, he writes, so this is just "a word in wilde haste" [sic]. Crowley's correspondence has been typed up by Karl Germer, so it is not clear whose slip this is; the most interesting possibility is that Germer, transcribing a huge amount of material in his second language, has copied a Freudian-style slip of Crowley's in the original letter. It is still perfectly possible that it is a typo of Germer's[5] but, in a life given so much to signs and wonders, it is like a curious little omen that deserves not to be ignored.

✛

5   Although it is a very clean copy, and the commonest typing error is transposed letters, not the neat addition of an extra letter on a word.

Crowley nevertheless sought to distance himself from decadence. Writing notes for an account of his life in 1924, Crowley claimed that he was really a Puritan: decadents like Wilde and Beardsley had cast an influence in his direction, he writes, but he had been "disgusted by their lack of virility". This seems sincere enough on one level, although you might not guess from it that Crowley had been in a passionate relationship with a female impersonator, or that the man in question – Herbert Pollitt – was a close friend of Beardsley. And, to make a complex relationship more complicated, Crowley says he lived with him as a 'wife'; which is to say, somewhat counter-intuitively, that he was the wife of the impersonator: "I lived with Pollitt as his wife for some six months".

Through Pollitt, Crowley commissioned a Beardsley bookplate and a book design (sick with tuberculosis, Beardsley died in 1898 before he could complete them). In the same circle he was well acquainted with Leonard Smithers, publisher of Wilde, Beardsley, Beerbohm and other figures of the period. Crowley also knew Wilde's friend Ada Leverson, known as "The Sphinx", with whom he had a brief sexual relationship, and describes her in strikingly *fin-de-siècle* terms: she was "one of the best and most loyal friends of Oscar Wilde. She was herself a writer of subtlety and distinction, but she filled me with fascination and horror. She gave me the idea of a devourer of human corpses, being herself already dead. Fierce and grotesque passion sprang up..."

More than just an immediate social network, the Nineties was a rich formative culture Crowley never quite lost, forming a larger background with lasting reference points. Compiling a list of people who might be encouraged to write about his own work, he includes Max Beerbohm, sensational novelist Marie Corelli, poet John Davidson, sexologist Havelock Ellis, Arthur Machen, Swinburne, and Arthur Symons. And hoping to start a new magazine in 1920, he suggests *The Yellow Book*, by then 25 years in the past, among its possible models.

+

The era's decadent tendency co-existed with an equally characteristic 'Counter-Decadence', associated with the poet W.E. Henley, and both tendencies are actively manifest in Crowley without neutralising each other. Henley is remembered for a single great poem, 'Invictus', and it made him a hero to Crowley. Suffering from bone tuberculosis at a young age, Henley had a leg amputated, nearly lost the second, and remained in agonising ill-health for the rest of his life, but 'Invictus' celebrated his unbroken spirit:

> Out of the night that covers me
> Black as the pit from pole to pole,
> I thank whatever gods may be
> For my unconquerable soul.
> [...]
> I am the master of my fate:
> I am the captain of my soul.

'Invictus' has been much admired by figures as disparate as Nelson Mandela and the Oklahoma bomber Timothy McVeigh. For Crowley, it "appealed to my deepest feelings about man's place in the universe; that he is a Titan overwhelmed by the gods but not surrendering." A real poem, he says, should produce "the definitely magical effect of exalting the soul to divine ecstasy", and "Henley's poem conforms with this criterion."

He was still praising it four decades later – along with Kipling's equally robust 1895 poem 'If' – by which time he couldn't recall the title, but cited both poems as the spirit that got London through the Blitz. It is in this sense that Crowley was no doubt quite sincere when he distanced himself from the hopeless pessimism of the decadents, even if the relationship is otherwise so close that any denial seems almost ironic. His admiration for Henley was so great that when he went out to Woking to have lunch with him he was overcome with shyness ("I have never lost the childlike humility which characterized all truly great men"). He later commemorated their meeting in a sonnet to Henley as high priest of Pan. A similar sense of man's place in the universe animates Crowley's poem 'The Titanic': the sinking is not a come-uppance for man's presumption (as in Thomas Hardy's poem on the same subject, 'The Meeting of the Twain') but a minor setback. Man will defy the gods, build more ships, and conquer the Atlantic again with his Promethean powers.

✛

The other great exhilarating inspiration was the German philosopher Friedrich Nietzsche: "Nietzsche was to me almost an avatar of Thoth, the god of wisdom". Nietzsche was a rising force in the *fin-de-siècle*: a translation of *Thus Spake Zarathustra* had been published in 1896 and Nietzsche's ideas on the *ubermensch*, the superman, became well-known in Edwardian London, together with his rejection of Christian values. George Bernard Shaw and others had engaged with his thinking, but few with the bloodthirsty force of Crowley's 1914 essay 'The Vindication of Nietzsche', intended as the introduction to his book of poems, *The Giant's Thumb*.[6] Exulting in the outbreak of the First World War, Crowley looks forward to the imminent annihilation of the British army and the defeat of Britain, seen as a country foolishly defending the values of the Victorian-Christian past against a Germanic-Nietzschean-Crowleyan future.

Apart from Charles Darwin and the poet Swinburne, both endorsed, Britain stands for everything Crowley dislikes: "Progress", "Humanitarianism"; even vegetarians and "Nut-foodists". Against all this – "the anaemia of the Humanitarian, and the hysteria of the Suffragist" – Crowley presents a 'might is right' philosophy of nature red in tooth and claw, as revealed to him in *The Book of the Law*.

"The Germans," writes Crowley, "were the only people who had the common sense, the clear sight, the ability to face, grasp

---

6   The title poem ends with a resurgent Pan triumphing over a dead Queen Victoria. Along with Crowley's best known poem, 'Hymn to Pan', the collection included 'The Titanic', 'Boo to Buddha!', 'Hymn to Satan', 'Eugenics', 'Morphia' and 'Charles Baudelaire'. Dedicated to Theodore Reuss and originally intended for British publication in 1914, it reached the proof stage in America in 1915, but was only published in 1992.

and use the facts which Nietzsche had thundered to the planet." The conquering German has "robbed...enslaved...and murdered" the defeated, "ravished their women and tossed their children on his bayonets, as it was in the beginning, is now, and ever shall be, world without end, Amen. Thus spake Zarathustra. Oh rapture!.... Baptism of rejuvenation! The old world is again bathed in blood; its limbs glow with crimson; it is the angry sunrise of a new aeon, and Apollo shakes himself clear of the dawn-mists, Nietzsche his morning star."

"And if Nietzsche be the dawn-star," he says, "shall there be no son of man to be a Sun of men?" This is Crowley himself as prophet, heralding the future and exulting in the start of the First World War, seen as a Darwinian conflict caused by over-population: "The Chinese (till Europe infected them) murdered all but a few selected female infants, and consequently lived in peace and prosperity for two thousand years. Civilization and the arts flourished...[but] Our squeamishness has forbidden us to take this elementary precaution."

Crowley's endorsement of Nietzsche is so strong it begs the question of why his readers should bother with his own *Book of the Law* in preference to Nietzsche himself, and he has the answer. Not only has Nietzsche become almost over-familiar, but Crowley's own book is more straightforward: "I quote it in preference to Nietzsche, not only because Nietzsche has penetrated from Prussia to Pimlico, and is quoted in Streatham as in Stuttgart, but also because it is simpler than Nietzsche, because there is no possibility of misinterpreting the doctrine..."

One of Nietzsche's most famous works, *Beyond Good and Evil* (1886, translated 1906) is already echoed in Crowley's 'The Stone of the Philosophers' (published in his 1907 book *Konx Om Pax*), and with reference to London housing. Several friends meet in the flat of Arthur Gray, a poet who lives in the proletarian dwelling of Holbein House. Still there near Sloane Square tube station, where Holbein Place meets Pimlico Road, Holbein House is a late-nineteenth-century tenement built by the Guinness Trust (a charitable and reforming initiative founded in 1890 to provide decent housing for the poor, akin to the Peabody Trust). It is now an attractive corner, with the antique shops of the Pimlico Road area in its ground-floor level, but in Edwardian times for Crowley, "Holbein House suggests rather Hogarth" – satirical artist of urban squalor, with works such as *Gin Lane* – "It is one of those sordid barracks where the Martinet of Realism, Society, pens his privates." To see an inhabitant of Holbein House is to understand "the predestination of the damned." At the end of the piece a Socialist has hanged himself with his red necktie, and Arthur Gray has exclaimed "We are all gods!… knowing good and evil, and that which is beyond. But I love Holbein House and London – dear vile London!"

✝

The late Victorian era seemed increasingly the age of the common people – Crowley's pale pigmies and beer-drinking apes, all slaving away in the great London ant heap – especially to those who disliked them. The reaction can be seen in the elitist strand that ran through aestheticism and decadence, with Arthur Symons still wondering in *London: A Book of Aspects* (1909) why ordinary people on Edgware Road "take the trouble to go on existing" given their vulgarity and lack of beauty. It continues into high Modernism,[7] with T.S. Eliot's flock of dead souls commuting to work across London Bridge in *The Waste Land*, and Ezra Pound (in a public park, Kensington Gardens) noting the "filthy, sturdy unkillable infants of the very poor."

Wyndham Lewis, Yeats and even D.H. Lawrence all felt oppressed by the masses, and John Carey comments that when Yeats joined the Golden Dawn in 1890 "it was part of a widespread revival of occultism, centred on Paris, which answered intellectual craving for a source of distinction and power that the masses could not touch." A few years later, further into the Modern period, Lawrence wrote in a letter that he would like to see private publication for an intellectual and spiritual elite: "I disbelieve utterly in the public,

7   See John Carey, *The Intellectuals and the Masses: Pride and Prejudice Among the Literary Intelligentsia 1880-1939* (Faber, 1992): a highly readable treatment of the subject, although inclining to the other extreme with a tendency towards inverted snobbery and 'toff-bashing'.

in humanity, in the mass. There should be again a body of esoteric doctrine, defended from the herd...the sheer essence of man, the sheer supreme understanding...It needs the sanctity of a mystery, the mystery of the initiation into pure being."

Crowley would have understood. In his commentary on *The Book of the Law* he noted that "Humanity errs terribly when it gets 'Education', in the sense of ability to read newspapers. Reason is rubbish; race-instinct is the true guide." This was one of the things he later admired in Hitler's table-talk, as written up by Hermann Rauschning: when Hitler (according to Rauschning) said education was a bad thing and we should keep the lower orders illiterate, Crowley wrote in the margin "Yes". Ordinary intellectuals ("left-wing high-brow Bloomsbury sissies" as he later calls them in *Magick Without Tears*) were no better, and he wrote in his commentary on *The Book of the Law* "the intellectuals are worse than the bourgeoise themselves: *A la lanterne!*" (i.e. "To the lamppost!", the cry of lynch-style hangings in the French Revolution). Or as we might say, "String them up!"

In a particularly intense backlash against the era's slide towards democracy, *The Book of the Law* looked forward to a society where the "few and secret...shall rule the many and the known." In fact, "On the low men trample"; "Ye are against the people, O my chosen!". This defiant elitism is intrinsic to Crowley and his identity as a spiritual aristocrat, from his cynicism about improving hopeless slum-dwellers in his poem 'Eugenics' to his disdain for the spectacular excitements of the popular press: "A piddling little quack-doctor" – Dr Crippen, in Islington in 1910 – "poisons his bitch of a wife and runs off with his fool of a typist – the business of the world is suspended until he is cinematographically hanged."

✢

Considered as an esoteric rejection of the era's rising mass culture, there are striking parallels with Sir Edmund Backhouse (1873-1944), now remembered for his pornographic fantasy memoirs: these are an *almost* plausible account of how he had sexual relations with everybody from Verlaine to the Empress Dowager of China, not forgetting the Prime Minister, Lord Rosebery. They are not the aspect I want to compare with Crowley, but instead his cultural background and stance, following Hugh Trevor-Roper's insight, in his classic study of Backhouse, *A Hidden Life*[8] that Backhouse was extraordinary but he was also a recognisable social phenomenon: "However eccentric... he belongs to a certain category and a certain date."

Backhouse had been an eccentric Oxford undergraduate, collecting gemstones and raising money for the defence of Oscar Wilde. And where Crowley left mundane Victorian Britain behind for the higher realms of the occult, Backhouse – esoteric in another key – left it by going to late-Manchu China and leading the life of a mandarin. In Trevor-Roper's disapproving account,

> From the middle-class traditions of his family he fled to an imaginary aristocratic world; the long Quaker inheritance was cast away; and from the materialism of late Victorian England, he took refuge in the fashionable non-conformity of his time and class; the 'aestheticism', the febrile eroticism, the aggressive, insolent deviation of the 1890s...

For Backhouse, says Trevor-Roper, "all English society, in the 1890s, was vulgar, bourgeois, materialist, and the duty of an aesthete, a superior spirit, was to set itself free from that society, and to signalise its freedom by outraging its conventions". In this reading, Backhouse rejected "the materialism, the philistinism, of Victorian England" in favour of the "elitism, the social and sexual non-conformity, of the

8   (Later editions are titled *Hermit of Peking*.) Trevor-Roper is hard on Backhouse in the book, but privately he may have had more sympathy: "I'm afraid I have a weakness for frauds like the Sobieski Stuarts [Jacobite imposters]; at least if they are *fantaisistes* who live their own fantasies, as they did. We need a touch of fantasy to irradiate this dull world of orderly, respectable virtues. My hero (if I can so describe him) Sir Edmund Backhouse, bart., [baronet] was another such...A certain amiable *snobisme* is, it seems, a necessary ingredient in the character; one escapes from the humdrum world into faery castles, invests oneself with glittering titles..."

1890s" – and the entwined "aestheticism", "sense of superiority" and hatred of "materialism" continued to be the central thread of his life in Peking, with a final transcendence into the high church, in this case deathbed Catholicism.

In later life Backhouse himself wrote of his hatred for "the sordid philistinism of the Victorian era and the drab self-satisfaction of the British middle-classes, scarce other than children playing at the edge of the abyss, into which they have now fallen". The abyss he rejoices in was the Second World War, which seemed to be going badly; again, there is a strong parallel with Crowley's joy at Britain's come-uppance, as it seemed, at the opening of the First World War. Pressing home his point, Trevor-Roper notes an overlap between the "aesthetic elitism" of the late nineteenth century and the "glittering sadistic elitism" of fascism: "It can be seen in Germany, in the Wagner circle."

✣

Crowley's later attitude to fascism is complex, but he was not a Nazi. Despite his Thirties fascination with Hitler (and even his claim to have given Nazism the idea of the swastika), the socialist aspect of National Socialism could never have appealed to him, and totalitarianism, whether fascist or communist, was too collective. He was an individualist, of an ultra-libertarian variety, staying faithful to his revelation of 1904: "Do what thou wilt shall be the whole of the Law."

As an extreme individualist Crowley was a right-wing libertarian, but with his lifelong love of monarchy and ease with slavery he wasn't a right-wing anarchist ("...the kings of the earth shall be Kings for ever: the slaves shall serve.") He was a romantic conservative, and this conservatism is one aspect where he didn't go against his family upbringing: as a teenager he canvassed door-to-door for the Tory party.

Crowley felt himself revolutionary in his militant anti-Christianity, but he is at pains to point out this is not the left-wing atheism of "sordid slum writers and Hyde Park Ranters" (i.e. preachers at Speakers' Corner). Instead, his politics and religion are one: "I hate Christianity as Socialists hate soap", and "it is no idle boast of the vermin socialists that their system is Christianity..."

His politics form a well-worn shape, but more extreme than usual. In the preface to his anti-Christian play *The World's Tragedy* (1910) he is outraged by the idea of state old-age pensions, which parliament was then debating. Pensions are outrageous because they discourage "honest ambition" (evidently old people who have failed to get rich should end up in the workhouse); because they increase taxation; and because the money could be spent on the army and navy. This whole package – no welfare, low taxes, high military spending – is familiar, and it only completes the picture that he advocated increased use of the death penalty and the expulsion of ethnic minorities.[9]

Paradoxically, having made elitism the core of his world view, the swingeing quality of these opinions collapses back into a populist simplicity. It would be naïve not to take the measure of these ideas, but they are not Crowley's most interesting aspect; when we consider him as a romantic conservative, the emphasis should perhaps be on romantic.

In its immediate context, this romantic conservatism includes his love of aristocracy and monarchy. He was a self-described "romantic Jacobite" (like MacGregor Mathers of the Golden Dawn), recognising Charles I as a royal martyr and his descendants as the legitimate monarchs. He similarly supported the Carlists in Spain, wanting to see King Carlos enthroned (one of history's lost causes, the remainder of the

9   Reading news of an Offences Against the Person Bill in the British Parliament (*Times*, 28 February, 1924), modifying the earlier Offences Against the Person Act, Crowley wrote in his diary "I would restore the death penalty for all crimes of violence". The previous year, in an 'Open Letter to Labour', he pontificated on the question of aliens: "Item 46. [The State] shall not allow aliens to possess property...or to live in it for more than one month in any year. Marriage with aliens shall forfeit citizenship. Aliens already domiciled when this constitution comes into force shall be expatriated, with full compensation. Aliens are defined as those whose race, sub-race, or nationality, is not that of the bulk of the citizens. Thus in Australia, all Chinese, Jews, naturalized Italians, and Indians although born in England, would go."

Carlist movement subsumed itself with General Franco in the Spanish Civil War). Crowley always claimed to have a Carlist knighthood for his willingness to participate in an abortive 1899 military coup: "I actually joined a conspiracy on behalf of Don Carlos, obtained a commission to work a machine gun, took pains to make myself a first-class rifle shot..."

More than that, Crowley is romantic in the larger sense, entwined with the Symbolist strand of the Nineties: symbolism was heir (like Crowley himself) to the more extreme aspects of romanticism, particularly in its darker and more gothic aspects. As a tendency which reacted against the progressive eighteenth-century Enlightenment, Romanticism stood for the exploration of the Self and the individual mind, intense extremes of subjective experience, and a strong spiritual aspect – the sense in which it has been labelled as "spilt religion"[10] – amounting to an attempt to recover the state of Man before the Fall, and to close the gap on Paradise.[11] Already spiritual, in its later Symbolist incarnation Romanticism overlapped more explicitly with the occult.

Crowley resonates with the major Romantics in almost every aspect, except one: he would have had no use for their left-leaning tendency or their sympathy for the French Revolution. But this leftward love of the common people had largely fallen away from Nineties romanticism and Symbolism (as in Villiers de L'Isle Adam's insanely aristocratic line "As for living, our servants can do that for

---

10   By T. E. Hulme, in his essay 'Romanticism and Classicism': intended to be hostile, it is perhaps a more resonant and thought-provoking description than Hulme realised. John Bramble, in his book *Modernism and the Occult*, notes the way that Romantic "natural supernaturalism" (another resonant phrase, this time associated with American romantic scholar M.H. Abrams) gave way in the late-nineteenth-century urban world to an "imperial-cosmopolitan supernaturalism" with new "mystico-hypnoid states of mind."

11   The gap is almost closed in this memorable Crowley observation from 1916: "I have been sucking up the vapour of Ether for a few moments, and all common things are touched with beauty...A million spent on objets d'art would not have made this room as beautiful as it is now – and there is not one beautiful thing in it, except myself. Man is a *little* lower than the angels; one step, and all glory is ours."

us.")[12] and it was possible to be a Tory romantic even in the early nineteenth century, notably in the case of Thomas De Quincey, author of *Confessions of an English Opium Eater*. Aside from their 'progressive' tendency, he fits an unmistakably Romantic profile, including their love of mountains and stars, their central subject of the self, their sympathy with Milton's Satan as the true hero of *Paradise Lost*, and their drug use; virtually all the key Romantics except Wordsworth were laudanum users.

This is the tradition where Crowley deserves recognition for his psychic voyaging, as a post-Nineties romantic: using a topaz as a magic gateway, like the mirror in *Alice Through the Looking Glass*, to explore a pre-Enlightenment otherworld last entered by John Dee and Edward Kelley,[13] or gazing at the sublimity of Aldebaran across a desert sky on ether.

Added to this is the sense that the real work of art is the life – a Wildean attitude, coming straight out of aestheticism and ultimately romanticism. The real work is not this painting or that poem, but the artist themselves ("To become a work of art is the object of living")[14]. This was fully in place at the *fin-de-siècle* and leads into the avant-garde project of abolishing the boundary between art and living, so that deliberately taking a walk or sharpening a pencil could be a work of art. The idea that living consciously can be art goes with Crowley's modest but radical claim that anything done deliberately is magic, "causing Change to occur in conformity with Will"; so to publish a book the magician begins with his "'magical weapons'" of "pen, ink and paper."

12   In his 1890 play *Axel*, which features occultism and Rosicrucianism, a castle with hidden treasure, and a romantic double-suicide. The critic Edmund Wilson alludes to it in the title of his study of Symbolism as the transitional movement between Romanticism and Modernism, *Axel's Castle*.

13   In North Africa in 1909, becoming *The Vision and the Voice*.

14   Wilde, cited Beckson, 1996, p.22. Compare "I have put my genius into my life; I have put only my talent into my works" (Gide quoting Wilde in an 1895 letter). This is the life Lord Henry congratulates Dorian Gray on living ("Life has been your art") in *The Picture of Dorian Gray*. Lord Henry also tells Dorian that "The aim of life is self-development. To realize one's nature perfectly – that is what each of us is here for."

Finally, perhaps, he is the most extreme manifestation of the Nineties current, and for this alone he would be significant. The critic Cyril Connolly injected an ominous note into this legacy when he described Crowley as bridging "the gap between Oscar Wilde and Hitler."[15] As we have seen, there is more behind this statement than chronology.

There is even something that chimes with Crowley's identity as "Beast", somewhere in the mix, within the larger ominousness of W.B. Yeats's 1919 poem 'The Second Coming'. This depicts the early twentieth-century world falling into anarchy and the arrival of an anti-Christ, a "rough beast". Against a background of the First World War, the troubles in Ireland, Bolshevism, and the lethal influenza epidemic then sweeping the world, this anti-Christ seems to represent the onset of horrifying times: Yeats had already ended his autobiographical essay 'The Tragic Generation' with the words "After us the Savage God" (arising from his shock at seeing Alfred Jarry's 1896 play *Ubu Roi*).

Yeats disliked Crowley, and if we take the entity in 'The Second Coming' to be entirely negative there might simply be an echo of him somewhere in the word "beast" (conscious or not, and subject only to whether Yeats had ever encountered the word in connection with Crowley – and it is likely he had, since he kept up with old Golden Dawn circles).[16] Along with the obvious echo of the Beast in the *Book*

15   As with Anthony Powell, the Wildean period aspect was more obvious to someone of Connolly's generation (born 1903); he never met Crowley, but Crowley sent him a poem after reading his book *The Unquiet Grave*.

16   After the schisms of 1900, Yeats became head of the Isis-Urania Lodge from 1901 until 1905. He was also associated with the Stella Matutina until it ended in 1923 (this continued the original magical emphasis of the old Golden Dawn, as opposed to A.E. Waite's more Christian-mystical turn) and he continued a friendship with Mathers's widow Moina (Mathers having died in the influenza epidemic). His prose work *A Vision* (1925) has a lengthy dedication to her. Yeats's father also met Crowley in the States and they compared notes. Meanwhile Crowley had adopted his Beast identity around 1904, gradually making it more public, and he solidly identified as Great Beast 666 by the time of his New York period and Magus initiation, 1915-18, taking the magical motto *To Mega Therion*: the Great Beast.

of *Revelation*, whose number is 666, the poem reflects the Golden Dawn background Yeats was steeped in. Its Egyptian mindscape (with a sphinx in a desert) is relatively uncommon in Yeats compared to his Celtic, Greek and Hindu imagery, but it revisits the world of the Golden Dawn, and one of the poem's autobiographical associations is Yeats's memory of a vision during his magical apprenticeship with Mathers. Sometime in 1890 or 1891 he was visiting Mathers down at Forest Hill, near the Horniman Museum, when Mathers asked him to concentrate on a card with an elemental fire symbol, and Yeats saw a Titan rising from desert ruins.

What makes the whole picture more complex is Yeats's ambivalence. The beast, although uncouth and terrible, is at the same time not to be wholly identified or confused with the "mere anarchy" at the beginning of the poem; it is also something that arrives to fill the vacuum, as if desperate times call for desperate remedies. And instead of being reducible to an apocalyptic ugliness on the horizon, some of Yeats's comments relevant to the poem show a greater sympathy with the coming era than a first reading might suggest.

Yeats believed history ran in cycles (as expounded in his monumental prose work *A Vision*, partly 'channelled' by his wife Georgie) and that the present Christian era would be replaced by an age of greater "personality" (after Christianity had tended to efface individualism). His further associations around the beast include "ecstatic destruction", and that the next era will bring the sudden reversal of "our scientific, democratic, fact-accumulating, heterogenous civilisation" into its opposite. As another admirer of Nietzsche, who also craved "a world made wholly of essences"[17] this reversal of a vulgarly democratic, rational, mongrelised and jumbled culture was hardly uncongenial to Yeats's thinking.

As the poem moves towards its climax, Yeats has a sudden vision from the words "The Second Coming!". It is "a vast image out

17   In his 1897 story 'Rosa Alchemica', the first of his fictions to feature Michael Robartes, a character inspired by Mathers, the Yeats-like narrator talks of his own magical-alchemical studies in terms of "the transmutation of life into art, and a cry of measureless desire for a world made wholly of essences."

of *Spiritus Mundi*" (the spirit of the world, described by Yeats as "a general storehouse of images", like a collective unconscious or neo-Platonic collective memory: a further legacy of his apprenticeship with Mathers). This image is the sphinx creature in the desert, awoken and coming into its own after a two-thousand year period.

Rather than 'being' Crowley, Yeats's beast is the spirit of an age, and the poem's undeniable confluence with a Crowley world – the Golden Dawn-style Egyptian imagery; the actual link with Mathers; the allusion to the Beast in *Revelation*; the end of Christianity; history running in distinct eras; the future anti-democratic and bloody, but not without a glory of its own – is the legacy of Yeats and Crowley's overlapping backgrounds in Nineties esotericism. And now, as one era leads into the spectre of another arising in the apocalyptic closing lines,

> ...what rough beast, its hour come round at last,
> Slouches toward Bethlehem to be born?

NOTES

"...'post-decadent...'": Anthony Powell, 'Life with Crowley' [rev. of Symonds *Great Beast* and Cammell *Aleister Crowley*], *Times Literary Supplement*, 14 December 1951, p.803.
"...as a 'Nineties' figure...": d'Arch Smith, *Times Deceas'd* p.111.
"...*fin de siècle* occultist...": Christopher Partridge, 'Aleister Crowley on Drugs', *Int. Jnl. for the Study of New Religion*, vol.7 no.2 (February 2017).
"...modus operandi...": Alex Owen, *The Place of Enchantment* (Chicago, 2004) p.213.
'Eugenics': in *The Giant's Thumb* (Thame, First Editions, 1992)
"...dark portion of the mind...": Yeats, 'The Trembling of the Veil' in *Autobiographies*, p.373.
"...bringing the unconscious...": Notebook, March 1920, Yorke collection OS A9.
"...sophisticated and even Satanic...": Richard Le Gallienne, *The Romantic '90s*, p.192.
"Dyahbolism": Max Beerbohm, 'First Meetings with W.B. Yeats', *The Listener*, 6 January 1955.

"Fra Angelico of Satanism": Roger Fry, 'Aubrey Beardsley's Drawings', *Athenaeum* no.4019, 5 November 1904.
"Catholic diabolist": Beerbohm, 'Enoch Soames', in *Seven Men and Two Others* p.15; good and evil pp.8-9; "Thou hast not…" p.17. His poem 'Nocturne' begins "Round and round the shutter'd square / I stroll'd with the Devil's arm in mine…"
"till you become as gods…"; "…which two also are one.": 'Absinthe: The Green Goddess', *The International*, February 1918.
"…take wine and strange drugs…": Liber AL II.22; "Burn to me perfumes!": Liber AL I.63. Francis King has also noted that *The Book of the Law* is written in "a heavily jewelled prose strongly reminiscent of some of the writers of the 1890s": *Magical World of Aleister Crowley*, p.35.
"Our Lady of Dreams": e.g. "Invocation of Our Lady of Dreams" [opium], 27 January 1918, *The Magical Record of the Beast 666*, p.69.
"Our Lady of Darkness"; "strange floating perfumes"; "epicene boy": 'At the Feet of Our Lady of Darkness', *The International*, February 1918.
Symons "a faint smell of patchouli", 'Being A Word On Behalf of Patchouli', preface to *Silhouettes* (1896).
'In Manu Dominae': in *The Winged Beetle* (1910).

✛

Letter to George V re Machen: diary draft, 2.vii.1930.
Wilde as rallying point: "Oscarizing" or to "Oscarize" became a period slang for sodomy. Crowley alludes to the scandal around Wilde's name in his parody of the *Looking Glass* court case:

> K.C: What was Mr Eckenstein's Christian name?
> Mathers: I – er – see there are ladies in court.
> Judge: Any ladies in this Court are probably beyond any scruples of that sort.
> K.C. Answer the question.
> Mathers: Oscar. (*sensation*)
> At this point Counsel fainted[…] (*The Rosicrucian Scandal*, in Robertson, *Scrapbook*, p.73)

The 'ladies in court' observation borrows something that was actually said in the case. More generally, as an indicator of early twentieth-century attitudes and notorieties, in 1930 a man named L.A.G. Strong, in a letter to Yeats, mentioned a lovesick chaplain whose loved one's parents thought he was so utterly, utterly frightful they regarded him as "a mixture of Wilde and Aleister Crowley": 3 April 1930, *Letters to W.B. Yeats*, Vol.II (Macmillan, 1997).
"…fight openly for that which no living Englishman dare defend….": 'Sodomy' section of the Preface to *The World's Tragedy*, p.xxvi.
'A Slim Gilt Soul': in *The Winged Beetle*.
"…to protest against decadence": 'A Galahad in Gomorrah', *The Equinox* Vol.I no.9 (1913).
1908 Ritz dinner for Wildeans: the seating plan is reproduced in *An Angel for a Martyr* p.4. Crowley was at a satellite table with Mr and Mrs Curtis Brown, J.C. Johnson and C.F. Richardson.

Harris's Wilde biography "sublime": written at the back of Crowley's December 1923 to February 1924 diary, Yorke collection OS A7. ("His biography 'Oscar Wilde' is a masterpiece utterly [illeg.] sublime and just.")
"a word in wilde haste": to Karl Germer from Tunis, 2 December 1925 {OTO}.

✣

"...by their lack of virility": point 11 in Crowley's numbered points for an account of his life, rue Vavin diary (March-April 1924), Yorke OS A12.
"...lived with Pollitt as his wife...": Crowley annotation to A.C. Benson's 1897 novel *The Babe B.A.*, which features Pollitt, Kac.40.
Commissioned Beardsley: Kac.38.
"...best and most loyal friends of Oscar Wilde...": Hag.558.
List of people to write about his work: 'Authors to write on AC', Yorke OS 23.
Models for magazine: 'Proposed new magazine', Magical Diary 1920, Yorke OS A9. The other two are the "old" *English Review* and the *New Yorker*.
Titan; poetry and ecstasy; Henley: Hag.345.
'Invictus', Kipling's 'If' and Blitz: *Magick Without Tears*. Ch.XVI 'On Concentration'.
"...childlike humility...": Hag.349.
Sonnet to Henley: 'W.E. Henley' in *Rodin in Rime* (London, S.P.R.T., 1907).
'The Titanic': *The Equinox* Vol.1 no.9.

✣

Nietzsche "almost an avatar of Thoth": Hag.746.
'The Vindication of Nietzsche', written as introduction to Crowley's book of poems, *The Giant's Thumb*, pp.vii-xxi of the1992 edition. All further quotes from these pages.
'The Stone of the Philosophers' [1907], in Crowley, *The Drug and Other Stories*, ed. William Breeze (Wordsworth Editions, 2010), pp.49; 75.

✣

"...trouble to go on existing": Symons, *London: A Book of Aspects* (Privately Printed [Chiswick Press, Took's Court], 1909) p.71.
"...a source of distinction and power that the masses could not touch": Carey, *The Intellectuals and the Masses*, p.71.
  Certainly some of the intellectual sentiments found by Carey make even *The Book of the Law* seem less out on a limb, from "The great mass of humanity should never learn to read and write", with schools closed, boys studying "primitive modes of fighting" and girls studying cookery and suchlike (D.H. Lawrence, cited p.15) to respected late 19th and early 20th century writer George Moore: "Art is the direct antitheisis to democracy"; "Pity, that most vile of all vile virtues, has never been known to me. The great pagan world I love knew it not... [nature decrees] the weak shall be trampled upon, shall be ground into death and dust"; "Injustice we worship; all that lifts us out of the misery of life is the sublime fruit of injustice. Every immortal deed was an act of fearful injustice...

What care I that some millions of wretched Israelites died under Pharaoh's lash or Egypt's sun. It was well that they died that I might have the pyramids to look on...What care I that the virtue of some sixteen-year old maiden was the price paid for Ingres' [painting] *La Source?*... Nay more, the knowledge that a wrong was done – that millions of Israelites died in torments, that a girl, or a thousand girls, died in hospital for that one virginal thing, is an added pleasure that I could not afford to spare.... Oh, for excess, for crime! I would give many lives to save one sonnet by Baudelaire..." (etc.: cited Carey pp.55-56).

"...esoteric doctrine, defended from the herd...": Lawrence, letter to Waldo Frank, 27 July 1917, *Letters of D.H. Lawrence* vol.VII November 1928-February 1930 eds. Sagar and Boulton (CUP 1993) p.143.

"Humanity errs terribly...": *Magical and Philosophical Commentaries on the Book of the Law*, ed. Symonds and Grant (Montreal, 93 publishing, 1974) Ch.II.27, p.203. Annotated Rauschning {OTO}.

"...Bloomsbury sissies": *Magick Without Tears* Ch.XVI 'On Concentration'.

"...*A la lanterne!*": *Magical and Philosophical Commentaries on the Book of the Law*, Ch.II.27.

"...the many and the known.": Liber AL I.10

"...low men trample": Liber AL II.24

"...against the people, O my chosen!": Liber AL II.25

"...little quack-doctor...": 'The Vindication of Nietzsche'

+

Trevor-Roper letters show sympathy: letter to James Stourton, 5 October 1986, *One Hundred Letters from Hugh Trevor-Roper*, pp.312-13.

"...certain category and a certain date": Hugh Trevor-Roper, *A Hidden Life*, p.294.

Gemstones, Wilde: Trevor-Roper op.cit. p.18.

"...middle-class traditions of his family...": op.cit. 279.

"...English society, in the 1890s, was vulgar...": op.cit. 280.

"...elitism, the social and sexual non-conformity, of the 1890s": op.cit. 294.

"...sordid philistinism of the Victorian era...": op.cit. 280.

"glittering sadistic elitism"; Wagner circle": op.cit. 296.

+

Claim to have given Nazism the idea of the swastika: "I personally suggested it to Ludendorff in '25 or '26": annotation to Rauschning p.212 {OTO}.

"Do what thou wilt shall be the whole of the law.": Liber AL I.40.

"...the kings of the earth shall be Kings for ever....": Liber AL II.58.

Canvassed door-to-door (in Cirencester, aged 14) for the Tory party: to Germer 2 December 1938 {OTO}.

"...slum writers and Hyde Park Ranters": Hag.539.

"...hate Christianity as Socialists hate soap": review of McTaggart, *Dare to be Wise*, in *Equinox* Vol.no.4 (1910), p.239.

"...boast of the vermin socialists...": 'Preface to *The World's Tragedy* (1910) p.xxxii.
"honest ambition" and pensions ("the official seal upon the survival of the unfittest"): op.cit. xxxii.
Death penalty: diary 28 February 1924, Yorke OS H4.
Ethnic minorities: 'Open Letter to Labour', Yorke OS H3.
"romantic Jacobite": Hag.121.
"...a conspiracy on behalf of Don Carlos...": Hag.121.
"spilt religion": T.E. Hulme, 'Romanticism and Classicism' in *Speculations* ed. Herbert Read, p.118.
"mystico-hypnoid...": Bramble, *Modernism and the Occult*, p.143.
"...sucking up the vapour of Ether for a few moments, and all common things are touched...": 'Diary of a Magus' (23 August 1916) {OTO}.
"...servants can do that for us": cited Edmund Wilson, *Axel's Castle* (Penguin, 1993) p.263.
Topaz: "...a part not unlike that of the looking-glass in Alice": Hag.616. The comparison with romanticism needs the caveat that Crowley seems to know what he wants to find in the world of *The Vision and the Voice* – a world Dee and Kelley would hardly have recognised – and it seems concordant with *The Book of the Law*, making these experiments as much a part of the history of "revealed" religion as of mental voyaging.
Aldebaran on ether: to Norman Mudd from Tunisia, October 1923, cited Symonds (1997) p.354.
"...put my genius into my life...": Gide quoting Wilde in an 1895 letter, cited Beckson p.75.
"Life has been your art": Wilde, *The Picture of Dorian Gray* ed. Isobel Murray (O.U.P., 1974) p.217.
"The aim of life is self-development. To realize one's nature..." Wilde op.cit. p.17.
"...to occur in conformity with Will"; "'magical weapons'"; "pen, ink and paper": *Magick* p.131.
"...gap between Oscar Wilde and Hitler": Cyril Connolly, 'Engendering Monsters', *Sunday Times*, 14 November 1971.
Crowley sent Connolly a poem after reading Connolly's *Unquiet Grave*: ibid.
"After us the Savage God": Yeats, The Trembling of the Veil' in *Autobiographies* (Macmillan, 1955) p.349.
Yeats's father met Crowley: John Butler Yeats to W.B. Yeats, 18 December 1914, in *Letters to W.B. Yeats*, ed. Finneran, Harper and Murphy (Macmillan, 1977) pp.309-10.
Yeats's vision of a Titan: *Autobiographies*, 185-6.
Age of greater "personality": Ellmann, *The Identity of Yeats*, p.258.
"ecstatic destruction": Yeats in Ellman op.cit. p.258 n.5.
"...scientific, democratic, fact-accumulating, heterogenous civilisation": Yeats's note to *Michael Robartes and the Dancer*, cited Ellman op.cit.p.258.
Yeats as admirer of Nietzsche: see e.g. Carey, *The Intellectuals and the Masses* p.4.
Yeats describes him as "a counteractive to the spread of democratic vulgarity."
"...world made wholly of essences": 'Rosa Alchemica', in Yeats, *Mythologies* (Macmillan, 1959) p.267.

Not without a glory of its own: despite Yeats's faith in the return of an ideal and peaceful past of "workman, noble, and saint" ('The Gyres', 1937), when he was asked in 1937 for a message for India he picked up a samurai sword and said "Conflict, more conflict!". See Joseph Hone, *W.B. Yeats 1865-1939* (Macmillan, 1962) p.459.

"storehouse of images": Yeats on *Spiritus Mundi*, "a general storehouse of images which have ceased to be a property of any personality or spirit", in his note to *Michael Robartes and the Dancer*, in Jeffares, *A New Commentary on the Poems of W.B. Yeats* p.204. There is a similar idea in his 1901 essay 'Magic'.

BIBLIOGRAPHY

Aberconway, Christabel, *A Wiser Woman?* (Hutchinson, 1966)
[Abramelin] Mathers, Samuel Liddel MacGregor (ed.), *The Book of the Sacred Magic of Abra-Melin the Mage* (Watkins, 1898)
Anand, Mulk Raj, *Conversations in Bloomsbury* (New Delhi, Arnold-Heinemann, 1981)
Anand, Mulk Raj, *Curries* (Desmond Harmsworth, 1932)
Anson, Peter, *Bishops At Large* (Faber, 1964)
Archer, Ethel, *The Hieroglyph* (Dennis Archer, 1932)
Baker, Phil, 'Secret City: Psychogeography and the End of London' in *London from Punk to Blair*, ed. Joe Kerr and Andrew Gibson (Reaktion, 2003)
Bankes, Viola, *Why Not?* (Jarrolds, 1934)
Bax, Clifford, *Inland Far* (Heinemann, 1925)
[Beardsley] *Aubrey Beardsley: A Catalogue Raisonné* ed. Linda Gertner Zatlin (Yale, 2016)
Beerbohm, Max, 'Enoch Soames', in *Seven Men and Two Others* (Heinemann, 1950) [1919]
Beerbohm, Max, 'First Meetings with W.B. Yeats', *The Listener*, 6 January 1955
Bogdan, Henrik, 'Aleister Crowley: A Prophet for the Modern Age' in Partridge (2015)
Booth, Martin, *A Magick Life* (Hodder and Stoughton, 2000)
Booth, Martin, *Cannabis* (Doubleday, 2003)
Bowker, Gordon, *George Orwell* (Abacus, 2003)
Bramble, John, *Modernism and the Occult* (NY, Palgrave Macmillan, 2015)
Brodie, Fawn M., *The Devil Drives: A Life of Sir Richard Burton* (Eyre and Spottiswoode, 1967)
Bromage, Bernard, 'Aleister Crowley', *Light* Vol.LXXIX no.3440 (Autumn 1959)
Brook, Peter, *Threads of Time: A Memoir* (Methuen, 1998)
Brooks, Collin, *Tavern Talk* (Barrie, 1950)
Brooks, Collin, *More Tavern Talk* (Barrie, 1952)
Brown, Mick, *Performance* (Bloomsbury, 2000)
Bulwer-Lytton, Edward, *Zanoni* (Saunders and Otley, 1842)
Burke, Thomas, *Living in Bloomsbury* (George Allen and Unwin, 1939)
Burnett-Rae, Alan, *A Memoir of 666* (London, Victim Press, 1971)
Burroughs, William, *Junky* (Penguin, 1977)
Burton, Sir Richard, *The Book of the Thousand Nights and a Night* (Benares, Kamashastra Society, 1885)
Caine, William, *The Author of Trixie* (Herbert Jenkins, 1934)
Calder-Marshall, Arthur, *The Magic of My Youth* (Cardinal, 1990) [1951]

Calder-Marshall, Arthur, 'Full of Rich Dirt' [rev. of *Magick and White Stains*] *Times Literary Supplement* 27 July 1973

Calloway, Stephen, *Aubrey Beardsley* (V&A, 2020)

Cammell, C.R., Aleister Crowley: The Man: The Mage: The Poet (The Richards Press, 1951)

Carey, John, *The Intellectuals and the Masses* (Faber, 1992)

Casaubon, Meric, *A True & Faithful Relation of what passed for many years between Dr John Dee and some spirits [...]* (T. Garthwait, 1659)

Chancellor, E. Beresford, *Literary Ghosts of London: Homes and Footprints of Famous Men and Women* (Richards, 1933)

Churton, Tobias, *Aleister Crowley: The Biography* (Watkins, 2011)

Churton, Tobias, *Aleister Crowley In England* (Rochester, Vermont, Inner Traditions, 2021)

Clayton, Antony, *Decadent London* (Historical Publications, 2005)

Cockren, Archibald, *Alchemy Rediscovered and Restored* (Rider, 1940)

Colquhoun, Ithell, *Sword of Wisdom: MacGregor Mathers and the Golden Dawn* (Spearman, 1975)

Connolly, Cyril, 'Engendering monsters', [rev. of Symonds' *The Great Beast* and other books] *Sunday Times* 14 Nov 1971

Coster, Iain, 'The Worst Man in London', *The Inky Way Annual II* (World's Press, 1948)

Cross, Harold H.U., *The Lust Market* (Torchstream Books, n.d. c.1950s)

Crowley, Aleister, *Aceldama* (privately printed, 1898)

Crowley, *De Arte Magica* (Edmonds WA., Sure Fire Press, 1988) [1914]

Crowley [and/or Izeh Krani], 'At the Feet of Our Lady of Darkness', *The International*, February 1918

Crowley, *Bagh-I-Muattar: The Scented Garden of Abdullah the Satirist of Shiraz* (Privately Printed, 1910)

Crowley, 'Behind The Front: Impressions of a Tourist in Western Europe', *The Fatherland* (New York) Vol.III no.21, 29 December 1915

Crowley, *The Book of the Law (Liber AL)*, ed. William Breeze (York Beach, Weiser, 2004) [1904; 1926]

Crowley, *The Book of Lies* (Wieland, 1913)

Crowley, *The Confessions of Aleister Crowley* ed. John Symonds and Kenneth Grant (Cape, 1969)

Crowley, *The Diary of a Drug Fiend* (Colins, 1922)

Crowley, *The Drug and Other Stories*, ed. William Breeze (Wordsworth Editions, 2010)

Crowley, 'Energized Enthusiasm', *The Equinox* Vol.1 No.9 (Spring 1913)

Crowley, 'A Galahad in Gomorrah', *The Equinox* Vol.1 no.9 (Spring 1913)

Crowley, *The Giant's Thumb*, ed. Anthony Naylor (Thame, First Editions, 1992) [1915]

Crowley, *The Goetia: The Lesser Key of Solomon the King*, ed. William Breeze (York Beach, Weiser, 1995) [1904]

Crowley, 'The Green Goddess', *The International*, February 1918

Crowley, 'The Herb Dangerous: The Psychology of Hashish', *The Equinox* Vol.1 no.1 (1909)

Crowley, 'The Initiated Interpretation of Ceremonial Magick', in *The Goetia* (1904; 1995)

Crowley, 'John St. John', *The Equinox*, Vol.1, No.1 (1909)

Crowley, *The Magical Diaries of Aleister Crowley: Tunisia 1923* ed. Stephen Skinner (Neville Spearman, 1979)

Crowley, *Magical and Philosophical Commentaries on the Book of the Law*, ed. Symonds and Grant (Montreal, 93 publishing, 1974)

Crowley, *The Magical Record of the Beast 666*, ed. John Symonds and Kenneth Grant (Duckworth, 1972)

Crowley, *Magick*, ed. John Symonds and Kenneth Grant (Routledge & Kegan Paul, 1973) [1911;1912; 1929]

Crowley, *Magick Without Tears*, ed. Karl Germer (Hampton NJ, Thelema Publishing Co., 1954)

Crowley, *Moonchild*, ed. John Symonds and Kenneth Grant (Sphere, 1972) [1929]

Crowley, 'My Crapulous Contemporaries: The Bismarck of Battersea', *The Equinox* Vol.1 No.7 (Spring 1912)

Crowley, 'My Crapulous Contemporaries: An Obituary', *The Equinox* Vol.1 no.8 (Autumn 1912)

Crowley, 'My Wanderings in Search of the Absolute', *Sunday Referee*, 10 March 1935

Crowley, 'The Revival of Magick' Part 1, *The International*, Vol. XI, no.8. August 1917

Crowley, *Rodin in Rime* (London, S.P.R.T., 1907)

Crowley, ed. Regardie, *Roll Away the Stone* (St. Paul, Minn., Llewellyn Publications, 1968)

Crowley, 'The Stone of the Philosophers', in *The Drug and Other Stories* (Wordsworth, 2010)

Crowley, 'The Temple of Solomon the King', *The Equinox*, Vol.1 no.3 (Spring 1910)

Crowley, *The Rosicrucian Scandal*, in Robertson 1988 [1911]

Crowley, 'The Titanic', *The Equinox* Vol.1 no.9 (Spring 1913)

Crowley, *The Winged Beetle* (privately printed, 1910)

Crowley, *The World's Tragedy* (Paris, privately printed, 1910)

[Crowley] ed. Frieda Harris, *Aleister Crowley, October 18th [sic] 1875 – December 1st, 1947. The last ritual, read from his own works, according to his wish, on December 5th, 1947, at Brighton* (privately printed, 1947)

Cullen, Tom, *The Man Who Was Norris* (Sawtry, Dedalus, 2014)

Curtis, Anthony, *Lit. Ed.: On Reviewing and Reviewers* (Carcanet, 1998)

Deghy, Guy, and Keith Waterhouse, *Café Royal: Ninety Years of Bohemia* (Hutchinson, 1955)

Driberg, Tom, 'A Mixed Bag of Early Birds', *Daily Express*, 23 December 1937

Driberg, Tom, *Ruling Passions* (Cape, 1977)

Ellmann, Richard, *The Identity of Yeats* (Macmillan, 1954)

Epstein, Jacob, *Epstein: An Autobiography* (Hulton Press, 1955)

Fabian, Robert, *London After Dark* (Naldrett Press, 1954)

Farson, Daniel, *Soho in the Fifties* (Michael Joseph, 1987)

Fitzgibbon, Constantine, *The Life of Dylan Thomas* (Dent, 1965)

Foster, Roy, *Yeats: A Life: The Apprentice Mage* (OUP, 1997)

Fry, Roger, 'Aubrey Beardsley's Drawings', *Athenaeum* no.4019, 5 November 1904

Fuller, Jean Overton, *The Magical Dilemma of Victor Neuburg* (Mandrake, 1990)

Fuller, J.F.C., [John Frederick Charles] 'Aleister Crowley 1898-1911: An Introductory Essay' in *Bibliotheca Crowleyana* [sale catalogue] (Tenterden, Keith Hogg, 1966)

Fuller, J.F.C., [as 'Sam Hardy'] 'Half Hours with Famous Mahatmas', *The Equinox*, Vol.1 no.4. (Autumn 1910)

Fuller, J.F.C., *The Star in the West: A Critical Essay upon the Works of Aleister Crowley* (Walter Scott Publishing Co., 1907)

Fuller, J.F.C., *Yoga: A Study of the Mystical Philosophy of the Brahmins and Buddhists* (Rider, 1925)

Gilbert, R.A., *The Golden Dawn Scrapbook: The Rise and Fall of A Magical Order* (York Beach, Weiser, 1997)

Gilbert, R.A., 'The Hermetic Order of the Golden Dawn' in Partridge (2015)

Gilbert, R.A., 'Seeking That Which Was Lost: More Light on the Origins and Development of the Golden Dawn', *Yeats Annual 14* (Basingstoke, Palgrave Macmillan, 2001)

Gilbert, R.A., *A.E. Waite: Magician of Many Parts* (Wellingborough, Crucible, 1987)

Gonne, Maud, *A Servant of the Queen: Reminiscences* (Gollancz, 1938)

Grant, Kenneth and Steffi, *Zos Speaks!* (Fulgur, 1998)

Greene, Graham, *Graham Greene: A Life In Letters* ed. Richard Greene (Little, Brown 2007)

Hamilton, Gerald, *Mr Norris and I* (Allen Wingate, 1956)

Hamilton, Gerald, *The Way It Was With Me* (Leslie Frewin, 1969)

Hamnett, Nina, *Laughing Torso* (Constable, 1932)

Harper, George Mills, *Yeats's Golden Dawn* (Macmillan, 1974)

Harper, George Mills (ed.) *Yeats and the Occult* (Macmillan, 1976)

Hawtree, Christopher [ed.] *Night and Day* (Chatto and Windus, 1985) [1937]

Heseltine, Philip, *The Collected Letters of Peter Warlock Vol. IV 1922-30* ed. Barry Smith (Woodbridge, Boydell Press, 2015)

Hoare, Philip, *Oscar Wilde's Last Stand* (Duckworth, 1997)

Hogg, Keith, *Bibliotheca Crowleyana* [sale catalogue] (Tenterden, 1966)

Hone, Joseph M., *W.B. Yeats 1882-1959* (Macmillan, 1962)

Hooton-Smith, Eileen, *The Restaurants of London* (London, Knopf, 1928)

Howe, Ellic, *The Magicians of the Golden Dawn: A Documentary History of a Magical Order 1887-1923* (Routledge & Kegan Paul, 1973)

Howe, Ellic, and Helmut Moller, 'Theodor Reuss: Irregular Freemasonry in Germany, 1900-1923', *Ars Quatuorum Coronatorum*, vol.91 (1978) pp.28-46

Hulme, T.E., *Speculations* ed. Herbert Read (Routledge & Kegan Paul, 1936)

[I Ching], trans. James Legge, 'Part II: The Yi King', in *The Sacred Books of China: Confucianism* (Oxford, Clarendon, 1882)

Irwin, Robert, *Satan Wants Me* (Dedalus, 1999)

Jackson, Stanley, *An Indiscreet Guide to Soho* (London, Muse Arts, n.d. [c.1950])

Jay, Mike, *Mescaline: A Global History* (Yale, 2019)

John, Augustus, *The Autobiography of Augustus John* ed. Michael Holroyd (Cape, 1975)

John, Augustus, *Chiaroscuro: Fragments of Autobiography* (Cape, 1954)

Josiffe, Christopher, 'Aleister Crowley, Marie de Miramar and the True Wanga', *Abraxas Journal* no.4 (2013)

Kaczynski, Richard, *Perdurabo* (Berkeley, North Atlantic Books, 2010)

King, Francis, *The Magical World of Aleister Crowley* (Weidenfeld and Nicolson, 1977)

King, Francis, *Ritual Magic in England: 1887 to the Present Day* (Neville Spearman, 1970)

King, Francis, *Sexuality, Magic and Perversion* (Neville Spearman, 1971)

La Fontaine, Jean, *Speak of the Devil: Tales of Satanic Abuse in Contemporary England* (Cambridge University Press, 1998)

Lachman, Gary, *Aleister Crowley: Magic, Rock and Roll, and the Wickedest Man in the World* (Penguin Tarcher, 2014)

Lachman, Gary, *Turn Off Your Mind: the Mystic Sixties and the Dark Side of the Age of Aquarius* (Sidgwick & Jackson, 2001)

Laite, Julia, *Common Prostitutes and Ordinary Citizens: commercial sex in London, 1885-1960* (Basingstoke, Palgrave Macmillan, 2012)

Lamburn, Joan, 'Letters to Alyse Gregory 1941-1943', *The Powys Journal*, XXVI (2016)

Laver, James, *Museum Piece* (Andre Deutsch, 1963)

Lawrence, D.H., *The Letters of D.H. Lawrence*, vol.7, ed. Sagar and Boulton (C.U.P. 1993)

Le Gallienne, Richard, *The Romantic '90s* (Putnams, 1926)

Levi, Eliphas, *Transcendental Magic: Its Doctrine and Ritual*, translated and introduced by A.E. Waite (Rider, 1923)

Lewis, Jeremy, *Cyril Connolly: A Life* (Pimlico, 1998)

London Encyclopaedia, The, ed. Ben Weinreb and Christopher Hibbert (Macmillan, 1993)

Macdonell, A.G., *England Their England* (Macmillan, 1933)

Machen, Arthur, *Things Near and Far* (Secker, 1923)

Maddox, Brenda, *George's Ghosts: A New Life of W.B. Yeats* (Picador, 1999)

Mannin, Ethel, *Confessions and Impressions* (Jarrolds, 1930)

Marlow, Louis [pseud. Louis Umfreville Wilkinson], *Seven Friends* (The Richards Press, 1954)

Marsh, Ngaio, *Death in Ecstasy* (Geoffrey Bles, 1936)

May, Betty, *Tiger Woman* (Duckworth, 2014) [1929]

Medway, Gareth, *The Lure of the Sinister: The Unnatural History of Satanism* (New York University Press, 2001)

[Montalban] 'Frontiers of Belief: Madeline Montalban', in *Man Myth and Magic* no.23, 1970

Morgan, Ted, *Literary Outlaw: The Life and Times of William S. Burroughs* (Bodley Head, 1991)

Murray, Paul, *From the Shadow of Dracula: a Life of Bram Stoker* (Cape, 2004)

Nelson, James G., *Publisher to the Decadents* [Smithers] (Pennsylvania State University Press, 2000)

Newnham-Davis, Lieut.-Col. N., *The Gourmet's Guide to London* (NY, Brentano's, 1914)

O'Donnell, Elliot, *Rooms of Mystery* (Philip Allan and Co., 1931)

Owen, Alex, *The Place of Enchantment* (Chicago UP, 2004)

Owen, Alex, 'The Sorcerer and His Apprentice: Aleister Crowley and the Magical Exploration of Edwardian Subjectivity', *The Journal of British Studies*, 1997-01, Vol.36 (1)

Owen, Lady Edmée, *Flaming Sex: Her Own Life Story* (John Long, 1934)

Owen, Lady Edmée, *The Sleepless Underworld* (John Long, 1935)

Partridge, Christopher, 'Aleister Crowley on Drugs', *Int. Jnl. for the Study of New Religion*, vol.7 no.2

Partridge, Christopher, (ed.) *The Occult World* (Routledge, 2015)

Pasi, Marco, *Aleister Crowley and the Temptation of Politics* (Durham, Acumen, 2014)

Pennington, Michael, *An Angel for a Martyr: Jacob Epstein's Tomb for Oscar Wilde* (Reading, Whiteknights Press, 1977)

Plomer, William, *At Home: Memoirs* (Cape, 1958)

Powell, Anthony, *The Acceptance World* (Heinemann, 1955)

Powell, Anthony, *Casanova's Chinese Restaurant* (Heinemann, 1960)

Powell, Anthony, *Faces In My Time* (Heinemann, 1980)

Powell, Anthony, 'Life with Crowley' [rev. of Symonds *Great Beast* and Cammell *Aleister Crowley*], *Times Literary Supplement*, 14 December 1951

Powell, Anthony, *Messengers of Day* (Heinemann, 1978)

Raine, Kathleen, *Yeats, the Tarot and the Golden Dawn* (Dublin, Dolmen Press, 1972)

Randolph, Paschal Beverly, *Eulis!* (Toledo, Randolph Publishing Co., 1874)

Rauschning, Hermann, *Hitler Speaks* (Thornton Butterworth, 1939)

Regardie, Israel, *The Eye in the Triangle* (Phoenix, Falcon Press, 1982) [1970]

Richardson, Maurice, 'Emperor of Hocus Pocus', *Observer*, 26 October 1969

Richardson, Maurice, 'Luncheon with Beast 666', in *Fits and Starts* (Michael Joseph, 1979)

Richmond, Keith 'Discord in the Garden of Janus' in *Artist Occultist Sensualist* eds. J. Bonner and G. Beskin (Beskin Press, 1999)

Robertson, Sandy, *The Aleister Crowley Scrapbook* (Foulsham & Co., 1988)

Seaman, Penelope, *Little Inns of Soho* (Saint Catherine Press, 1948)

Self, Helen J., *Prostitution, Women and Misuse of the Law: The Fallen Daughters of Eve* (Frank Cass, 2003)

Semple, Gavin, and Austin Osman Spare, *Two Tracts on Cartomancy* (Fulgur, 1997)

Sieveking, Lance, *The Eye of the Beholder* (Hulton Press, 1957)

Simpson, Colin, Lewis Chester and David Leitch, *The Cleveland Street Affair* (Weidenfeld and Nicolson, 1976)

Skilton, David, 'Contemplating the Ruins of London: Macaulay's New Zealander and Others', *Literary London: Interdisciplinary Studies in the Representation of London* Vol.2 no.1 (March, 2004)

Smith, Barry, *Peter Warlock: The Life of Philip Heseltine* (OUP, 1994)

Smith, Timothy d'Arch , 'Aleister Crowley's Aceldama (1898): the 'AB' Copy', (*The Book Collector*, Vol.56 no.2, Summer 2007)

Smith, Timothy d'Arch, *The Books of the Beast* (Oxford, Mandrake, 1991)

Smith, Timothy d'Arch, *The Times Deceas'd* (Settrington, Stone Trough Books, 2003)

Stephensen, P.R., *The Legend of Aleister Crowley* (Mandrake, 1930)

Summers, Montague, *Antinous and Other Poems* (Sisley's, 1907)

Sutin, Lawrence, *Do What Thou Wilt: A Life of Aleister Crowley* (NY, St. Martin's Press, 2000)

Symonds, John, *The Beast 666* (Pindar Press, 1997)

Symonds, John, *Conversations with Gerald* (Duckworth, 1974)

Symonds, John, *The Great Beast* (Rider, 1951)

Symonds, John, *The Great Beast* (Macdonald, 1971)

Symons, Arthur, *London: A Book of Aspects* (Privately Printed [Chiswick Press, Took's Court], 1909)

Symons, Arthur, *Silhouettes*, Second Enlarged Edition (Leonard Smithers, 1896)

Thomas, Dylan, *Collected Letters of Dylan Thomas*, ed. Paul Ferris (Dent, 2000)

Thompson, Jason, 'Burton, Sir Richard Francis', *Oxford Dictionary of National Biography* (OUP, 2004)

Thornton, R.K.R., (ed.) *Poetry of the 'Nineties* (Penguin, 1970)

Todd, Ruthven, *Fitzrovia and the Road to the York Minster* (Parkin Gallery, 1973)

Trevor-Roper, Hugh, *A Hidden Life* (Macmillan, 1976)

Trevor-Roper, Hugh, *One Hundred Letters from Hugh Trevor-Roper*, ed. Richard Davenport-Hines and Adam Sisman (OUP, 2014)

Urban, Hugh, *Magia Sexualis: Sex, Magic, and Liberation in Modern Western Esotericism* (University of California Press, 2006)

Urban, Hugh, 'Magia Sexualis: Sex, Secrecy and Liberation in Modern Western Esotericism', *Journal of the American Academy of Religion*, Vol.72, no.3 (September 2004)

Waite, A.E., *The Book of Black Magic and Pacts* (George Redway, 1898)

Waite, A.E., *Shadows of Life and Thought* (Selwyn and Blunt, 1938)

Waugh, Evelyn, *A Little Learning* (Chapman and Hall, 1964)

Wheatley, Dennis, *The Devil and All His Works* (Hutchinson, 1971)

Wheatley, Dennis, *The Devil Rides Out* (Hutchinson, 1934)

[Wheatley, Dennis] *A Catalogue of Books from the Library of Dennis Wheatley* (Oxford, Blackwells, 1979)

Whineray, E., review of *Chronicles of Pharmacy* by A.C. Wotton, *The Equinox*, Vol.1 no.6 (Autumn 1911)

Whineray, E., 'A Pharmaceutical Study of Cannabis Sativa', *The Equinox*, Vol.1, no.1 (Spring 1909)

Wilde, Oscar, ed. Karl Beckson, *I Can Resist Anything Except Temptation* (Columbia University Press, 1996)

Wilde, Oscar, *The Complete Letters of Oscar Wilde* (Fourth Estate, 2000)

Wilde, *The Picture of Dorian Gray* ed. Isobel Murray (O.U.P., 1974)

Wilson, Edmund, *Axel's Castle: A Study in the Imaginative Literature of 1870-1930* (Penguin, 1993)

Winnicott, D.W., *Playing and Reality* (Tavistock Publications, 1971)

Yeats, W.B., *Autobiographies* (Macmillan, 1955)

Yeats, W.B., *The Collected Letters of W.B. Yeats: Vol. II 1896-1900*, ed. John Kelly (Oxford, 1997)

Yeats, W.B., 'Magic', in *Essays and Introductions* (Macmillan, 1961)

Yeats, W.B., *Mythologies* (Macmillan, 1959)

[Yeats] *Letters to W.B. Yeats*, ed. Finneran, Harper and Murphy (Macmillan, 1977)

Yorke, Gerald, ed. Keith Richmond, *Aleister Crowley, The Golden Dawn and Buddhism: Reminiscences and Writings of Gerald Yorke* (York Beach, ME, The Teitan Press, 1997)

ACKNOWLEDGEMENTS

I am above all grateful to William Breeze, Hymenaeus Beta of Ordo Templi Orientis, for his gracious permission to quote unpublished Crowley diaries and other OTO copyright material, and for his great kindness in making the OTO archives available to me in digital form; I am also grateful for the pleasure of contributing a little input, mainly on London and London people, to the ongoing Crowley diaries and biographies project. I must also especially thank Mark Watson for his sleuthing wizardry with genealogical sources and other records, digging out addresses and back stories, particularly of forgotten women.

A host of other excellent people have helped in various ways, small and large, including Richard Bancroft, Michael Bracewell, Alastair Brotchie, Stefan Dickers, Geoffrey Elborn, Jake Fior, Clive Harper, Mike Jay, Chris Josiffe, Gary Lachman, Darcy Moore, Peter Parker, Jim Pennington, Mark Pilkington, Stephen Pochin, Robert Rickard, Sandy Robertson, Suzy Robinson, Anthony Sillem, Timothy d'Arch Smith, Tom Symonds and Viktor Wynd.

I wrote this book largely during the covid lockdown – a good time for walking through deserted streets – and used libraries far less than usual. The London Library, sterling as ever, sent books by post. But working largely without libraries I became more aware of a handful of exceptional websites and their masters, notably Steve Brachel's Crowley project at 100thmonkeypress.com, a thing of bibliographical excellence and extremely useful; Keith Richmond at Weiser Antiquarian (weiserantiquarian.com), whose originally researched catalogue entries are more impressive than several of the Crowley biographies; and the Aleister Crowley Society's website LAShTAL (lashtal.com), brainchild of Paul Feazey, which manifests the continuing vitality of Crowley's legacy.

✢

I should also acknowledge certain things about the book. It is essentially a book about London 'then', not primarily a visiting guide to London now. A number of sites have disappeared (the Chancery Lane address has been completely redeveloped, for example, as has Langham Buildings and All Souls Place) so please check before visiting anything. Much of central London is nevertheless intact in terms of buildings, but businesses have often changed. Pubs frequently remain, but restaurants tend to go.

Further, it is not a study of Crowley as the prophet of a revealed religion. It will be clear that I do not believe in Crowley in that sense, any more than I believe in Christ or Mohammed, because I don't believe in 'revealed' religion on the Middle Eastern model. Nor is it about Thelema, and what at its heart was a sincere vision of untrammeled freedom and individual excellence, and it is only very glancingly about the significance of his rationalised or even secularised approach to spiritual experience ("We place no reliance / On Virgin or Pigeon; / Our method is science / Our aim is religion"). For better or worse it is about Crowley the man, within the culture that produced him; an Englishman of a certain class and generation, rooted in the rich matrix of a particular time and place.

INDEX

STRANGE ATTRACTOR PRESS 2022